We Can Work It Out

We Can Work It Out

MAKING SENSE OF MARITAL CONFLICT

*Clifford Notarius, Ph.D.,
and
Howard Markman, Ph.D.*

G. P. PUTNAM'S SONS

New York

G. P. Putnam's Sons
Publishers Since 1838
200 Madison Avenue
New York, NY 10016

Library of Congress Cataloging-in-Publication Data
Notarius, Clifford I.
We can work it out : making sense of marital conflict / Clifford
I. Notarius & Howard J. Markman.
p. cm.
Includes index.
ISBN 0-399-13866-8
1. Communication in marriage. 2. Interpersonal communication.
3. Marriage. I. Markman, Howard J. II. Title.
HQ734.N8   1993   93-8572 CIP
646.7′8—dc20

Printed in the United States of America
1   2   3   4   5   6   7   8   9   10

This book is printed on acid-free paper.
∞

To Joyce Notarius for sharing with me her love, friendship, and understanding and for teaching me to feel all that lies beyond words.

CIN

To my family, Fran, Mathew, and Leah, and my parents, Claire and Arnold, for their support and guidance.

HJM

ACKNOWLEDGMENTS

WE FIRST met as clinical psychology graduate students in 1972 at Indiana University. There began a collaboration and friendship that are the foundation for this book. Along with our advisor and friend, Dr. John Gottman, we launched a series of studies on marital satisfaction. More important than the specifics of any study, John's enthusiasm for the research enterprise and the trust and confidence he placed in us started us on the path to the scientific study of relationships that we remain on today. For this and all that goes into a successful mentoring relationship, we are grateful.

Over the years, we have also been fortunate to work with and learn from very talented groups of students at Bowling Green State University, the Catholic University of America, and the University of Denver. Charleana Arellano, Adriana Balaguer, Paul Benson, Susan Blumberg, Karen Boeke, Jane Buongiorno, Tom Burns, Karen Cammuso, Mari Clements, Margaret Cunningham, Jennifer Cummings, Sara Dimitri, Karen Jamieson-Darr, Margie Dominguez, Wayne Duncan, Joyce Emde, Frank Floyd, Cindy Galinski, Paul Howes, Donna Jackson, Matt Johnson, Danielle Julian, Paul Haefner, Lisa Herrick, Lynne Hornyak, Lisa Hoyer, Ruth Ann Irwin, Santi Karamchetty, Shelle Kraft, Doug Leber, Hal Lewis, Kristen Lindahl, Savanna McCain, Lisa Martin, Beth Moses, Michele Piquet, Lydia Prado, Naomi Rather, Mary Jo Renick, Julie Lee Richter, Jennifer Sade, Chris Siaz, Scott Stanley, Ragnar Storaasli, Jim Sucich, Nelly Vanzetti, Brigit VanWidenfelt, Wendy Wainwright, and Elise Zamsky are students who worked along with us on various research projects reported in this book. These students—many

7

of whom are now colleagues—are one of the best reasons for being a professor.

No one can know just how labor intensive the interactional study of couples and families actually is without seeing the painstaking efforts that go into each study. The students and colleagues mentioned above know. The work that forms the backbone of this book could simply not have been done without the dedication and effort from these students and the dozens of research assistants who worked on our projects. And as the artisans who lay a single mosaic tile into what will become a large mural take on faith the integrity of the finished whole, staff on our projects have worked with a similar faith that the whole would come to justify the effort spent on behalf of placing each piece. This book is a first step away from the wall to see the current form of the "big picture."

Advances in the scientific understanding of close personal relationships have occurred through the coordinated efforts of an extraordinary group of researchers scattered coast-to-coast in the United States, Europe, and Australia. Every contemporary book on marriage that draws upon recent studies for its content will reflect the contributions of these scholars—ours is no exception. Don Baucom, Andy Christensen, Phil Cowan, Carolyn Pape Cowan, Steve Duck, Norm Epstein, Frank Fincham, John Gottman, Bernard Guerney, Kurt Hahlweg, Kim Halford, Jill Hooley, Ted Jacob, Neil Jacobson, Gayla Margolin, Sherrod Miller, Pat Noller, Dan O'Leary, David Pellegrini, Cas Schaap, and Bob Weiss are among our colleagues in the field who have enriched us professionally and personally and we wish here to credit their work and their influence upon us and this book.

The research reported in this book has been supported by grants from the National Institute of Mental Health, National Science Foundation, and in a variety of ways by the Catholic University of America and the University of Denver. We appreciate the ongoing support we've received from these institutions over the years. We also owe a special thanks to Research Press for their permission to use some material from our previous book, *A Couple's Guide to Communication*, written with John Gottman and Jonni Gonso.

Earlier drafts of this book have been used in some of our courses we've taught on Understanding Human Conflict and Marital and Family Interaction and Therapy. Comments from students in these classes have been helpful and valued.

The clients with whom we have worked over the past years have made a special contribution to this book. Therapy is never easy, often entails struggle, and occasionally there are some minutes that transform both client and therapist. This book reflects all of these moments. The case histories in this book have been significantly altered to disguise individual clients. During the preparation of this book, we each had on several occasions the uncanny experience of reading a case history that the other had written and finding that the case described too closely a client that the other of us was seeing. This speaks to the universality of issues and processes that predominate in couples and it is in the spirit of this universality that all case material is offered. Case detail presented in the book is not intended as, nor is it in fact, a disclosure of confidential material from any one client or couple.

The writing of this book has been a team enterprise. We are sincerely grateful for the expert guidance and support we have received nearly every step of the way in bringing this book from the point of interesting discussion to published reality. Our agent Chris Tomasino at RLR Associates is a special person to us. She has been an invaluable resource during all stages of this book. We feel very lucky to have benefited from her warmth, wisdom, guidance, sense of humor and friendship. Writer Henry Dreher took our drafts and found words to sharpen our ideas. In the process he transformed some of our tortured sentences into graceful prose. Our editor at Putnam, Laura Yorke has been terrific. From the start, her vision for the project helped define the overarching structure of the book and her careful reading and adept editing of the chapters made our efforts the best they could be. We appreciate her enthusiasm for and dedication to our work. Chris, Henry, and Laura have given graciously of their talent, experience, time, and we sincerely appreciate their contributions.

Finally, we extend our heartfelt appreciation to the couples and families who volunteered to participate in our research studies. Without the willingness of individuals to openly share their relationships with us, the scientific study of families would not be possible. Many participants in our research stated that their decision to volunteer was based on a wish that other families could learn from their experiences—good and bad. We hope that with this book, we have fulfilled some of these wishes.

CONTENTS

Part I: Relationships Made Easy
13

CHAPTER 1 *Relationships Made Easy: An Overview*   *15*
CHAPTER 2 *The Six Simple Truths of Marriage*   *26*
CHAPTER 3 *For Better or for Worse*   *37*
CHAPTER 4 *For Richer or Poorer—Your Relationship Bank Account*   *68*

Part II: Better Understanding
93

CHAPTER 5 *Making Sense Out of Nonsense*   *95*
CHAPTER 6 *Hot Thoughts: The Fuel of Destructive Relationship Conflicts*   *135*
CHAPTER 7 *Sweaty Palms and Racing Hearts*   *159*

Part III: Better Talk
189

CHAPTER 8 *A No-Nonsense Guide to Talking Sense*   *191*
CHAPTER 9 *A No-Nonsense Guide to Resolving Problems*   *217*

CHAPTER 10 *Blinded by a Blizzard: Overcoming Anger on the Path to Change*　237

CHAPTER 11 *From Repair to Revival*　257

References　275

Index　281

PART I

Relationships Made Easy

Chapter 1

RELATIONSHIPS MADE EASY: AN OVERVIEW

Do YOU remember when you were first getting to know your partner? Most of us have very fond memories of these times. Think about how the two of you met, out of all the people in the world. When was the first time you saw each other? The first time you spoke? What was the first "date" like? The first time you kissed? Made love?

Even if this period does not last long, memories of how sweet these times can be are stored away forever. For some, these positive memories contrast so sharply with the pain of current relationship difficulties that immediate relationship challenges seem overwhelming. If that is the case for you, we encourage you to accept the challenge to make the relationship better, and we hope to help you through the program we present.

In our view, most people who are partners in a couple have no more important goal in their lives than relationship success. As psychotherapists, teachers, and researchers, we listen every day to our patients, students, and research participants speak of how important their personal relationships are to their sense of well-being. When a relationship is going well, partners are happier, healthier, both physically and mentally, and there is more energy for life.

Unfortunately, for about one out of every two marriages these benefits are never realized. When a relationship is deadened by anger or detachment and withdrawal, partners can find themselves ill, depressed, and dissatisfied with many aspects of their lives. A variety of national surveys collected by the National Center for Health Statistics have found that people immersed in relationship conflicts are more likely to need medical attention and more likely to find themselves in a hospital bed, for either medical or psychiatric reasons, than are those who are happily married. Relationship problems also touch more than two million children a year, and they too will bear the wounds of relationship distress.

But people don't get married for the health benefits. They marry for love, companionship, for a family. They marry for friendship and intimacy. Even though nearly one out of every two marriages will end in divorce, marriage remains the life-style of choice. Most people don't know it, but the divorce rate in the U.S. actually *declined* about 10 percent during the 1980s and has remained at a twenty-three-year low through 1992. So there is reason for hope. Yet when a marriage ends, people tend to jump back into another relationship within three years; and, on the average, these new relationships stand an even greater chance of encountering serious conflict than do first marriages.

So why do most of us desire to be in an intimate relationship when it is so often fraught with difficulties? The strength of these desires lies in the promise of happiness that comes along with relationship success. With this book, you can increase your chance of seeing that promise fulfilled—and of being in the 50 percent of couples who make it.

If preventing and curing relationship conflict seems like an impossible dream, it's because counselors and other books have been setting their sights too low. All too often, they discuss why relationships are doomed to fail rather than teaching couples how to succeed. They argue that men and women are fundamentally different rather than helping women and men discover their similar needs. They teach couples how to "fight fair" instead of how not to fight. They tell couples how to make their relationships marginally better, instead of how to make them wonderfully successful. We believe this book presents a new kind of model for you to follow, with a focus on optimism.

In these pages, we will unveil the mysteries of good and bad relationships, conveying tested remedies for making the bad ones good and the good ones better. Diagnostic questionnaires will enable you to pinpoint your relationship trouble-spots, and clearly defined, readily applied skills of communication and conflict management will empower you to remake your relationship—or just to make it the loving union you had always hoped it to be.

COUPLES RESEARCH MADE EASY

With the results of over twenty years of research with thousands of couples, we can now share with you the *precise factors* that make a relationship satisfying to both members. Our studies have involved diverse groups of happy and unhappy couples at all stages of the life cycle— from those planning marriage, to those getting ready for their first child, to those looking back on thirty-plus years of marriage. Couples from all walks of life, from large cities to small communities, and from a variety of ethnic backgrounds and socioeconomic classes have shared their lives with us in over twenty-five separate investigations. We have analyzed how they talk, how they think, and how they handle conflict. Through our research we have developed a *language* to describe and understand relationship success. And we have learned that relationship success depends on the ability of two people to *manage* the conflicts that inevitably occur in all relationships. Partners are often very motivated to work on their marriage but simply do not know how to transform their motivation into meaningful action. Without that capacity, some of the solutions become part of the problem instead of the remedy.

Our studies have identified the real-life communication skills of successful relationships. Based on what we have learned about the key features of loving, effective, harmonious long-term relationships, we have developed clinically proven methods to steer couples toward success and away from common pitfalls. In effect, we have found that destructive marital conflict can not only be "cured," it can also be prevented.

In our studies we put marriage under a microscope. We invited couples to our research centers to focus in on how they communicated while handling conflict. Each couple was interviewed, completed a series of questionnaires (similar to those you'll fill out in chapter 3) and, most importantly, were videotaped discussing their most intense relationship issues. The videotapes were transcribed and then objective observers, trained by us, meticulously analyzed what partners said to each other and how they said it. All told, it took about twenty-four

---

Box 1.1
Why Study Both Happy and Unhappy Couples?

One of the most important decisions we made when we began our search for the keys to relationship satisfaction was to base our therapeutic strategies on scientific findings and clinical experience, not just one or the other. We also knew that we had to study not only unhappy and distressed couples but also happy and nondistressed couples. By comparing the characteristics of both groups, we could discover the essential differences between them.

Some of the greatest sport coaches in history claim that their coaching methods were derived from the careful study of the most and least successful athletes in their sport. For example, while we were graduate students at Indiana University, our swimming team routinely won the national championship. The coach, "Doc" Councilman, would intensively study his Olympic-class swimmers like Mark Spitz to figure out what world-class swimmers were doing right and then teach all swimmers these skills. Our study of successful couples followed a similar path.

Just as Doc Councilman studied the natural stroke mechanics used by his best swimmers, we set out to discover the natural communication patterns used by happy couples to resolve their differences. When couples came to our laboratory, we asked them to discuss a current relationship problem for about fifteen or twenty minutes. These conversations were videotaped for the detailed kinds of study you will learn about in this chapter.

Often people wonder if couples speak and behave in the same manner in front of us as they do at home. Will couples try to fool us into thinking they are happier than they really are? On the other

continued

hand, will some partners try to convince us that they are more miserable, as they might in a plea for help? Human beings do naturally attempt to manage the impressions they make on others, and the couples we studied could have made such attempts.

However, it is much more difficult for a couple to manage the impression they are creating than it is for an individual. We were most interested in observing the subtle way partners talk to each other, patterns that cannot so easily be altered.

Once partners start talking about their major issues, most begin focusing on the discussion at hand and ignore the camera. If you saw these videotapes, you would observe firsthand how passionate and intense couples often become when they discuss or argue about real-life issues. While we recognize that couples do not talk at home in *exactly* the same way that they do in our research centers, the couples' conversations that we observed did appear to reflect the couples' ability to communicate effectively and to manage conflict in their real lives.

hours of study to make sense out of each hour of videotaped interaction.

We also studied how a group of 135 happy premarital couples changed over time. If we had just compared groups of happy and unhappy couples, we wouldn't know if differences between them resulted from current distress or from communication patterns already in place before the distress became evident. By studying how happy premarital couples changed over the first ten years of their marriages, we sought to discover what individual or relationship characteristics—present while couples were still happy—ultimately led to distress, divorce, or continued happiness. Thus we asked couples in 1980 to complete many questionnaires. The couples were also interviewed and observed while privately discussing an unresolved relationship issue. Approximately every year after 1980, we went back to each couple to determine if they were still together and, if so, how happy each partner was with the relationship and where they stood on their conflict-ridden issues. We used the information gathered in 1980 to test all the popular explanations for relationship stability and success over the next ten years.

WHAT WE FOUND

Our discoveries have been striking. Using information gathered in 1980, we were able to predict with over 90 percent accuracy which couples were distressed or divorced, and which continued to have enduring relationship success in 1990. The discoveries have also gone against the grain of conventional wisdom. We realized that traditional views of relationship success had to be redefined, and new visions created. In so doing, we have become able to help couples avoid common mistakes and embrace new techniques to solidify or repair the foundations of their relationships.

Here, set off against accepted bits of conventional wisdom about relationship success, are our major findings:

- *Conventional wisdom:* Whom you marry has a lot to do with how happy your marriage will be.

OUR FINDING: Marital happiness has little to do with whom you marry and everything to do with how you cope with conflict.

- *Conventional wisdom:* Personality flaws—his insensitivity, her insecurity—are the underlying cause of marital distress.

OUR FINDING: Personality traits do not predict marital happiness or marital stability.

- *Conventional wisdom:* How compatible and alike you are to your partner is an important ingredient to relationship success.

OUR FINDING: It's not how similar or different you are, it's how you *handle differences* when they arise that counts.

- *Conventional wisdom:* Problems early in marriage tend to get better with time, so it is best to ignore them at the beginning.

OUR FINDING: Problems tend to worsen over time, so it's best to deal with them early in the relationship, when they are easier to handle.

• *Conventional wisdom:* Men and women have different needs in a relationship and have different approaches to intimacy.

OUR FINDING: The major difference between men and women in marriage lies in the way they handle conflict and not in their ability to be intimate.

• *Conventional wisdom:* If there is enough love and commitment between two people, nothing can get in the way of happiness.

OUR FINDING: Love is needed to get a relationship off the ground, but it doesn't provide enough fuel to keep a marriage flying toward success over time—nor does commitment. Again, it's how couples manage conflict that makes the difference.

As you can undoubtedly tell from our six findings, relationship success for today's couples depends on being able to communicate effectively with your partner. For any two people living together in the culture of the 1990s, there will always be differences of opinion on likes, desires, and plans to get things done. Setting up a home together will provide fertile ground for disagreements. The couple will have to figure out ways to earn and spend money, to keep house, to raise children, to enjoy free time, and to meet each other's needs for both intimacy and privacy. In decades past, the potential for conflict was mitigated by the easy way individuals could fit into society's prescribed roles. Couples had clear cultural prescriptions for dealing with their differences, many of which were gender related. For example, husbands earned the bacon and wives cooked it. There were no arguments about who would stay home with Timmy when he had a sore throat and could not go to school.

While contemporary couples tend to embrace more egalitarian goals for their relationship, the tasks of a life together clearly have not changed. With no prescribed way of meeting these challenges, each couple today must work out their own unique compromises. The only way to achieve these compromises and maintain relationship satisfaction is through the use of *effective communication and conflict management skills.* Our ability to identify the premarital communication problems that lead to future relationship grief, after years of marriage, offers hope to all couples. Based on our research findings, we have developed and evaluated the "Better Talk" program that is presented in this book. This program teaches couples how to use the communication and relationship skills we identify, and they need, to improve unhappy marriages and prevent the declines in happiness that directly stem from poor communication. In one study, premarital couples who were taught the Better Talk tools had a 50 percent lower rate of breakup and divorce than those couples not participating in the program.

The easiest time to learn these skills and methods is early in a relationship, before destructive arguing patterns have solidified. But it is never too late; any couple can master the skills we teach. An essential element of success is to start applying these skills in low-conflict, controlled situations, and then gradually to start applying them in the major, powder-keg areas of conflict that may exist between you and your partner. By the time you finish this book, we believe you will have mastered the critical skills we have identified as essential to relationship success in the 1990s and beyond.

HOW TO USE THIS BOOK

We are going to provide you with the two essential resources: the tools to make positive changes and the knowledge required to use those tools creatively. Neither one of these is sufficient by itself. You would not attempt to fix a car engine without fully understanding its complex mechanisms. Nor could you use even the most elegant and sophisticated set of tools to fix a breakdown if you did not know how to apply them. Armed with the instruments of change as well as an in-depth understanding of how and why these changes will improve your relationships, you will be able to achieve the goal of relationship success.

Part 1 of this text, Relationships Made Easy, introduces you to our key findings on how and why relationships run smoothly or begin to break down and allows you to identify pivotal issues in your relation-

ship. Part 2, Better Understanding, enables you to see the inner workings of communication and conflict management through examples of
other couples and the methodical outlining of the dynamics present between them. It begins giving you the tools you will need to put this
understanding to use in your relationship. Part 3, Better Talk, builds
upon the understanding and tools mastered to this point and provides
a detailed plan to work through each problem confronting your relationship.

In the next chapter, The Six Simple Truths of Marriage, you will learn
six simple truths of marriage culled from our research. These simple
truths make easy the task of understanding the causes of marital discord as well as providing the seeds for how to treat and prevent relationship problems. In chapter 3, For Better or for Worse, you will learn
to pinpoint the troublesome issues in your relationship and discover
which side of the "for better or for worse" balance your relationship is
perched upon. You will also learn to identify your typical style of handling conflict. In chapter 4, For Richer or Poorer, you will learn about
our "bank account" model of relationships, enabling you to determine
if your relationship is overflowing with deposits or headed toward
bankruptcy. You will also learn how to tap into what we call your "reservoir of hope" for a better relationship, by translating good intent into
positive change.

In part 2, we will assemble all the pieces of the puzzle that make up
the picture of relationship happiness or distress, giving you a deeper
understanding of the issues identified in part 1. In chapter 5, Making
Sense Out of Nonsense, we contrast the specific types of messages that
leave partners feeling close with those that we call "zingers," which
tear at the very fabric of the relationship and leave people feeling isolated, hurt, and hopeless. We then offer beginning strategies on how to
limit zingers and enhance positive messages. In chapter 6, Hot
Thoughts: The Fuel of Destructive Relationship Conflicts, you will discover how your thoughts promote or limit the small, but significant,
changes you must make on behalf of the relationship. Most people simply assume that events cause their feelings. We will help you to discover that events trigger thoughts, and it is these triggered thoughts
that lead to feelings of well-being and openness to change, or to despair

and rigid refusal to change. You will also discover how your thoughts determine if differences between you and your partner represent a strength or a weakness in the relationship. In chapter 7, Sweaty Palms and Racing Hearts, we fit the final piece of the relationship "puzzle" into place with a discussion of how your thoughts, messages, and actions are affected by your nervous system and how, in turn, your nervous system affects everything you do or say. Not surprisingly, the nervous systems of men and women seem to react differently to relationship conflict, and so any differences we have with our mates must be examined in this context. With "Better Understanding" of the relationship puzzle, you will see that you have control over the future course of your relationship.

Everything you learned in the first two parts is essential to being able to maximally benefit from part 3 of the book, Better Talk. You will not be able to easily learn the skills presented here unless you have mastered chapters 5, 6, and 7 and learned how to recognize your good and bad communication habits as well as contain your hot thoughts and physiological arousal. As we've mentioned, our research findings presented in parts 1 and 2 led us to conclude that the key to marital success was to teach couples how to handle conflict—*to talk without fighting*. This led us to develop "Better Talk"—our step-by-step program that offers you a proven set of communication and conflict-management skills and principles.

In chapter 8, A No-Nonsense Guide to Talking Sense, we encourage you to take each of the issues in your relationship, identified in chapter 2, and talk about them—not trying to solve them—in a way that facilitates understanding and keeps the lid on destructive conflict. We provide you with additional skills to meet this goal. Then in chapter 9, A No-Nonsense Guide to Resolving Problems, we enable you, without fighting, to work together as a team to develop creative solutions for solving these hot-button issues. We have found that most marital problems can be managed by the plans laid out in chapters 8 and 9. "Better Talk" guarantees that each person's thoughts and feelings will be expressed and understood. In this context of increased understanding, a form of team spirit will develop between you and your partner.

At times, despite their best efforts, some partners will still experience stubborn obstacles in their path to relationship harmony. In chapter 10, Blinded by a Blizzard: Overcoming Anger on the Path to Change, we focus in on one of the major themes plaguing most relationships— anger. We help partners trace the roots of anger to issues of hurt and self-esteem and then help them talk about and resolve anger-related issues.

After the fires of conflict are cooled, partners often need to stoke the warmth of intimacy and closeness. In the final chapter, From Repair to Revival, we present a set of exercises designed to increase closeness, sensuality, and fun in a relationship between partners who have successfully reached the goals set forth previously. Our goal here is to help partners learn how to prevent a downward drift in their relationship over time.

Throughout the book we will emphasize that partners must *practice relationship skills* if they are to become adept at using them when the going gets tough and conflict erupts. Exercises are an important part of this book; if you apply the same discipline to your relationship that you might to a diet or fitness regimen, you will be on your way toward a healthier and happier relationship as well.

In the next chapter, pay close attention to the six simple truths about relationships drawn from our research. They will guide you through the book, and we will be referring to them in later chapters.

Chapter 2

THE SIX SIMPLE TRUTHS
OF MARRIAGE

SINCE WE have spent twenty years in scientific investigations of marriage, the first question we are usually asked is "So what did you find?" In this chapter, we sum up the results of our research and clinical work by presenting the six simple truths of relationship happiness. Without underestimating the effort it takes to create a genuinely happy relationship, or the complexity of the problems couples typically encounter, here are the facts partners need to know in order to sustain a happy marriage or to repair and revive an unhappy one. As you'll see, the findings chart a new course to relationship happiness. These simple truths are the beacons of optimism that will guide you through the sometimes turbulent waters that beset all close relationships.

Simple truth #1: *Each relationship contains a hidden reservoir of hope.*

Our research has shown that even the most destructive fights and conflicts start with *good intentions*. These good intentions form the basis for a *hidden reservoir of hope* that a fully satisfying relationship can be achieved. The key: how to tap into the good intent and the reservoir of hope.

Chuck and Barbara were married for less than six months and although both had good jobs, they were already fighting about money. When we attempted to help them resolve the problems they were having about money, it took less than ten minutes for them to get into a heated argument. If you were observing the couple, you would probably notice immediately that Chuck and Barbara were both trying to get their way and were not at all concerned about the other person's perspective. In our therapy program, we gave Barbara and Chuck the opportunity to tell us whether their intentions were good or bad right after they had made just one statement to each other.

Barbara and Chuck used an exercise we will describe for you in chapter 3. When Barbara said "I feel you monitor every purchase I make, and it upsets me to have you checking up on me. You know, I work just as hard as you," Chuck immediately felt the comment was negative. Yet we asked Barbara to declare her intent, and she said it was "definitely positive." We discussed the discrepancy between Barbara's positive intent and the negative impact the statement had upon Chuck. We discovered that Barbara's intent was positive because she felt she was finally expressing a very important feeling that she thought would help solve the problem. And we learned that the impact on Chuck was negative because he felt attacked. When Chuck spoke, his intent was also positive because he wanted to avoid a fight with Barbara; however, his words had a negative impact on her because she felt he was trying to dodge the issue. They soon realized that both had very good intent despite the negative impacts.

We helped Chuck and Barbara discuss their money problem so that the speaker's positive intent would result in a positive impact on the listener. (We cover these issues in chapter 4.) Chuck and Barbara left the session with increased understanding of why fights started and heightened hope that they could begin talking and listening better to each other.

In the heat of conflict, statements made might appear to others as though the partners were trying to pour gasoline on a fire already burning out of control, when in truth the speaker actually means for the statement to douse the fires of conflict. One of our tasks, in therapy and in this book, is to break this important good news to couples. It would be much harder to help couples improve their relationship if partners were actually trying to be destructive and had no hope for change. Instead, we find that most partners retain their wish for relationship improvement even when the going is toughest. In fact, people believe they are acting according to that positive wish despite appearances to the contrary. This is a hidden reservoir of hope that we will teach you to tap into to improve your relationship.

Simple truth #2: *One "zinger" will erase twenty acts of kindness.*

Our research has shown that it takes one put-down to undo hours of kindness you give to your partner. This principle is comparable to the fact that it takes twenty minutes of exercise to work off a candy bar and it takes but a minute to eat another one. The key: Intimate partners must learn how to manage their anger and control the exchange of *negative* behavior.

Betty and Steve were an attractive young couple with high hopes for the future. They had been dating for two years, and for the last six months were working hard to improve the relationship and convince themselves that marriage was a good idea. One Saturday, they decided that they would spend the day together shopping and then go out to dinner and a movie. When they first started dating, this was a favorite way to spend a day together, and they both had good memories of these times. But the good times had diminished over the last six months, as fights had started to erupt. With high expectations of breaking out of what they hoped was a slump, the day started off well enough. Both Betty and Steve were invested in having a good time themselves and in showing kindness and consideration to the other. By late afternoon, they stopped for coffee and shared with each other how much they had missed these fun times together. Yet no more than an hour later, the couple suddenly found themselves in a heated argument about where to have dinner. Neither could recall exactly how it started except that Steve remembers, "Betty got angry really fast and called me an inconsiderate dictator who always had to have my way." But Betty remembers, "Steve made reservations at this restaurant he knows I hate, didn't tell me at first he had reservations, and when he just tried to steer me to this grease pit I told him I'd rather eat elsewhere. Then he wouldn't talk to me." The weekend was ruined, and each partner's many acts of kindness were rendered meaningless as they were swallowed up by unbounded conflict.

In our therapeutic program, Betty and Steve learned that twenty acts of kindness cannot take away the sting of one good "zinger." Often partners try to be extra nice to each other after a tough conflict. Although this can be helpful, if it is part of a larger pattern of "Nasty → Nice → Nice → Nasty" the relationship is still going to suffer. It is better to figure out ways to manage the zingers than to cope with their consequences.

Another lesson Steve and Betty learned was to pause right before they zinged their partner and consider what they hoped to accomplish with their words. Partners in a healthy relationship realize that zingers have a strong impact, and that it is unrealistic to expect their mate to have "tough skin" and be able to tolerate the barbs. Instead, when a partner has a zinger on the tip of the tongue, he or she is better served by finding a way to express the feelings in a constructive manner. Constructive expression of gripes, criticisms, and annoyances is a matter of knowing how to express oneself and choosing the appropriate time and place for the conversation. In part 2 of the book, we will provide you with the guidance and skills you need to express "negative" thoughts and feelings constructively.

Simple truth #3: *Little changes in you can lead to huge changes in the relationship.*

We began our research thinking it would be easy to detect differences between happy and unhappy couples. Although it turns out to be true that there are clear and reliable differences, those differences tend to be small and subtle. For example, unhappy couples may use only one or two more zingers a day. But multiply that by 365 . . . The implication is that small changes in behavior—listening to your partner rather than walking away or yelling just once in the heat of an argument—can produce substantial changes in marital happiness.

Most couples in trouble think that for things to improve, extraordinary changes—if not a miracle—would have to take place. And human nature being what it is, most of us who have relationship troubles think those major changes need to be made by our spouse, not ourselves. But we often don't realize that we have no control over our partner's behavior. As a result, we develop a sense of hopelessness and helplessness about the relationship. If only he (or she) would change, everything would be fine—or so we think. The breakthrough comes when we realize that by making even small changes in ourselves, we can effect big, positive changes that make us more optimistic and open to our partners.

Eileen and Allen were both on their second marriage by the time we saw them. As in their first marriages, they often got into fights because they could not seem to agree on anything. She wanted a light blue synthetic carpet for the den; he wanted a light green wool. She wanted wallpaper; he wanted painted walls. For a vacation, he wanted to go to the beach, and she wanted to go sightseeing in big cities. Allen began to feel that Eileen had to have everything her way and that she was trying to control him. He felt hopeless and began to wonder about separation. In talking with Allen, it became clear that he expected that he and Eileen would agree on most things in life, and that such agreement would be the true source of their intimacy. With so much disagreement about so many things, Allen felt, with great sadness, that the relationship no longer had any basis for closeness and intimacy.

We helped Allen work to understand his own needs for agreement and to recognize how deeply he felt the power of Eileen's disagreements. He began to experiment with a small change in how he perceived his disagreements with Eileen. He began to understand that their disagreements simply meant that they were two different people with different backgrounds and needs. There was no reason that they should agree on everything. Allen began routinely to expect that they would differ on many issues, and that they only had to agree when agreement was essential—for example, when the couple had to decide on a school for their son. He learned that they could allow their differences to stand when a consensus was unnecessary. For example, when Eileen thought he should drive to work on the highway and he preferred to go through the city, there was no need for a summit conference. As Allen continued his experiment with small changes, he began to see significant positive changes in how Eileen was responding to him. Discussions took the place of arguments, and the couple learned to accept each other. A new degree of closeness was beginning to emerge from the cold isolation that had come to characterize Allen and Eileen's marriage.

At the beginning of therapy, couples like Eileen and Allen tell us they feel hopeless and overwhelmed. Many say to us, "Give us something specific to do to make our relationship better." As we told Eileen and Allen, you can each start right now by making small changes in *your own* behavior. "Planting" small changes in behavior today brings a relationship in bloom tomorrow. To do this you need only follow our formula of relationship addition and subtraction: *Add* to your relationship acts of thoughtful kindness—complement your partner on how he or she looks, touch your partner's back when you walk by—and *subtract* from your relationship acts of thoughtless nastiness—ignoring your partner when you are angry, calling your partner names. As you live and breathe this formula, you can rediscover and preserve feelings of love, attraction, and satisfaction in your relationship.

Simple truth #4: *It's not the differences between partners that cause problems but how the differences are handled when they arise.*

Many partners think that their relationship woes are the result of differences between themselves and their mate. We've heard many couples say "We're not compatible, he likes to be on the go, I like to stay at home," or "She goes to bed early; I'm a night person." This reasoning is an understandable effort to explain the causes of unhappiness. However, since marital conflict does *not* stem from the differences but how those differences are handled, partners must learn how to manage differences between themselves. Rather than focusing on areas of agreement and disagreement, partners in happy relationships develop good listening skills. These skills have nothing to do with eliminating differences, forcing consensus, or giving advice. Listening skills involve understanding and acceptance of differences in personality and taste. Having a good listener is having a good friend. In a happy relationship, a partner can count on his or her mate's being a good friend and never a judge or counselor.

Eileen and Allen, the couple who made small changes with big results, learned this simple truth in therapy. If they hadn't, their focus on differences might have cost them their marriage. Along with learning that differences are the rule and not the exception, Allen and Eileen mastered new ways of managing differences and were so successful in this endeavor that their uniqueness became a strength rather than a liability of their relationship.

Among the many differences challenging this couple, Eileen and Allen had divergent philosophies of child rearing. For instance, Allen wanted the children in bed by 9:30. When they were told to turn the lights off, he expected them to obey. Eileen also wanted the children in bed by 9:30, but when they didn't obey she preferred to avoid a scene. "Kids will be kids," she thought, and she was content to think that they'd fall asleep within an hour or two after having been told to go to bed. In fact, both Allen and Eileen agreed that there should be only a few nights a month when the children could stay up past 10:15.

All attempts to talk about this problem had previously disintegrated into vicious arguments about child rearing, with both partners blaming the problem on their respective experiences growing up. Allen accused Eileen's parents of catering to the kids, and Eileen accused Allen's parents of making him and his brothers live in fear. When we helped Allen and Eileen to listen to each other's desires, it was apparent to both that they simply wanted to provide the best possible conditions for their children at bedtime. Once they were helped to listen to each other without judgment or analysis, they were able to develop a common plan for bedtime rituals that was flexible enough to please both of them. As Allen and Eileen learned to manage their differences, everyone benefited—including their children.

As was true of Allen and Eileen, partners in today's relationships have more options than ever before, leading to natural conflicts. The key to relationship success is how these disagreements are handled by couples when they arise. Unfortunately, partners do not receive basic training in how to deal with differences. As you read on, you will learn how to avoid blaming each other when problems arise and strategies for handling the differences that inevitably occur.

Simple truth #5: *Men and women fight using different weapons but suffer similar wounds.*

Not only do men and women suffer similar wounds, they also sustain these wounds trying to accomplish the same objectives: acceptance, support, and affection. When partners try to understand what is not going right in a relationship, they tend to examine the current weapons that are being used rather than the ultimate goals that are so strongly desired by both people. When we have focused our research on the goals men and women share for their relationship, we have exposed many common misconceptions about the differences between men and women in marriages.

Contrary to the conventional wisdom that men "have a problem with intimacy" and women "tend to overreact," men and women differ little in their desire for intimacy and connection. For a variety of reasons, both biological and cultural, men have a harder time handling conflict, while women have a harder time tolerating emotional distance. Thus, men often *withdraw* from uncomfortable arousal associated with marital discussions while women sometimes feel a need immediately to *resolve* every conflict through discussion. In part 1 you will discover how and why each of these strategies can be harmful to relationships, and in part 2 you will learn how to monitor and contain your own responses.

Jack and Diane, a middle-aged couple, had been struggling for years in what they believed was a battle of the sexes. Jack thought that Diane was too emotional and often attributed her outbursts to "hormones." Jack even thought that Diane was not as interested in sex as he was, and he often felt rejected when his initiations were turned aside. Diane was troubled by the way Jack stormed around the house and continually felt that he was angry with her about something she had done. Diane was equally troubled by the absence of a good sex life and began to wonder if Jack was having an affair. The couple's sex life had been put on hold in the face of Diane's occasional outbursts of rage and Jack's simmering anger. Although both Jack and Diane were desperate for a return of caring romance to their relationship, they were unable to break through the barriers they had erected.

In our program, Jack and Diane came genuinely to understand that they had similar goals but often chose different ways to express their disappointment when the goals were not realized. Once they accepted that their gender-associated differences were superficial compared to their shared goals of good sex and caring concern, they had taken the first big step toward working as a team to achieve common goals.

Throughout this book, you will learn more about the surprising similarities and differences between men and women in marriage. The appreciation of how each gender faces conflict is the first step to healing the negative feelings—derived from disputes based on differences— that both sexes share. This task is made easier when partners realize that their wants and needs are similar, even though prior attempts to meet these needs were met by failure and frustration. We will provide specific strategies for helping partners work together to create the type of relationship most men and women want and need.

Simple truth #6: *Partners need to practice relationship skills in order to become good at them.*

Many partners seem to live their lives by playing at the game of marriage. We are bombarded by celebrities making jokes about their fifth, sixth, or seventh spouse and the hope that after the first half dozen partners, maybe, now that they've practiced enough, they will get it right. Little chance! Instead of continually changing partners in the quest for a happy relationship, people should be learning to manage the conflicts, angers, and disagreements that are common to all relationships.

Unfortunately, partners enter into relationships with no agreed-upon rules or skills for handling the strong negative feelings that are an inevitable part of all relationships. Without rules, in the face of conflict, partners often resort to forms of guerrilla warfare with random sniping that can seriously wound their mates. Instead of taking control of conflict, partners let conflict take control of them.

Carl and Myra were married for ten years and had two daughters: Beth, six, and Ellen, three. After the first three years of marriage, neither partner was very happy, but each felt this was the best marriage had to offer. After six years, Carl and Myra became increasingly miserable and sought help, first from their pastor and then from a therapist. They were given some suggestions to improve their marriage, but these were not effective and the partners grew even more angry with each other. For the first time, Carl and Myra begin to think about separation and divorce. At the same time, they kept trying as well as they knew how to heal the relationship. Carl would call home from work every day to show Myra he was thinking about her; but Myra felt Carl was merely "checking up" on her. Consequently, she was annoyed by the calls and showed her negative feelings.

On the other hand, Myra knew that Carl did not like taking care of the household bills, so she decided to manage the family budget. Carl liked the fact that he no longer had to worry about utility bills but was often annoyed that he had no input into financial decisions affecting the family. Myra and Carl tried to talk about their efforts on behalf of the relationship, but these discussions rapidly degenerated into an argument that made each feel worse not only about the issue but also about the marriage as a whole.

On the brink of divorce, Myra read an article about our therapy program, and Carl agreed to give counseling one more try because he liked the idea that the program was research based. Early in the program, we helped them identify which issues in the relationship were hotbeds of conflict and which areas they managed well. We then taught Myra and Carl the tools of effective communication and the mechanisms responsible for destructive conflict. Week by week, we attacked first the less-volatile marital issues and gradually the most explosive ones. Each week Carl and Myra practiced structured exercises to master the skills they were learning. Soon they needed us less and less as they became more adept at managing their own conflicts.

Myra and Carl continued to have weekly meetings to review current relationship concerns and progress with their new set of skills. At one meeting they sat down to talk about a brief argument they had had the day before about money. They had been able to stop-short the quarrel by agreeing to talk about the issue in the meeting scheduled for the next day. For the first time, Carl and Myra were able to express their feelings about the money issue and have the other person listen. In this supportive climate, each said things that he or she had never said before. Myra revealed that part of the reason she wanted to pay the bills was that this was one way for her to help out in the money arena, adding that "I've never really said this to you, but since I quit practicing law when we had Beth, I've felt guilty that I stopped bringing home a paycheck." Carl revealed that he also had feelings that he had not expressed about her working outside the home. He said: "I don't want you to take this the wrong way, but part of me felt angry when you decided to stop work, because I expected us always to have two paychecks to handle all our bills." Although they didn't try to solve the problem in this meeting, they left the talk feeling they had made progress. After several more talks about money and careers, Myra decided to seek a part-time job at her old law firm and Carl decided to spend more time at home with Ellen and Beth.

As they continued to practice and use their new relationship skills, they were able to deal with many of their old issues as well as new ones that emerged. When we last heard from them, they felt that they had achieved a new and more deeply satisfying level of relationship happiness.

THE SIMPLE TRUTHS IN ACTION

In the midst of a relationship fight, when words and deeds are flying fast and furiously, when tensions are running high, it is easy to feel lost and to have no idea how to find your way out of the emotional storm. At these times, we want you to use the six simple truths that you learned in this chapter as beacons to guide you toward more effective communication and conflict management.

The simple truths were designed to make easy the task of understanding the causes of marital conflict as well as providing the seeds for how to treat and prevent relationship problems. We will refer back to the simple truths and show you how they have been useful in our work with couples. After you've read this book, you will be able to use the simple truths to remind you of what you have learned.

The rest of parts 1 and 2 of this text expands on each of the simple truths we've discussed so far. In the next chapter, you will learn to pinpoint the troublesome issues in your relationship and discover which side of the "for better or for worse" balance your relationship is perched upon.

Chapter 3

FOR BETTER OR FOR
WORSE

WE ARE all familiar with that phrase from marriage ceremonies, "For better or for worse, for richer or poorer . . ." It is the phrase signifying that healthy marital commitment requires acceptance of good times and bad, strengths and weaknesses, healthy traits and unhealthy ones. What the marriage vows *don't* tell us is that embracing our differences and riding the highs and lows won't work if we deny the difficult aspects of our most intimate relationships. Our research and clinical experience have revealed that awareness and acceptance of our strong suits *and* vulnerabilities are the *sine qua non* of marital satisfaction. But awareness comes first. We must willingly take a hard though nonjudgmental look at our characteristics as couples. That enables us to pinpoint the trouble spots and then apply tested and proven methods for change, resolution, and healing. Thus we are saying that accurate diagnosis of relationship difficulties is a key first step of the relationship change process. This chapter will enable you to take a reading of where your relationship stands and set the stage for relationship change.

PREDICTING THE FUTURE OF A RELATIONSHIP

When couples reach the point where they are contemplating marriage or when they are having their first child, their relationship is generally happy and satisfying. The partners are optimistic about their future together. Sadly, about one in two of these couples will eventually lose their dream of long-term happiness by intensifying relationship tension and perhaps divorce.

We have conducted a series of studies in which we have observed and interviewed couples at two key early transition points: when they were planning marriage and when they were having their first child. We gathered lots of information on these couples right at the start of these major stages of the family life cycle.

Then, after letting time run its course, ten years in one study and five in another, we contacted the couples again to learn which ones stayed happy, which ones grew unhappy, and which ones split apart. Our question was simply: Now that we knew what happened to each couple, could we discover the subtle signs within the relationship that could foretell the ultimate outcome? The results across our studies have been remarkably consistent. The research revealed that it wasn't how much the partners loved each other or how good their sex lives were that was associated with future satisfaction.

Instead, as we noted earlier, our research showed that relationship happiness or downfall starts and ends with the precise manner in which couples discuss issues and handle conflict. Using our measures of the specific strategies each couple was using to handle conflict when we first met them, we were able to classify correctly, *with over 90 percent accuracy*, what group (happy versus unhappy or divorced) each couple fell into after five or ten years. It became evident that with successful discussion of disagreements partners grow confident of their abilities to tackle whatever is required of them to find mutual happiness. On the other hand, when disagreements lead to chronic fights and discord, partners become more pessimistic about their relationship and lose confidence in their ability to make the relationship work for them.

RELATIONSHIPS CHANGE OVER TIME

It is commonly believed by couples and therapists that relationship happiness peaks before marriage and steadily declines over time. Our research indicates this to be true only for couples who wind up divorced or chronically and severely distressed! Happy couples do experience shifts in satisfaction, but we did not find any steady decline over time. Our key point here is that change and adaptation are an important part of every successful relationship. Couples who fail to realize this are bound to react to any change as a disaster and the beginning of the end.

Instead of viewing problems as a relationship weakness that must be avoided at all costs, successful couples use relationship problems as signals of where to invest energy for change and adaptation. Ignore the signals by denial and withdrawal, or turn them into crises characterized by escalation and attack—and you have the recipe for marital distress.

Keep in mind that people do not fall out of love the way they do out of trees! Relationship decline is neither a sudden nor an inevitable process. When love and happiness do decline, it usually follows a steady and relentless erosion of satisfaction due to unbounded and destructive conflict. Our message is: You can stem the tide of erosion by learning to handle conflict constructively.

Previous research has indicated that husbands were happier with their marriages than wives, leading to the conclusion that marriage was better for men than women. Our long-term follow-up study of 135 premarital couples conducted during the 1980s and early 1990s allowed us to examine whether husbands tend to be more satisfied in marriage than wives. We found that women were more satisfied with their marriages than were the men at every point when we evaluated them—a contradiction of the previous findings of earlier researchers.

The relatively greater happiness of wives may reflect that the changing roles of women are providing them with opportunities to pursue careers and reduce dependence on their marriage. Also, bringing home the bacon is no longer the defining role of men in relationships. Today, men share child-rearing responsibilities, household chores, and give emotional support. These added contributions to the well-being of the couple may leave men feeling somewhat less satisfied—or at least confused—than in previous generations. Most importantly, these findings confirm that change and adaptation are a way of life. Men and women today will need to work hard to learn the special relationship skills required to negotiate successfully the challenges posed by these social and cultural changes.

Of course, whatever is happening in the culture at large, it's what's happening under our own roof that ultimately matters most. In this chapter, we offer you two relationship quizzes to help you identify your trouble spots and strong suits. You will learn how you typically communicate and how you handle conflict in relationships. You'll also learn whether your relationship is closer to the "better" or "worse" end of the marital spectrum and why. These quizzes will help you gauge where you stand in terms of the factors that predict future happiness. Their purpose is not to make you feel guilty or hopeless about your relationship problems.

Although it's possible that some people may feel guilty or upset when confronting relationship trouble spots directly, our goal is to help partners feel optimistic about improving their relationship and optimistic that they can prevent future problems. Hundreds of couples in our program have used similar quizzes to help unravel the seemingly tightest relationship knots. We will provide you with instructions on how to score the questionnaires and use the results to start building a better relationship.

The first questionnaire is called Predict and is based on our longitudinal research on the factors that predict future marital problems and divorce. We prepared the Predict questionnaire to help you take a peek at how the inevitable challenges that confront all relationships are experienced in your home. You will discover whether your typical responses to relationship conflict are more or less likely to lead to future difficulties. Predict will take you only a few minutes to complete, yet what you learn here can affect how you and your partner react to the very next disagreement that surfaces between you. Take the time now to complete the Predict questionnaire.

PREDICT

To complete this questionnaire, we first want you to recall recent conversations during which you talked about a disappointment, an annoyance, a problem, or a gripe. Determine whether each statement is a true or false description of your typical reactions during these types of discussions.

1. I sometimes nag at my partner in order to get him/her to talk.
   True_____ False_____
2. It is very easy for me to get angry at my partner.
   True_____ False_____
3. My partner does not try very hard to understand me.
   True_____ False_____
4. When my partner does something that makes me angry, I usually let him/her know about it.
   True_____ False_____
5. I often push my partner to talk about issues even when it is clear that my partner doesn't want to talk.
   True_____ False_____
6. I feel good after getting angry.
   True_____ False_____
7. If I had my choice I'd avoid conflicts and disagreements.
   True_____ False_____
8. When my partner brings up a relationship issue, I tend to withdraw, become silent, or refuse to discuss the matter further.
   True_____ False_____
9. I often find myself saying "I don't care. Whatever you want is fine with me" when I am asked for an opinion.
   True_____ False_____
10. I often agree with my partner's wishes just to end discussions.
    True_____ False_____
11. Sometimes I don't talk to my partner because I've noticed that talking leads to fighting.
    True_____ False_____
12. I often sit and stare at my partner, not saying anything.
    True_____ False_____
13. During problem discussions, my stomach often feels as if it's all tied up in knots.
    True_____ False_____

14. I often feel a lump in my throat when I argue with my partner.
    True_____ False_____
15. My body often becomes tense during a relationship problem discussion.
    True_____ False_____
16. My heart often speeds up or races during our conversation.
    True_____ False_____
17. I often feel very anxious at the start of a problem discussion.
    True_____ False_____
18. I would describe myself as very emotionally charged or tense whenever there is a major disagreement.
    True_____ False_____
19. I am basically unhappy with my relationship.
    True_____ False_____
20. I have often felt like leaving my partner.
    True_____ False_____
21. I often don't feel close to my partner.
    True_____ False_____
22. We hardly ever do any fun things together.
    True_____ False_____
23. I'm not sure I really love my partner anymore.
    True_____ False_____
24. I am not satisfied with our sex life.
    True_____ False_____
25. I often do not feel supported by my partner.
    True_____ False_____
26. At the beginning of most conversations about typical relationship problems, I believe that we will not be able to get close to a satisfying resolution.
    True_____ False_____
27. I have little confidence in being able to discuss a significant relationship problem with my partner without fighting.
    True_____ False_____
28. In five out of ten disagreements with my partner, I will be unable to make any headway in reaching a happy solution.
    True_____ False_____

Scoring Predict

There are actually five different scores we want you to find. Give yourself one point for each "true" and fill out the following table:

1. Tendency to pursue: Number of "true" statements in questions 1–6 _____
2. Tendency to withdraw: Number of "true" statements in questions 7–12 _____
3. Tendency toward arousal: number of "true" statements in questions 13–18 _____
4. Current unhappiness: number of "true" statements in questions 19–25 _____
5. Current expectations: number of "true" statements in questions 26–28 _____

How to Interpret Your Predict Scores

In his famous book *Anna Karenina*, Leo Tolstoy asserted that happiness in marriage comes in a only a few forms but that "every unhappy couple is different each in its own fashion." Our research has shown that Tolstoy was wrong! It is more accurate to say that marital distress comes in only a few forms whereas marital happiness is a many-splendored thing.

Your Predict scores will do three things. First, they will help you pinpoint your typical style of conflict interaction and allow you to determine if it places you at risk for relationship problems over time. Second, they will point out the contribution your body and mind—in terms of your level of arousal during conflict and your expectations for resolving conflict—are making to the long-term future of your relationship. And third, Predict lets you determine on which side of the "for better or for worse" balance your relationship currently falls.

Now we'll introduce you to the four styles of conflict interaction so you can determine which of these patterns are operating in your relationship. You will begin to see how long-term relationship happiness depends on the successful management of conflict and avoidance of these specific styles of destructive conflict management.

THE FOUR STYLES OF CONFLICT INTERACTION

Despite the positive *intent* that we know partners have when confronting relationship conflict (as we discuss in the next chapter), once conflict gets going it will leave partners feeling aroused and perhaps overwhelmed. When our emotions run high and our communication and conflict-resolution skills are low, we tend to handle marital disagreements the way people classically handle threats to security and well-being—we put up our fists to fight or we put on our running shoes to flee. In couples, there will always be two strategies that guide the response to conflict—his and hers.

If we consider the possible pairing of his and her strategies, we can summarize the four types of relationship conflict as follows:

Her Strategy	+	His Strategy	=	Relationship Conflict Type
Fight	+	Fight	=	Escalation
Flee	+	Flee	=	Withdrawal
Fight	+	Flee	=	Pursuit ↔ Withdrawal
Flee	+	Fight	=	Withdrawal ↔ Pursuit

When any one of these four conflict types becomes the standard way of reacting to disagreements, some relationship misery will occur over the long run. We count pursuit ↔ withdrawal patterns twice because couples function very differently depending on who is placed in which role, the man or the woman. In our experience, it is far more common to see female pursuers and male withdrawers than it is to see these positions reversed.

As long as one partner adopts one of these destructive strategies, the relationship will be placed at risk. Every couple from time to time may find themselves embroiled in an escalating fight, chilled by the emotional coolness created by mutual withdrawal, or maddeningly frustrated by the relationship tug-of-war that results when one partner pushes for peace through talk, and the other pushes for peace through avoidance of conflict.

Over time, if these patterns become ingrained, the couple will become *controlled* by their typical response to relationship disagreements. The pattern will seem to take on a life of its own. You may already have a strong sense of which strategy best describes your usual response to conflict. In the next section you can check out your guess by examining your answers to the Predict questionnaire.

Pursuit versus Withdrawal

Are you a relationship partner who often feels an urgency to express anger and deal with upsetting events sooner rather than later? Are you unable to leave a problem unsettled for even an hour, even if your partner is not interested in talking? If so, then you are using increasingly ineffective strategies to get your partner's attention. We call partners who engage in these type of behaviors "pursuers," or "escalators." If you answered true to four or more of Predict questions 1 through 6, then you are someone who tends to play the pursuer role when conflict occurs.

On the other hand, are you a partner who wishes to maintain peace and harmony above all else? Is it your tendency to see everything as a really small problem, so small that you feel it does not merit discussion? If so, then your overriding goal in relationships is to avoid conflict. We call partners who engage in these types of behavior "withdrawers." If you answered true to four or more of Predict questions 7 through 12, it is likely that you often withdraw when conflict occurs.

We call couples in which both partners rely on escalation as their typical response to conflict *explosive boilers.* By contrast, partners who rely on withdrawal as their typical response to relationship conflict are the *silent steamers.* When one partner tends toward escalation and the other tends toward withdrawal, the couple will join a group we call the *vicious cyclers.*

Explosive Boilers and Silent Steamers

If both partners in a couple are attacking and vigorous *pursuers,* the relationship will tend to be explosive and dissatisfying. Such partners are very good at speaking their minds, but they are not as good at listening. If you've ever participated in or observed a conversation with two speakers and no listeners, you know that communication is impossible in such circumstances. Relationships with two pursuers are characterized by patterns of attack and counterattack. We sometimes call these types of couples *explosive boilers.*

When Kenny and Beth first came in for help with their marriage, our staff quickly learned that they were explosive boilers. Their shouting match began as soon as they settled into their chairs, and it carried throughout the office suite. It rarely mattered what exactly they were yelling about. One day it was about mowing the grass, another it was about driving the kids to a birthday party, and on another day it was about vacation plans. Listening to Kenny and Beth was difficult, but it was clear that beneath their anger each person had something important to say. And although the therapist could read through their individual anger to discover the underlying caring and concern that each had for the other, what was really important was getting Beth and Kenny to experience the caring and concern directly. They learned to control their explosive tendencies during their therapy, and later they described the first part of therapy as having helped them install a volume-control knob that helped them listen to each other for the first time.

When both partners tend toward patterns of *withdrawal,* the relationship will be characterized by low levels of intimacy and fun. Just below the surface, an uneasy tension is ever present, and the partners invariably feel distant from each other. Often, withdrawn partners have a bit of a martyr complex. They derive strength from believing themselves "right" and their partners "wrong" for specific actions. Rather than work toward consensus, they would rather stew about how wronged they feel and how unjustly they are being treated. We call relationships characterized by mutual withdrawal the *silent steamers.*

Occasionally, a couple that is experienced in the art of explosive boiling realizes that their anger is not getting them anywhere. In their attempt to remedy this situation, the couple goes to the opposite extreme and enters the domain of the silent steamers. Dan and Paula were such a couple. Several times a week they would have a riotous fight with each other. Usually these fights had to do with Dan feeling unappreciated and Paula feeling criticized. The last fight we heard about started when Paula came into the kitchen, saw Dan doing the dishes, and asked him in an angry tone, "Don't you have anything better to do with your time?" Although the events sound innocent enough, Paula felt that Dan was redoing already clean dishes because he didn't like the way they were originally done, and Dan felt attacked because he was merely trying to do his fair share of housework.

Over the next few months, the couple evolved into silent steamers. The same events that previously triggered a riot, now triggered an icy cold distance. When Paula didn't get their car inspected as she had planned, Dan didn't talk to her for three days. When Dan painted the porch green instead of brown as Paula had expected, Paula went around the house slamming doors but never said anything to Dan. The strength that Paula and Dan had was in trying to work on their difficulties. They learned the hard way that neither explosive boiling nor silent steaming were up to the task of dealing with their differences. In therapy, Dan and Paula came to understand the source of each other's anger, and they learned new tools to settle their disagreements constructively.

In addition to your Predict scores, you can also gauge if your relationship is characterized by explosive boiling, silent steaming, or some healthy middle ground, simply by looking over the following descriptions. Explosive boilers:

- Argue about the same things over and over again, but get nowhere.
- Have discussions that often get out of control and leave both partners angrier than when they started.
- Are seldom able to reach satisfying resolutions about common issues (e.g., money, household tasks).
- Have repetitious fights about "stupid little things."

By contrast, silent steamers:

- Rarely if ever express their negative feelings to each other.
- Seldom fight, but instead live with constant tension.

- Often feel that they are walking on eggshells.
- Typically brush issues under the rug rather than face them.

If you don't fall squarely into either camp, you may be among those fortunate individuals who have learned to express personal gripes, disagreements, disappointments, and needs in appropriate ways that do not foster blame and alienation. These healthy methods of conflict management increase the chance of finding satisfying resolutions while maintaining balance in the relationship.

More often than not, relationships are paralyzed by the presence of one pursuer and one withdrawer. In this unfortunate but all-too-common combination, both partners feel that they have a right to their own particular style of coping with conflict, and neither wants to compromise. Such relationships are like democracies that don't work. Each partner has one opposite vote for every matter requiring action, and so the result is relationship gridlock.

When Pursuers and Withdrawers Meet: Vicious Cyclers

In our culture, although it is true that females often play the role of pursuer and males the role of withdrawer, the gender linkage to these roles isn't at the heart of the matter we want to discuss at this point. What is very important to realize is that these roles feed off each other. There can be no pursuer without a withdrawer, and there will be nothing to withdraw from if there is no pursuit. Put them together and you have a system spiraling out of control. When one person in a couple pursues and the other withdraws, the pursuer is likely to step on the accelerator and become increasingly more aggressive or attacking. The withdrawer is now even more likely to shut down and avoid conflict. As a result, the conversation tends to escalate into battle, especially if the withdrawer feels cornered and then begins to counterattack. Thus, couples who get stuck in pursuit/withdrawal are likely to exhibit patterns of escalation and arousal similar to explosive boilers.

PURSUIT ↔ WITHDRAWAL

Withdrawers often feel betrayed by their partners. They cannot understand why their partner gets upset by the "little" things that they have decided to let slide by them. In fact, however, withdrawers rarely if ever find any problem big enough to discuss. Peter, a thirty-year-old medical resident, felt he was always doing something wrong in the eyes of his wife, Jean. After stopping at Food Mart on the way home from the hospital to pick up a few groceries that Jean had asked him to get, he received the following greeting when Jean saw the Food Mart bags: "Why didn't you go to Safeway?" Peter was irritated, but he didn't say anything. After dinner, he decided to wash clothes piled in the hamper and loaded up the washing machine with whites and some Wisk. When he came up from the basement, Jean said, "I hope you didn't use the Wisk; I've been using the powdered Tide now." Again, Peter walked away without saying anything. But now he was fuming inside. Jean followed him into the living room and asked him, "What's wrong?" Peter continued his journey and headed for his den, acting as if he hadn't heard her. Jean exploded, "Why don't you just talk to me for once?" He parried, "Leave me alone!" Heading for the den, Peter popped some Rolaids and stifled his anger toward Jean.

When Peter began having an affair, Jean was completely stunned and through her tears cried, "But you never even said anything was bothering you." Shortly after Jean discovered Peter's affair, the couple entered our program to work on their marriage.

We told Jean that it was Peter's responsibility to express his irritations to her. By relentlessly pursuing him—continuing to ask what's wrong and trying to get him to talk—she actually accomplished the opposite of what she wanted: his continued withdrawal. We told Peter that by avoiding conflict, he was hurting himself and the relationship. We also stressed that by withdrawing, he, too, was accomplishing the opposite of what he wished for. Instead of avoiding conflict, he was participating in a cycle that always yielded arguments. After they learned our rules for conflict management, Peter started to withdraw less and Jean started to pursue less, resulting in more constructive discussions and a return to days of greater harmony.

The curious thing about pursuit and withdrawal is that in their nonextreme form, each tendency is actually very positive. For a relationship to be successful, issues must be discussed but not escalate into fights. If neither partner ever exhibited some degree of pursuit, then issues would never get discussed. If neither partner ever exhibited some degree of withdrawal, then neither person would be able to restrain his or her emotions and relationship discussions might quickly turn ugly. In general, when high levels of pursuit *or* withdrawal are present, relationships will suffer.

Withdrawal ↔ Pursuit

Ginny and Hank both worked for local government, and each supervised three people below them. One of the things that really confused them was the contrast between their relationship with co-workers and their relationship with each other. At work, everything seemed to go smoothly with their staffs working together as a team. But at home, day-to-day living was punctuated by long bouts of tension and open warfare. Weekends were the worst. One weekend in June, Hank was in the den paying bills and Ginny was gardening. Hank saw a couple of charges on the Visa bill that he did not recognize and went out to the garden to ask Ginny about them. Ginny said she didn't remember the exact charges but she was sure they were right. So far, so good. Hank asked again, "Come on, you must remember a $123 charge to Sears." Ginny didn't look up from her gardening. Hank walked up closer and repeated himself, "One hundred and twenty-three dollars? Sears?" Ginny looked up at Hank but didn't say anything. She went back to pulling weeds. Hank walked back to the den, looked at the checkbook, and stomped back out to the garden to try to engage Ginny one more time. When she saw him coming, she stood up, walked past him into the house, and slammed the door behind her. Hank followed, yelling "Don't run away from me. We said we'd talk these things out. Come back here. Ginny, I can't take this." By then, Ginny was locked in their bedroom where she stayed for the next three hours.

Ginny and Hank were a little unusual in that they were each very adept at both pursuit and withdrawal. In the above conflict, Hank played pursuer to Ginny's withdrawal, but often it was Ginny who was in pursuit. To help them avoid their destructive conflict patterns, we first taught them to recognize how they repeatedly brought to life the roles of pursuer and withdrawer. They were soon able to see that despite variations in role and problem area, the underlying pattern of pursuit and withdrawal was the same. Using our Better Talk program presented later in part 3, Ginny and Hank learned how to use regular "Couple Meetings" to discuss any concern that mattered to either of them. This structure works to disrupt the pursuit-withdrawal cycle because it guarantees the pursuer that his or her concerns will be listened to and the withdrawer that discussions will not escalate into a loud brawl.

WHAT'S INSIDE COUNTS, TOO

If you find yourself among the ranks of pursuers or among the legions of withdrawers, and yet you are very satisfied in a long-term relationship, the reason may be that you are nonreactive to relationship conflicts. Most pursuers and withdrawers are quite uncomfortable when they anticipate a conflict or find themselves embroiled in one. The discomfort of conflict includes a response from our sensitive nervous system that is often experienced as "arousal." The arousal may be felt as a racing heart, sweaty palms, a tense stomach, or even shortness of breath. Different people will experience different bodily reactions, but all of them represent arousal.

If you answered true to three or more of Predict questions 13 through 18, then you are likely to be physiologically aroused when you discuss problems with your partner or argue. This arousal is a sign that past conversations have not gone well and a fear that future discussions will end in a fight. High scores are a warning sign of future relationship difficulties. If partners are aroused when they discuss salient relationship issues, they will find it difficult to work as a team.

From time to time, we all get aroused during relationship discussions. But constant arousal during sensitive efforts toward conflict management becomes totally counterproductive. Imagine being in the unfortunate situation of watching an eye surgeon performing a very delicate operation on someone you love. The surgery has been in progress for some time, and the surgeon's steady hands are working diligently to repair the eye. While watching the operation, you overhear two people talk about the surgeon and learn that she holds some political views that are diametrically opposed to yours. You're so offended by her views that your heart starts to race with anger, a sure sign of arousal. At this time, would you run into the operating room to berate the surgeon and question the legitimacy of her political outlook? Of course not. You have control over your emotions and would not risk the eyesight of your loved one by venting your anger. Nor should you let arousal get the better of you during delicate attempts to resolve conflict with your mate.

Some people constantly risk the future of their relationship by creating conditions that promote arousal in themselves or in their partner. This arousal must be controlled, and it takes teamwork to accomplish it. The teamwork must create a safe and encouraging environment for working on conflict so that pursuers can feel that there is engagement and so that withdrawers can feel that peace will be maintained. We will give you the tools to implement these changes in chapter 7.

LOW EXPECTATIONS, DASHED HOPES

In relationships characterized by chronic patterns of pursuit, withdrawal, or arousal, partners begin to expect the worst. On the other hand, when couples believe they can change these patterns, they've taken a big leap toward transformation. Jackie Gleason, the famous comedian, once said that good comedy is 10 percent skill and 90 percent confidence. Athletes know that the "mental game" is at least as important as the physical game at the top levels of performance. The same is true for relationships. Partners' faith in their abilities to talk about important relationship issues without the talk turning into a fight is crucial to relationship well-being in the present and the future.

Questions 26 through 28 tap into your expectations for being able to discuss relationship issues in a mutually satisfying manner. If you answered two or more of these questions true, you currently expect most discussions to turn into a fight. These expectations can turn into a self-fulfilling prophecy and guarantee the very outcomes that you don't want. Left unchecked, these negative expectancies predict declines in relationship satisfaction over time. These negative expectations may also go hand in hand with bodily arousal. If you expect problems to increase rather than decrease through discussion, it is no wonder that you begin to get aroused just anticipating the dreaded conversation. These are more trouble-signs of a relationship headed toward increasing dissatisfaction.

Janice and Quinn began therapy by filling out a form similar to Predict. From their answers, it was obvious that they had very low expectations for being able to discuss their disagreements in a way that brought them closer together rather than pushed them further apart. One of their big disagreements had to do with the family budget. Janice felt she had no money to spend on clothes for the kids, and Quinn felt Janice was spending beyond their means. When they were asked to show us what a typical discussion about the family budget was like, they each threw up their hands and said, "Why bother." When partners in a couple feel hopeless right at the start of the conversation, this despair will guarantee a disappointing outcome. One of the characteristics of these types of arguments is that both partners listen more to the voice inside their heads speaking of hopelessness and despair than they do the actual voice of their partner, which often speaks of reason and hope. The best way to build positive expectations is to experience success. Janice and Quinn learned and practiced the skills discussed in chapter 8 of this book and finally were able to have problem discussions about money that were free of conflict. As a result, their confidence soared at being able to tackle any disagreement that arose between them.

FOR BETTER OR FOR WORSE

By now you can see that pursuit, withdrawal, arousal, and low expectations are all signs of relationship difficulties. To take a reading of how these tendencies fit together, we have included questions 19 through 26 in Predict. These questions determine if your relationship is closer to the "better" side of the relationship balance or to the "worse" side. Politicians often ask voters the question: Are you better off now than you were four years ago? This is also an important question for partners to ask themselves. If you've answered five or more of questions 19 through 26 true, then your relationship tends toward the worse side of "for better or for worse," suggesting that you are not communicating effectively. If you've answered fewer than five of these questions true, you are currently communicating and managing conflict well in your relationship. If this happiness is maintained with few significant lapses into pursuit or withdrawal, slight arousal, and a strong belief in your ability to resolve relationship difficulties, then you have built a solid foundation for the relationship. You can use this book to fortify that foundation and turn a good relationship into a great one. If you currently lack a solid relationship foundation, this book will help you construct one that will allow you to build a stable and satisfying relationship over time.

Targeting the Issues in Your Relationship

Now that you have had the opportunity to identify your style of handling conflict, your tendency to get aroused, and your expectation level for discussions, as well as the degree to which your relationship is "for better or for worse," you are ready to take a look at the issues about which you and your partner typically disagree.

THE RELATIONSHIP ISSUES PLANNER (RIP)

The Relationship Issues Planner (RIP) is based on our longitudinal research on the problem areas that couples typically encounter *over time* in their relationship. We've concluded that *all* relationships must deal with certain issues that stem from living together. By completing our second questionnaire, you will be able to identify which issues you and your partner currently are facing and the extent to which they are problem areas. Later on, we will ask you to rank-order your issues from low to high conflict. When you start our Better Talk program, you will begin by dealing with your low-conflict issues and work your way up through your list to your most difficult problem areas.

You may be wondering why we have couples in experiments talk about high-conflict areas but direct couples to start working out issues with low conflict. In research, studying couples under high-conflict conditions reveals the most about their ingrained interaction styles. However, couples are best able to change these styles when they first experience success learning new skills under low-conflict conditions. Once learned, the skills can be generalized to higher-conflict issues.

Completing the RIP

Listed below are the common relationship issues that most couples will encounter from time to time over the course of the relationship. You can write out the list on a separate sheet of paper. Please rate how much of a problem each issue is by writing in a number from 0 to 10 next to it. A 0 would indicate that the issue is not at all a current problem for you, whereas a 10 would indicate that the issue is a severe current problem. (A 3 would indicate that the issue is somewhat of a problem, whereas a 7 would indicate that the issue is quite a bit of a problem.) If you wish to add other areas not included in our list, please do so. Examples of other issues that partners have noted include: sleep habits, illness, and life priorities. Partners should fill out the RIP separately and not discuss any of the issues before completing their own ratings.

PROBLEM AREA

Alcohol and drugs
Careers
Children (or potential children)
Communication
Friends
Home chores
Money
Recreation

Relatives

Religion

Sex

Other_____

RESEARCH ON RELATIONSHIP ISSUES: WHAT DO COUPLES IN AMERICA FIGHT ABOUT?

After completing your RIP you may be wondering how you compare to other couples. We have found that both happy and unhappy couples say they are struggling with the same issues; however, the struggles differ greatly in intensity and frequency. This is another example of how differences between partners are just not as important as how those differences are handled. Let's see what issues are at the top of partners' lists, and see how these issues vary over the course of the relationship.

Money—The Root of Many Struggles

You probably won't be surprised to learn that our research has found that money is the number-one issue among married couples. Money is followed by a tie between communication and sex. For some couples, communication is number two and sex number three whereas for others sex is number two and communication number three. We initially hypothesized that money would only be a problem for couples struggling to make ends meet. We learned that this was not so when we took into account how much money people had. Regardless of income levels, money was still the number-one issue.

There are several reasons why money is the number-one problem for couples. First, couples are constantly faced with financial decisions. Some of these decisions are everyday, minor ones; others are long-range, life-altering ones. And many of us know firsthand how times of financial stress can strain even the strongest relationship.

A second reason that money is the most important problem for couples is that it is an arena in which many hidden issues are played out, unbeknownst to the couple. These issues usually involve power, control, status, and influence. For example, in Bob and Linda's relationship, Bob was not only the primary wage earner, he was also the money manager in the family. On the surface Linda accepted this arrangement, but over the years she developed a great deal of resentment toward him. This hostility existed because of the way the arrangement played out. When he wanted to buy new work tools, that was okay; but when she wanted to spend money on clothes, she felt disapproved of and monitored. The hidden issue was one of power and control and, until therapy, they did not deal with it directly. With some guidance, Linda was able to let Bob know how strongly she felt controlled by him and how powerless she felt when it came to spending money. We helped Bob listen to Linda's concerns and understand how hurt she felt when he challenged her purchases. Together they worked out a satisfactory budget for personal purchases that would guarantee Linda's participation in family monetary affairs and grant both of them freedom to spend money as each saw fit so long as it stayed within their agreed-upon budget.

Communication and Sex over Time

Our research has shown that the issues that afflict *married* couples tend to remain stable over time: couples tend to be affected by the same issues whether they've been married for ten years or two. This finding should tell you that once a problem is present in a relationship, it is unlikely to go away by itself.

In contrast to married couples, however, problem areas *do* change over time from the engagement period to early marriage. The major problem for premarital couples, like married couples, is money. However, communication and sex are not major issues before marriage.

Why do communication and sex jump from being very low to very high problem areas on couples' problem lists after marriage? Pleasurable sex and satisfying communication are two of the major reasons that couples decide to marry and are a joyous part of the early stages of a relationship. When couples in therapy go back to this stage, they often talk about how easy it was to communicate with the other person: "We were able to share things that we never could share with other people." They recall how much fun they had together, and how the sexual, sensual part of their relationship was natural and always pleasurable. Even the most distressed spouses in therapy can reminisce about this period in the relationship and suddenly show a warmth and kindness toward each other that may have been long absent from the relationship.

Box 3.1
Rediscovering Romance

Think back to the first time in your relationship when you experienced a special joy with your partner. The first time you talked till the early hours of the morning, had a romantic dinner together, explored each other's bodies, took a trip together, or walked hand in hand and it didn't matter where you were or where you were going. As you recall these times, think about how you behaved toward your partner—how you looked at each other, what you were thinking, how you spoke, and how polite you were. During this period of getting to know him or her, you were most likely very considerate, unlikely to start an argument even with cause, and very likely to be kind, gentle, and romantic. Those actions are what made those times so special; and even though the two of you may have been through a lot together since, you can still rekindle the feelings from the courtship. We would like you to try a little exercise in reliving an afternoon, evening, or perhaps even a day from those times.

Ask your partner out on a "date into the past" with the understanding that each of you will strive in your own way to re-create the feelings of romance from a special time in the relationship. If this exercise seems impossible to you now, that's okay. Some couples have built up so much anger that they cannot set it aside even for a few hours. If that is you, you will need to work first to reduce the anger. Continue reading through part 1 of this book and begin to work through the exercises in part 2. When you are ready, return to this exercise and see if you and your partner can rediscover, even if only for a few hours, the romance that brought you together.

Jealousy

In contrast to sex and communication problems, which rise over time in intensity, jealousy is the number-two problem for dating and engaged couples but drops toward the end of the list after marriage. The rise and fall of jealousy reflect the struggles that dating couples often have forming a "couple identity." Part of this process involves making a commitment to one person, and partners often move at different paces through this process, sparking issues of jealousy.

Karen and Ron met in a continuing-education class at a local college and became engaged after dating for three months. They were very excited about planning a small wedding for the following June, but the issue of jealousy soon reared its ugly head and disrupted these plans. During the first six months of their engagement, they frequently found themselves in the middle of arguments that usually began when Ron contacted a former girlfriend. Karen could not understand why Ron continued to call former girlfriends on their birthdays. Ron felt that he had a right to talk to whomever he wished and he was not willing to give up these calls to women he considered his friends. Karen suspected that there was something more going on and was puzzled why Ron never called his male friends on their birthdays. In our program, Ron discovered that his calls to ex-girlfriends were motivated by his desire to keep these past relationships alive and by his need to retain a sense of independence from Karen. We helped Ron and Karen discuss and settle this issue. Karen acknowledged that Ron had a reasonable desire to maintain some independent friendships outside of the marriage and Ron acknowledged that he had a responsibility to make sure that these friendships never crossed over very specific boundaries (e.g., Ron would keep no secrets from Karen and Ron would never consent to any sexual intimacies with a former girlfriend). We agreed to revisit this issue if it surfaced again in the future, but it never did. June came and they were joined by their immediate family and a few close friends, to become happily married in an intimate ceremony in the mountains of Colorado.

Children

Contrary to popular belief, children (or decisions about having children) is not rated as one of the major issues that couples face and argue about. Typically, couples rate children as a middle-level problem (4 or 5 on inventories like the RIP). We find that couples are able to work better as a *team* when dealing with issues having to do with children, than when dealing with other issues.

Connie and Paul's eight-year-old daughter Claire was healthy, bright, articulate, full of energy, and simply refused to keep her room tidy. Although both Connie and Paul felt that Claire was old enough to assume responsibilities around the house, including keeping her room clean, they disagreed on strategies to accomplish this common goal. Connie felt that Claire should simply be told to clean up her room and punished if she failed to obey. Paul believed that his daughter was old enough to do it by herself, and he feared that Connie's plan would continue the frequent squabbles that he wanted to avoid. After talking about this problem in therapy, Paul and Connie realized that their goals for Claire were nearly identical. To accomplish their common goals, they agreed to a plan that involved creating a "star chart" for Claire. During a family meeting, they told Claire how important it was to them that she clean up her room every day and to do so without being asked. They proposed that they would check her room after dinner each night and if it was clean, they would thank her for doing her chore and paste a big star for the day on a calendar that was kept in her room. If it was not clean, she would simply be told that she'd get no star for the day. After every ten stars were earned, Connie was able to trade them in for a little present or a special outing. Connie and Paul reported that in just two weeks, Claire was straightening her room on most nights and was enjoying having control over her ability to earn stars for special rewards. Connie and Paul were delighted that a frequent source of family tension had ended.

Relatives

One of the surprises from our research on marital problems is that relatives, a group that many people believe are a major source of conflict in marriage, actually represent a mid-level problem. As with many problem areas, issues revolving around relatives usually come up at predictable times of the year, such as holidays and vacations.

David and Elaine were dreading their upcoming vacation. When asked why, it turned out that they always took one week of their two-week vacation and spent it with his family, who lived near a mountain resort. His mother and Elaine would frequently argue about what activities they should engage in, with Elaine feeling that she had no input or control, particularly when it involved the children's plans. David's retort was always that his mother was old and set in her ways, and that she had been trying to take control of situations for as long as he could remember. This attitude came across to Elaine as if her husband were siding with his mother, and this provoked major conflicts between them.

We decided to do some anticipatory planning, given that they knew the dynamics of this particular issue. It was clear that David was trying to play the role of mediator between his mother and his wife, and was feeling that he was in a "no-win" situation. By doing this and putting himself in a referee position, he was not siding with his wife, which was what she really wanted. We suggested that David abandon his "no-win" role of referee and join with his wife, at least by listening supportively to her concerns. Once he did, the relationship dynamics changed and David was able to let Elaine know that he more or less agreed with her feelings about the intractability of Grandma's behavior. Once they started working together as a team, David and Elaine were able to generate a whole set of potential solutions to the problem. In fact, the teamwork and consensual solutions brought about greater closeness between them.

DEVELOPING A PERSONAL PROBLEM PLAN (PPP)

One of the most important uses for the Relationship Issues Planner is to help you develop a set of priorities for tackling difficulties in the relationship. We call this set of priorities your Personal Problem Plan, or your PPP. You now know the problem areas that most couples find difficult, but there will be many readers with different lists. We want you to work with your own unique ratings of each relationship issue. More specifically, we would like you to work with the unique list that develops from rank-ordering your own responses.

Here is how to develop your PPP. Based on your RIP scores, rank-order the problems from 1 to 10—1 being most intense to 10 being the least intense. Some of the issues toward the bottom of your list may be marked with zeros, indicating they are not at all currently conflict issues in the relationship (although they may have been in the past). For example, Elaine's (from our last case history) problem list and rankings looked like this:

Issue Area	RIP Score	Rank Order
In-laws	10	1
Money	9	2
Communication	9	2
Sex	6.5	4
Jealousy	5	5
Recreation	3	6
Household chores	3	6
Children	2	8
Alcohol and drugs	0	9
Religion	0	9
Career	0	9

The last three would all be tied for last place.

When you are doing this with your partner, you should compare your individual RIP scores and come up with a PPP for the relationship. You can do this by reserving about fifteen minutes for a discussion at a time when you know you won't be interrupted and can devote your full attention to this task. Sit down with each of your lists and come up with a joint list that describes the order of problems in the relationship that you both agree on. If there are some areas that you absolutely cannot agree on, enter these onto a special list and keep at the task of developing a joint ranking list.

As you read and work your way through this book, we will ask you to use your PPP to identify the topics you will talk about with your partner. We want you to start talking about issues near the bottom of the list as you learn and practice new skills for talking about relationship problems. We will help you understand why the skills are important and give you explicit instructions on how to implement them.

When you successfully master the skills at low levels of conflict, we will have you gradually move up your list to start tackling the major issues that are robbing your relationship of happiness and stability.

Resist the notion that it is silly to work on minor problems when "major" problems cry out for your attention. When you start with issues high in conflict intensity, it is hard suddenly to engage new skills, manage arousal, and avoid old habits like pursuit and withdrawal. When it comes time to confront the deeper issues facing the relationship, it is desirable to be buoyed by hope and the sense of accomplishment that follows from successfully tackling the smaller issues first.

Predict AND RIP TOGETHER

Now let us introduce you to Betty and Phil. Their story illustrates how Predict and RIP can be used in tandem to help couples set goals for relationship improvement. Betty and Phil came to therapy because Betty had found out that Phil was having an affair. The other woman, Alice, had called Betty at home to tell her. Betty felt betrayed; she felt that affairs were things that happened to other couples, not to her and Phil. However, upon reflection, she knew something was very wrong with their relationship. Looking back over the last months, Betty remembered that Phil had been working late more often, had a new style of haircut, and had bought a set of new clothes. He also had been more distant with her. The distance itself was not surprising because during the last three years, they had grown increasingly far apart, particularly after the birth of their first child.

Phil's affair began the way so many affairs do. He was not actively looking for an alternative partner but became acquainted with Alice over a period of months after seeing her frequently at work. The fun talks and positive times that he began having with Alice stood in sharp contrast with the distance, hostility, and lack of sexual closeness that he had been increasingly experiencing with Betty.

As with many couples in this situation (although certainly not all), Phil interpreted his affair as at least partially due to the distress in his marital relationship that had developed since the birth of their first child three years earlier. As we found out in our history of the couple, the early signs of marital conflict were present even sooner. To help us (and them) assess the degree of distress and the core issues in the relationship, the couple completed the Predict and RIP question-naires.

On the Predict inventory, Betty answered "true" to most of the questions on the pursuit scale and Phil answered "true" to most on the withdraw scale. This suggested that Betty and Phil were caught in the pursuit ↔ withdraw cycle. The arousal scale showed that Phil was clearly very aroused by conflict, and, although Betty tended to be less so, she was still aware of changes in her body brought on by distress. Neither expected to get anywhere when they discussed important relationship issues. Both scored at the very low end of the "for better or for worse" scale.

These diagnostic findings provided a picture of a relationship in trouble—and these were patterns that had not developed overnight.

Their high scores on the pursuit ↔ withdrawal scales were indicative of the fact that the more Betty pushed her case for communication, the more Phil would withdraw in order to attempt to manage conflict. And while Betty felt that Phil was coldly ignoring her, the arousal scale indicated that he was actually heated up inside. He cared about her and the issues they were facing, but he handled his arousal differently than she managed hers—he turned inward, while she turned outward. Their low scores on the expectations for resolution scale indicated that they hardly ever talked about their problems, because they were so fearful of a fight breaking out. Over time, they argued more, talked less, and each became very dissatisfied with their relationship. Consistent with his tendency to withdraw, Phil's affair was a destructive way of han-dling the problems inherent in their relationship.

Even before the affair, Betty and Phil were clearly dissatisfied with their marriage, and they needed to take some steps to get it back on track. As is the case for many couples, the affair was a *symptom* of a floundering relationship—and made a bad situation even worse.

The problem list filled out by Betty and Phil indicated that her issues were communication (10), money (8), and sex (8); his were money (7), sex (5), and recreation (4), with communication (3) being number 4. Even though Phil began to have an affair and was obviously unhappy with his marriage, his RIP ratings were slightly lower than Betty's. This is very common, and it went along with Phil's withdrawing tendencies and his need to minimize conflict, even if it meant losing motivation to have his needs met in the relationship. Betty and Phil's PPP included communication, money, recreation, and sex.

During one of their first therapy sessions, Betty and Phil separately completed a brief questionnaire that we use to determine which goals they each wanted to work on first. Because their RIP ratings could have taken us in several different directions, we wanted to see what Betty and Phil's priorities were for starting therapy. Phil's primary goal for therapy was to stop fighting with Betty, whereas Betty's first was to talk more and to feel understood. Phil's second goal was to feel closer to Betty, and her second goal was to fight less. If you ignore the ordering of their respective goals, their top two goals for therapy were in perfect agreement. Phil and Betty were very surprised to learn how close their goals were, and a new sense of optimism emerged about the possibilities for working things out.

This situation is also indicative of a very important factor: Joint goal setting for the relationship is essential as a first step in diffusing conflict. Unfortunately, many couples do not get past arguing about their *primary* goals and thus get stuck on their differences instead of discovering their commonalities. Typically, women come to us with their primary desire being more communication, whereas men come in with their primary desire being less fighting. As in the case of Betty and Phil, the second major goal for most women is less fighting and the second major goal for most men is better communication. However, when push comes to shove, as it often does in relationship conflicts, each person lobbies hard for his or her top priority or goal.

By giving Betty and Phil information on their communication patterns, each other's problem list, and by having them talk about their goals for their relationship, we were able to start the process of relationship change. We helped them see that even though their conflict-management styles and priorities may have differed, better communication and decreased conflict were both very important to each of them. In this context, it was also important for them to share their common desire for enhancement of the positive side of their relationship, a side that had eroded over time. Both Betty and Phil wanted more intimacy, fun, sex, and romance.

As they came to understand the causes of their relationship difficulties and realized that they had a large degree of overlap among their goals, they were ready to work together to begin to communicate and resolve conflicts more effectively. They could begin to build on their similarities and to handle their differences.

FROM INSIGHT TO CHANGE

Like Betty and Phil, you can use the questionnaires in this chapter to help you pinpoint your typical responses to relationship conflict. Predict and RIP will also help guide you through the exercises that appear throughout this book. If you read but did not complete the questionnaires in this chapter, now would be a good time to complete Predict and RIP. Remember, the questionnaires will help you to identify relationship issues that are appropriate for beginning work as opposed to those that are too hot to handle. As you learn to recognize the "fight potential" that lies hidden in a problem area, you move a step closer to learning how to master current—and prevent future—relationship difficulties.

No matter where you came out on Predict and RIP, this information is essential for making your relationship the best it can be. We have yet to find a couple whose problem areas were too severe or whose style of conflict resolution was too troublesome to benefit from our program.

Having completed Predict and RIP, you are armed with precise diagnostic information on the strengths and weaknesses in your relationship. In the next four chapters we will help you gain an in-depth understanding of the fuel that maintains your particular conflict-resolution strategies, and then we will begin to show you how to convert this fuel into the energy you need to transform your relationship into the one you want.

In the next chapter, we introduce a model that we've developed to help couples start the process of dealing with disagreements more constructively. Through it, you will learn how to understand your partner's intentions better and to read each other more accurately.

Chapter 4

FOR RICHER OR POORER—YOUR RELATIONSHIP BANK ACCOUNT

IN OUR view, past efforts to search for the key causes of relationship problems have been misdirected. The spotlight of psychotherapy often focuses on the area of partner choice and the fact that there are always unconscious factors that help to determine whom we select. The process of uncovering these "keys" can sometimes be illuminating. But, in our experience, it has been far more fruitful to improve the communication process with the partner we have selected (for whatever reasons) than to find new partners. Hence, in this chapter we focus not on our reasons for picking our mates, but rather on how we can overcome our inevitable differences.

This is very good news for couples. If you believe that partner choice is the most important ingredient of a happy relationship, then the only way to remedy serious problems is to change your partner's personality traits (an endeavor doomed to failure), or to initiate a breakup/divorce and start again. Yet, even that strategy doesn't seem to work out very well—the rates of divorce are 10 percent higher for remarriages than first marriages. On the other hand, communication processes *can* be changed and once changed can lead to happier and more satisfying relationships. Our simple truth #4 (see chapter 2)—the fact that it's not the differences between partners that cause problems but how these differences are handled—should be a source of hope.

Nevertheless, partners often come to us with the mistaken belief that similarity with their mates is the basis for success. When we *ask* partners why they selected the person they decided to marry, we hear the following reasons:

- Physical attraction
- Enjoying being with each other
- Having fun together
- Being in love with the other person
- Having a lot in common with each other
- Feeling ready to be married
- Feeling at ease being with each other

A powerful force underlying much of this list is the role of *perceived* similarity. Partners often think someone they love is similar to them, whether or not this is objectively true. In fact, perceived similarity is much more important than actual similarity in terms of whom we choose to marry.

Why? Because when faced with reality, the perceived similarity quickly wears thin and couples are faced with differences that they are often unprepared to handle. *Then the true test of the relationship begins.* So often we hear couples say that after marriage things that were not problems earlier suddenly became issues. A wife who did not previously complain about the amount of time her husband spent watching television—particularly sports—suddenly finds herself feeling terribly annoyed. The new husband, in turn, is unpleasantly startled by his wife's criticisms and wonders what became of the pleasant companion who used to watch television with him. Thus, *the factors that bring people together, that determine whom we select as our life partners, are not good predictors of how the relationship will develop over time.*

We suggest a way of thinking about relationship development that focuses on the key factors that *do* predict the future of the relationship—the actual and perceived qualities of the interactions between partners. Again, the best way to handle differences—the key to relationship happiness—is to enhance communication and understanding. So, keep in mind that although you can never change your partner's personality *directly*, you *can* change how you and your partner communicate. This in turn can lead to changes in your partner's personality, in you, and in the relationship.

The first step toward better talking and listening is to use a new research-based model that we've developed called the "relationship bank account."

YOUR RELATIONSHIP BANK ACCOUNT

Like any bank, the balance in your relationship bank account is constantly changing with deposits and withdrawals. A deposit in the relationship bank account can consist of anything from a little act of kindness to a grand gesture of love and affection, or anything in between. Withdrawals can be small, like those associated with a little annoyance or irritation, or large, like those following a serious and unresolved fight. But in general, emotional deposits and withdrawals are made up of little exchanges. Each day, partners add to and subtract from their account balance through their interactions with each other.

The bank account metaphor not only instructs you to make more deposits, it also helps you learn how to identify *attempted* deposits, how to avoid withdrawals, and heightens awareness of your "overall account balance"—an index of how happy you are in your relationship at any given time. Moreover, the model helps you better understand your mate's intentions and enables you to read each other more accurately. This will serve to increase the chances of attempted deposits making it into the account and potential withdrawals remaining in the account, drawing interest.

On any day, the greater the balance in your account, the "healthier" the bank. Happy relationship partners are backed by a strong relationship bank with healthy reserves, whereas unhappy partners struggle to make relationship ends meet with no resources left in the relationship bank.

Most couples (at least those who marry for love, and that is most of us) start the relationship off with a sizable deposit. Acts of love, both major and minor, are plentiful. However, the currency might be inflated by idealization, by being "in love with love," and by powerful sexual attraction. This can lead to letdowns when, later on, the "currency" deflates and expectations decline.

As with a real bank, the relationship bank must deal with different currencies—his and hers. Because the two currencies may have different valuations, and each may fluctuate from day to day, the value of any deposit or withdrawal at any given time is always set by the "teller"—the receiving partner.

Joe and Donna are a couple with a healthy relationship who have kept the currency alive, the deposits flowing, and the withdrawals limited. They liked to surprise each other frequently with little acts of thoughtfulness. One week, Joe got up early every morning to make breakfast. Another week, he arranged to bring Donna's car in for inspection so that she would not have to take time off to get it done. Donna realized Joe was having a hard week at work and so decided one Thursday night to make one of his favorite dishes, a lamb curry. Another time, Donna beat Joe to the weekly task of mowing the lawn. He usually did it, but neither of them enjoyed yard work. Donna and Joe acknowledged each other's "deposits" and appreciated their partner's caring.

Donna and Joe also had sufficient "reserves" that enabled them to maintain good balances despite occasional difficulties. In relationships without sufficient reserves, frequent withdrawals might lead to a "run" on the relationship bank account.

Kathy and Luke are a young, troubled couple whose constant quarrels have depleted their bank account. During a lull between one of their frequent marital storms, Luke and Kathy tried very hard to repair the damages done to their relationship. Kathy went to the Hallmark shop in the mall and bought a card that said "Even though these have been rough times, I still love you." Luke went to the flower shop and bought one red rose and wrote on the card "I hate it when we fight—let's have a nice dinner tonight and go out to the movies afterward." They exchanged gifts that afternoon and made love for the first time in months.

However, on the way to dinner, Kathy asked Luke to slow down and drive more carefully. Luke heard Kathy's request as a criticism, starting boiling inside, and drove even faster. Then Luke almost collided with a truck and Kathy screamed for him to pull over. He started swearing at her, suddenly stopped, and ordered her to "get out!" Unfortunately, the "acts of kindness" exchanged that afternoon were not enough to prevent the destructive battle that destroyed all hopes for a nice dinner and evening.

As with Luke and Kathy, when reserves go out faster than deposits come in, eventually the bank will experience a deficit and the partners will find themselves unhappy and wondering when the next deposit will be made. At this point, partners must take special care to refinance the relationship. Showing you ways to turn relationship bankruptcy into relationship growth and stability is an important goal of this book.

In the last chapter, we had you take a peek at the *balance in your relationship bank account* (your standing, "for better or for worse") when you completed the Predict questionnaire. It is just as important to know the balance in the relationship bank as it is to know the current balance in your real savings and checking accounts. You couldn't plan a budget, pay bills, or go on a shopping spree if you did not know the bottom line of your reserves.

And just as the balances in your actual savings and checking accounts are likely to influence how you feel about any given withdrawal or deposit, so, too, will the balance in your relationship bank account influence how you feel about specific withdrawals and deposits. When the account balance is well in the black, with lots of reserves, the impact of any single withdrawal or deposit is not likely to be strongly felt. When couples have developed a reservoir of good will, then minor irritations will be just that—minor. However, if the account balance is hovering around zero or is in the red, even a small withdrawal is likely to have significant impact.

Often unhappy partners compare themselves to other couples and wonder why the same action has so much more impact in their own relationship than it does on those of their friends. Matt comes home from work late and his wife, Hillary, gets very upset. Matt's colleague, Jim, also worked late, but his wife, Lisa, takes it in stride. When they talk the next morning, Matt is mystified about why the same acts had different consequences. Part of the reason may be that there are different relationship economies operating in each marriage.

Unhappy couples often find themselves on a roller coaster of emotion as the relationship balance fluctuates around zero. If a day passes with instances of caring outweighing acts of hostility, the partners are likely to feel satisfied about the relationship. If a day passes with more angry exchanges than acts of kindness, partners are likely to report that they are unhappy with their marriage. At such times, partners, like Hillary and Matt, are likely to be extremely *emotionally reactive* to each other. They're hardly likely to "cut each other any slack." For all relationships, it is healthier to build a substantial relationship bank account through acts of caring and kindness than it is to experience sharp day-to-day fluctuations in relationship happiness as the balance "dances" around zero.

THE BANK ACCOUNT MODEL IN ACTION

We have used the bank account model in our research to help understand how couples send and receive messages. In one of our studies, we had couples participate in an exercise in which only one partner speaks at a time, while the other *only* listens.

After the first partner made a statement, we wanted to see how positive, negative, or neutral the speaker *intended* his or her message to be and exactly what *impact* (positive, negative, or neutral) this message had on the listener. Therefore, right after the first message, the speaker privately rated his or her intent (positive, negative, or neutral) and the listener privately rated the actual impact of the message upon him or her (positive, negative, or neutral). We then had partners switch speaker and listener roles, and this process continued throughout the entire conversation.

Two very surprising results emerged from our research. First, happy *and* unhappy partners had *identical* and *positive* intents! The desire to communicate positively to one's partner, despite whatever balance there might be in the relationship account, can be seen as a "reservoir of hope" for the relationship—providing evidence of a will to improve the relationship. With positive will, there is almost always a way.

Box 4.1
Don't Use Positive Intent as an Excuse

We want to make sure some readers are not interpreting our findings on positive intent as a license to get away with unkind or thoughtless deeds. Our fear is grounded in the way some partners excuse any of their behavior that comes across as undesirable by saying "Oh, I didn't mean it." For example, the husband who forgot to call home when he was late for a dinner date as per a prior agreement says: "Oh it was a terrible day and it just slipped my mind. It's not like I remembered and blew it off. I just forgot. I didn't mean to mess up your plans." The impact of this message is likely to be negative, especially if it is part of a long-standing pattern of behavior. Although it is better that the husband's forgetfulness wasn't a deliberate act, just pleading the marital version of the Fifth Amendment is not enough.

A more constructive response is to say (and of course mean): "I blew it, I forgot, it was a terrible day, but I realize that we had an agreement and I broke it and it cost you. I will make every effort to live up to the agreement in the future." You can see that here the husband is taking responsibility for his actions and the impact of his behavior on his partner. Perhaps more important, he should make every effort to listen to his partner's feelings about the event. His partner's job is to be able to accept his apology and not use it as an opportunity to unload on him.

Even children seem to learn early about using positive intent as an excuse. One night, Howard's seven-year-old son, Mathew, was taking a bath with his sister, Leah. He picked up a toy nuclear-powered submarine in order to destroy Leah's dolls and proceeded to dump water all over the floor. Mathew said that it was not his fault, and he didn't mean it, and proceeded with his attack plans on his sister. Howard said, "I didn't say you meant to do it, but it happened . . . Will you please clean it up." He went on to explain why Mathew needed to take responsibility for his actions, even though he didn't intend to flood the house. Howard must not have been overly clear, because after listening to him, Mathew said, "You clean it up. You're the grown-up!"

Fortunately, in marriage, both partners are grown-up and need to take responsibility for their own behaviors as well as to let others take responsibility for theirs.

Second, although both happy and unhappy partners exchange many messages that are received positively, the unhappy couples exchange just a few more messages that have a negative impact. As simple truth #3 states: Small differences in behavior can make a big difference in how partners feel about the relationship. If interactions are positive except for one good "zinger," that one zinger may be enough to cause significant strife. If significant strife occurs once a week, that may be enough to cause continuing relationship distress.

Now let's take the two findings together: (1) During a conversation, happy and unhappy partners both express the wish that their messages will be received by their partner as positive, and (2) overall, for both happy and unhappy partners this wish comes true except that in unhappy relationships, there are just a few more interactional zingers that a listener registers as negative. In other words, the big difference between happy and unhappy partners is that happy couples make *fewer* withdrawals from the relationship bank account by limiting the interactional zingers. Once couples have learned to curtail zingers, they then can go on to make positive deposits that will have more lasting effects.

IRA AND TRISH: LEARNING TO CONTROL ZINGERS

Trish and Ira were one of the many couples we've seen whose positive acts of kindness were overwhelmed by zingers. They had been married for over two years, and for the last six months they were both miserable with each other. Ira felt he was walking around on eggshells, and Trish kept wondering if she had made a mistake marrying him. Trish and Ira tried so hard to make the relationship work, yet they still found themselves tense and bedraggled.

One day, Ira left work early in the pouring rain to meet Trish's bus so she would not get soaked coming home from the office. After dinner, Ira cleaned up the kitchen because he knew that Trish liked to come down to a clean kitchen in the morning. On the weekend, Trish suggested that they go over to Ira's brother's on Sunday to watch a football game because that was something he often liked to do. Trish volunteered to pick up Ira's shirts at the cleaner's to save him a special trip. Their week was filled with many of these kindnesses.

Unfortunately, many of their weeks were also filled with one blow-out fight. One week it had to do with Ira's accepting an invitation to an office party without checking out the date with Trish. Over dinner, he casually mentioned that Don and Dale were having the party next weekend, and that he'd promised to be there with Trish. Trish fell quiet when she heard this, then erupted angrily: "I don't understand how you can be so inconsiderate. I'd never accept an invitation without checking it out with you first. How do you know I want to go to Don and Dale's? I hate your office parties. And next week is my birthday. I don't exactly want to spend the night at a party with your office people."

Ira took the bait. He yelled back, "I'm going to the party. I don't give a damn what you do. Why do you have to make everything so difficult?" In the five minutes it took to have this argument and exchange a few good zingers, the hours of effort on behalf of the relationship were trashed. For Ira and Trish, these cycles were all the more exasperating because they came out of the blue and seemed to destroy so much.

In our program, we taught Ira and Trish three specific techniques to help them control zingers. First, we instructed them how to use our "stop-action" tactic. Whenever they felt the impulse to sling a hostile barb, they were to have their inner voice yell "Stop!!!" and then add, "If I say this negative thing, I will only make things worse." The stop-action method taught Trish and Ira to avoid making inflammatory statements. However, the negative feelings were still there. We stressed to them that they needed to replace the negative thoughts that fuel conflicts with more positive ones. (We'll discuss this in detail in chapter 6). We then taught them how to express their negative feelings in a constructive manner by using the second technique, the Speaker-Listener tool. Introduced later in this chapter and described in detail in chapter 8, this method enables the person with the gripe to speak while the other partner only listens, making sure the speaker feels heard and understood. Finally, we provided Ira and Trish with our No-Nonsense Guide to Politeness (see box 4.2). Trish and Ira were able to use these

---

Box 4.2
A No-Nonsense Guide to Politeness

One of the sad facts of life in close relationships is that we treat the ones we love worse than we treat just about anyone else. We are more likely to hurl insults at, push, shove, hit, and slap our lovers than any other person in our life. We are even more polite to acquaintances than we are to our mates.

Why are we at times so nasty to our loved ones and so nice to others? Barry once excused his rude behavior to his wife, Becky, by saying, "After a hard day at work pleasing others and being on good behavior, I need to be able to be myself." Like many partners, Barry seems to believe that social norms of politeness should not operate at home. We strongly disagree! Given the high cost of rude or hostile behavior upon relationships, it's critical for us to learn to edit out such remarks and treat our partners with respect and politeness.

Imagine having a grab bag over one shoulder containing an unlimited number of things you could say to your partner at any time or on any occasion. At the most general level, the sack is filled with polite remarks and with zingers. Next time you are with your partner, imagine reaching into this grab bag for something to say. If you reach into your grab bag and pull out a zinger—throw it back into the sack before speaking and keep on picking until you have something polite to say.

Below we provide seven specific suggestions for helping you to recognize and throw back a zinger and find politeness.

1. When asked to do something, say what you can or want to do rather than what you can't or don't want to do. For example, if your partner asks if you want to go the movies and you are feeling tired, you might say, "I'd love to go to the movies tomorrow" rather than "I'm too tired."

2. When you first notice that your partner has done a chore, always show appreciation for the job even if there are aspects of the way in which it was done that do not meet with your approval. Say

continued

"Thanks for washing the counter" rather than "You missed a spot." If you routinely don't like the way your partner does a task, you should have a discussion about it at a time specially set aside for this purpose (see chapter 8).

3. Take note of departures from and reunions with your partner. Always greet each other with an acknowledgment and warm hello, and mark a leaving with a tender good-bye. You should not come home, go to bed, or leave the house in silence.

4. Avoid being a "psychopest." Psychopests try to offer insight into their partner's behavior under the guise of being helpful when in fact they are merely being critical. Don't say things like "You're behaving just like your mother" or "Do you know you're being anal retentive about the den?"

5. Always speak for yourself and avoid speaking for your partner. Say "I really want to go to the picnic" rather than "I know you will have a good time at the company picnic."

6. When you have an opinion on something, say what it is rather than fishing around with questions to get your partner to guess what it is. Try "I'd really like to eat at Captain Bob's tonight" instead of "Do you want to eat out tonight?"

7. When all else fails, fall back on ancient wisdom: "If you don't have anything nice to say, don't say anything."

three techniques to decrease the frequency with which they threw zingers at each other. Instead of zingers, the couple learned how to express gripes and disappointments and to deal with conflict in a constructive fashion.

Although we believe that damming the flow of withdrawals needs to be your priority, you and your partner also have a special obligation to cultivate deposits to the bank account. The small acts of kindness, empathy, and generosity bolster the foundation of your relationship.

When your account balance is higher, you'll be able to weather the turbulence produced by a period of significant withdrawals more easily.

HE SAID—SHE HEARD, SHE SAID—HE HEARD

As was all too obvious with Ira and Trish, communication between two people, no matter how much in love they are, is an imperfect process. One of the key contributions of the bank account model is that it focuses attention on the process of how we misinterpret and misread our partner's messages: *All too often when you are trying to make a deposit, your mate interprets it as a withdrawal.* This is a particularly critical insight because it explains why partners say to us: "I've been trying to make things better, but it hasn't worked." Anyone who has tried hard, but failed, tends to get very frustrated, depressed, and eventually gives up. It's the "American way" that trying will yield results . . . it's also the American Way that when partners try and fail in marriage—divorce quickly follows.

To get a better idea of how the bank account metaphor helps to explain common miscommunications, just think about the party game "Telephone." One person tells a little story to a second person, the listener tells the story to a third person, and so on down the line until the last person to hear the story finally retells it aloud. The game is fun because it is certain that the story produced at the end will only vaguely resemble the story at the beginning. Why? People "filter" what we say through the screens of current-life events and past experiences. In the case of couples, a similar process goes on with nearly every message spoken and heard. Thus, interpersonal communication is simply fraught with opportunities for creeping contradictions between what a speaker says and how a listener interprets. This is even more true of close relationships than relationships with strangers or acquaintances, because our filters are more likely to operate under conditions of high intimacy and high conflict.

Using our research-based concepts of intent and impact, we can define miscommunication as occurring when the speaker's intent does not equal the impact upon the listener—and miscommunications often are due to filters.

Filters can interfere with the speaker's intent being clearly expressed, as well as with the listener accurately understanding what the speaker is saying. The result: intended deposits in the relationship bank account turn into withdrawals.

For instance, when you've had a tough day and come home exhausted, you may say to your partner: "How was your day?" Your message may come out more negatively than you've intended, due to your current mood. Similarly, after a tough few hours with three difficult kids, you may *hear* your partner's question, "What's for dinner?" as "How come dinner isn't ready yet?" and then react in anger. Such situational or emotional filters help explain why intent is often more positive than impact. As we all know, simple miscommunications can often lead to complicated fights—and to a run on the relationship's account.

Over the years, in our workshops and therapy sessions, we observed two major types of listener filters that clearly influenced how marital messages are received. For some couples, the filters worked on behalf of the relationship. For instance, when partners were "blinded by love," they typically experienced all messages and kinds of behavior in a positive light. For other couples, filters worked in the opposite direction. It was as if they were "blinded by hate" and therefore routinely saw all messages and behaviors in a negative light.

Until recently, we were not sure if or how these different types of filters were involved in the development of marital problems. Therefore, we embarked upon two studies to try to uncover whether happy versus unhappy couples have specific filters or mental biases that contribute to their relationship success—or lack of it.

In both studies, we systematically analyzed partners' intent while speaking as well as the impact on the listener. We also videotaped these sessions, which allowed unbiased observers to assess the speaker's intent and impact. This enabled us to find out whether our couples' views of themselves were in sync with those of objective observers.

The first thing we discovered was that there was *overall agreement between objective observers and spouses in* happy *relationships.* This process was clearly seen in the interactions of Gerry, an accountant, and Pat, an attorney. Happily married for sixteen years, they had two children ages ten and fourteen. They were asked to discuss "communication," their top issue from their PPP (Personal Problem Plan). Pat told us that she was upset because she and Gerry no longer adequately planned their week together. She recalled their regular Sunday-evening talks over a glass of wine during which they chatted about the coming week and their schedules. Pat liked that they used to make plans for some "alone time" and missed that they no longer did this. As with many husbands in a satisfying relationship, Gerry had difficulty identifying areas of the marriage that would benefit from greater attention. But he did know exactly what Pat was talking about and agreed to discuss this issue.

Pat and Gerry talked about their problem area with some humor and made sure that they each understood what the other was saying. As they processed their issue, most of their ratings of each other's messages were neutral or positive. Our objective observers saw their discussion as just a little less positive than the partners themselves. Like all happily married partners, Gerry and Pat saw the relationship through filters that acted as "rose-colored glasses." This positive bias results in more deposits and fewer withdrawals in the relationship bank account.

Leslie and Michael's conversation was quite different. They had been married for fourteen years, had one child, age eleven, and both were very discouraged about their relationship. They were asked to talk about conflicts over household chores, their most intense problem. (Each had rated this area as a 10 on their RIP.) Leslie felt that Michael didn't do anything around the house other than take care of himself. If he went shopping, he bought food for himself but never household supplies or staples for the cupboard or refrigerator. Michael disagreed. He felt he did more than his share of housework but that Leslie never acknowledged his efforts.

As they discussed their issue, most of Michael's ratings were neutral or positive, with just a few negative ones. In contrast, Leslie rated most of Michael's messages as negative. Our objective observers *disagreed* with the couple. The observers saw Michael as negative, but less negative than did Leslie. Most importantly, the observers saw Leslie's comments very much more negatively than did Michael.

The second thing we discovered, just as with Leslie and Michael, is that *for all distressed couples there was little agreement among husbands, wives, and observers*—they all were on different wavelengths. Observers saw the wives as mostly negative: they were often critical of their husbands and sounded angry. Thus the distressed wives saw the relationship through "black-colored glasses" that filtered out positive acts. For them, things were worse than they appeared to observers. For example, after a week during which a husband was very positive (e.g., buying roses, cleaning the bathroom) his wife said: "He's only doing this because you told him to." Later she said, "Well, if this is real change, why didn't he do this ten years ago?" This negative bias results in fewer deposits and more withdrawals to the bank accounts of unhappy couples.

In sharp contrast, unhappy husbands rated their wives' negative messages as neutral or positive. They saw the relationship through a "denial" filter—they seemed to have erected some kind of defense against their wives' negative statements. Below, we apply these findings to help us understand why Leslie and Michael, and many other unhappy couples, often get stuck when they try to resolve conflict.

MICHAEL AND LESLIE: WHY THE "DENIAL FILTER" DOESN'T WORK

When Leslie is troubled by some aspect of their relationship, she attempts to talk this over with Michael. Michael perceives difficulties as well, but he is less likely to bring them up. This pattern by itself—typical of the pursuit ↔ withdrawal mode of interaction—is problematic, but we will maintain our focus here on what happens in the conversation when Leslie brings up the gripe. When Michael finds himself confronted with Leslie's gripe, he is thinking two things. First, because he seldom talks about what bothers him, he wonders why he has to listen to Leslie. He may not bring things up because he would rather live with what he considers minor disappointments than risk a big argument by coming to Leslie with a gripe of his own. This leads him to his second thought: If he gets into a conversation with Leslie, he anticipates a fight with her and he wants to avoid these fights more than anything.

So what does Michael do? He perceives Leslie's statements (the same ones that our observers see as critical and angry) as neutral or positive. Seeing the statement as more positive than it appears, Michael then goes on to treat it as "no big deal," and he offers explanations for why the issue should not concern Leslie. In terms of the bank account model, Michael's denial operates like a temporary and illusory "inflation" of their relationship currency that is bound to lose its value when the time comes to spend it.

In the same vein, Michael also offers some "quick fixes" for the problem in the hopes that the conversation will end quickly on a good note. Neither of these strategies works very well because they leave Leslie feeling that she is talking to a "brick wall." In turn, she increases the ferocity of her statements to make sure she gets through. Then Michael's worst fears are realized . . . he finds himself in the middle of a full-blown argument with Leslie.

Notice how Michael and Leslie, *together*, guarantee that the other person will exhibit the very behaviors they like least. Their conversation is another good example of how painful it is to observe the pursuit ↔ withdrawal pattern in action. In the end, observers see Leslie (the pursuer) as angry and demanding and Michael (the withdrawer) as uninvolved and uninterested.

FROM OPPONENTS TO TEAM PLAYERS

In therapy, part of the goal was to help Michael and Leslie work more like a team and less like opposing players. We showed Leslie how to present her concerns, gripes, or disappointments in such a way that she increased the likelihood that she would be heard. With Michael, we concentrated on developing his listening skills so that he could accurately detect and appreciate Leslie's current concerns. As his listening skills improved, he was able to detect and respond to Leslie's concerns when they were still minor and easier to deal with. We also helped him to take more responsibility by being a relationship spokesperson. (By never being the one to bring up gripes, he had always been the one who felt criticized.)

By taking the "bull by the horns" Michael was able to bring up the issues when he was prepared to do so. With Michael sharing in the responsibility to bring up relationship issues and Leslie discussing gripes and concerns in a constructive manner, the couple was able to feel more like a team and less like rivals.

The patterns displayed by Leslie and Michael are quite similar to those of other distressed couples in our studies and practices, enacting the modes of conflict interaction we observed in chapter 3. Certainly, in the case of some couples, the wife would behave more like Michael and the husband more like Leslie (withdrawal ↔ pursuit). And other couples show other variations, such as when *both* partners recoil from conflict, like Michael, and wonder why the relationship seems to have died and neither has much energy to do anything about it.

Whatever the precise patterns that characterize your relationship, we want your relationship to function more like a team with common goals and less like a battleground with opposing forces. If there is any opposing force, it is the problem area that is robbing you of intimacy, closeness, and love—it is not your partner. We'll detail ways to work as a team in part 3 of this book.

Working as part of a team means taking control of the only person you have control over—yourself. If you identify with Leslie, begin to experiment with ways to get yourself heard without forcing your partner to retreat or leave the "playing field." If you identify with Michael, begin to share your thoughts, concerns, and feelings with your partner as you pay more attention to your partner's needs and concerns. Listen to what your partner is saying *without* trying to resolve any issue, and without trying to take away your partner's feelings. If you get stuck, stop the conversation for now and come back to it later, using the floor exercise described in box 4.3. This exercise provides a safe place to experiment with all the changes suggested above, because this technique provides a clear set of rules for ensuring that good communication occurs between partners. By ensuring that positive intent has its desired effects, you will be able to "earn interest" on an already large bank account and reinvest in an account that is low.

Box 4.3
The Floor Exercise: Diagnosing Your Communication
Problems

To complete this exercise you will need seven small index cards. On one of the cards, write down the words *the floor* and set this card aside. Now, on two of the other cards, write down a plus sign (+), on two other cards a minus sign (–), and on the remaining two cards a big *0*. Divide the six cards into two even three-card decks consisting of a plus card, a minus card, and a *0* card. One deck is for you and one is for your partner. In each deck, you have one card to signify "positive message received," one card to indicate "negative message received," and one card to reveal "neutral message received."

Take out your Personal Problem Plan (PPP) completed in chapter 3. Select one of the problem areas that you have identified as meaningful, but not at the top of the list. Agree to discuss this topic (or another you both agree on) with your partner and then take a minute or two to define it a little bit more precisely. For example, if "money" were the topic area, you might focus on the time last week when you discovered that your partner had invested $1,000 in a friend's stock tip and did so without consulting you. This would be better than talking in the abstract about "money."

You should reserve about fifteen minutes when you will be able to devote your entire attention to this conversation. *Throughout the entire conversation, you will use the* floor *card to determine who is the speaker and who is the* listener. *The listener will use the +, –, and 0 feedback cards to provide the speaker with a continual readout of how positively (or negatively) each message is received.*

One of you will start with the floor, and this person will be in the role of speaker. The partner will be in the role of listener. The speaker will begin by saying whatever is on his or her mind. The job of the listener will always be to show the speaker one of the three feedback cards to reveal how the messages are being received. The listener can change the cards as often as desired to reflect changes in how each part of the message is being received.

The speaker should take note when a negative impact is registered

continued

by the listener. Right at that point in the conversation, something was just said to cause a withdrawal from the relationship account. To understand exactly what it was that caused the withdrawal, the speaker might give up the floor and let the listener have an opportunity to say what caused the withdrawal.

There are two goals for this exercise. First, we want you to have some practice talking about relationship issues while you and your partner frequently switch between the roles of speaker and listener. Second, we want to increase your understanding of the types of statements that result in both deposits and withdrawals in the relationship bank. Almost everyone who does this exercise discovers something new about their communication. In the role of speaker, partners are surprised to see which of their statements provoked a negative reaction from their mate. In the role of listener, partners are struck by how often they needed to switch between feedback cards to keep up with their changing reactions to the speaker.

The goal of this exercise is *not to solve the problem*. In this first communication exercise, we don't want you working to reach some compromise to whatever issue you are discussing. Instead, *we want you to understand the ways in which you and your partner communicate*. This exercise provides an opportunity to observe your own, relationship-specific communication patterns. As you observe the conversation, you are beginning the process of discovery to learn how specific messages are linked to specific withdrawals from and deposits in your relationship bank. For now, it is enough simply to observe this process. You need not be concerned with trying to change it.

Here's how the first few floor switches went with Karen and Ron. Karen started the conversation with the floor and Ron was holding up the neutral card to start the conversation. She said: "I want to talk about your diet." Karen gave Ron the floor, she held up the neutral card to signal she was ready as listener, and Ron said: "Okay, what about my diet do you want to talk about?" Karen took the floor, Ron held up the neutral card, and she said: "I'm really annoyed that you are not following the doctor's . . ." At this point, Ron switched from showing Karen the neutral card to showing her the negative card. Karen continued: ". . . orders. You've got this really high cholesterol

continued

and you still eat a lot of fatty stuff. It's not good for you. Why are you holding up the negative card?" Ron took the floor and said: "I held up the negative card because I feel like you are constantly watching over me." Karen switched from the neutral to the negative card when Ron added: "I will take care of this problem myself." Karen, taking the floor back, responded, "Listen, I am not trying to be critical. I am just worried about you. I want you to be around for a while longer. I'm scared that you're going to have heart troubles just like your dad, and they started when he was only forty-five." Ron holds up the positive card, Karen gives him the floor, and the conversation continues. If Karen and Ron had not been using the floor, we think there would have been a much greater chance that they would have thrown many more stones and barbs each other's way. This would have been a shame because there was, as is so often the case, positive intent at the start of the conversation.

From watching many couples use this exercise, we can alert you to a few pitfalls that can be avoided. On the speaker side, some partners hang on to the floor for dear life and engage more in a monologue than a conversation. For some couples this is understandable. If the speaker has been holding on to something that she or he wanted to tell the partner, then it seems only natural once the speaker has a captive audience that the words and feelings pour out. This can be avoided by keeping each person's time on the floor limited to a few sentences, and by trading the floor often. It is also a good idea to limit the first few floor exercises to about ten to fifteen minutes. You can always come back and continue a conversation if it feels as though it ended prematurely.

On the listener side, the most common pitfall is to forget to show a feedback card at all times while the speaker is talking. Right at the beginning, you might be holding up the "neutral" card. As soon as you, the listener, receive your partner's message as positive or as negative, be sure to change the card displayed in order to keep up with your actual receipt of your partner's messages.

As a result of using the floor exercise you will learn a technique that will, with practice, enable the two of you to talk constructively about relationship issues. The use of the speaker and listener roles

continued

slows down the communication process to the point where fights are unlikely to occur. Of primary importance, you will learn about the types of statements that leave your partner feeling happy or sad, angry or content, disappointed or encouraged, or disgusted or pleased.

One fun way to use the floor exercise is to have a ten-minute discussion and try to exchange as many positive statements as you can with your partner. So that you each have equal opportunity to accumulate positive "points," try to exchange the floor often. Limit each speaker's turn on the floor to only a few sentences before a floor switch. The points you earn can be viewed as deposits in your relationship bank account.

THE "SLEEPER EFFECT"

When we observe couples like Ira and Trish or Leslie and Mike, we are examining characteristics of couples who are *already* unhappy. When we compared them to partners like Donna and Joe, the couple discussed earlier in this chapter who had a healthy relationship bank account, we were able to learn how the unhappy couples differ from the happy ones. But this first set of studies did not tell us if the tensions set in *after* couples were already unhappy, or if the problem areas were there, lying dormant, years before a couple actually experienced relationship distress. This was a burning question for us. If we could detect factors associated with relationship unhappiness *before* they took their toll on a couple, we might be able to prevent the onset of distress in the first place.

Our long-term follow-up research has shown that couples who communicated well before marriage had better relationships up to ten years later than did the couples who showed problems in communication before marriage. More importantly, we discovered a "sleeper effect." It takes about two and a half years for the withdrawals from the relationship bank account to deplete the positive balance that usually is present in the marriage-planning stage of a relationship.

The "Sleeper Effect" in Action

When Dan and Nancy came to our research center for the first time, before marriage and with a large bank account, they reported that one of their major problem areas involved conflict with relatives. As with so many couples who have this difficulty, holiday times tended to breed dissension. So it was no surprise that when Dan and Nancy entered our study in January, they had just experienced a particularly hard Christmas season. Both partners came from strong Catholic backgrounds and had established traditions of celebrating the holidays together with their families. As you might expect, Dan and Nancy had a disagreement over whose family they would spend the holidays with, which was intensified for them because both families lived in town.

When we listened to their first conversation, it was evident that each partner assumed that the other would naturally understand how important it was to spend Christmas at her/his family's home. Yet they had never talked about this issue and were not prepared for the disagreement that surfaced around Christmastime. As they talked about this fight in their first research session, Nancy expressed her feelings about the importance of spending Christmas with her parents and her disappointment that they'd ended up with Dan's family. Dan was fairly hostile and withdrawn when Nancy spoke. Interestingly, when *he* spoke he was more disturbed by how upset *she* was than about the actual issue of where to spend the holidays. Both Dan and Nancy evaluated several of each other's messages as negative. However, as with most premarital couples, their overall satisfaction with their relationship was high. From their perspective, the upset about the holidays was merely a blip on a basically happy curve. However, from our research perspective, the negative ratings of each other's messages forecasted problems to come.

They got married in June and did not discuss the relative issue again until the following January when they returned to our research center for their second-year appointment. This second holiday season did not bring them better tidings. The same general pattern of conversation and impact ratings continued, but Dan was more withdrawn, disengaged, and hostile in the conversation and started to say things like

"You're right; you're right. Whatever you want, I'll do it." He didn't really want to compromise but was so anxious to put a stop to the disagreement with Nancy that he caved in. As you would expect from our findings, after one year of marriage the couple still reported a high level of marital satisfaction.

The third January we saw them, Nancy was extremely angry. She told us that last year Dan had agreed that he would go with her this year to spend Christmas Day with her family. Well, when this year rolled around, Dan kept his bargain but he was hostile, withdrawn, and negative. Once again, he said he'd change. She said, "We'll see," and the couple ended their conversation. As we would have predicted, Nancy's impact ratings were lower than Dan's. Her negative ratings reflected her anger at Dan's passive participation in the conversation on top of her troubling feelings about how he behaved toward her parents.

They did not come in for their annual appointment the next January because they became the first separated couple in our study, and by the five-year follow-up they were divorced.

As was the case with Dan and Nancy, we have found that many couples ignore the seriousness of these early negative ratings and thus the sleeper effect is able to take hold. Only after several years of these types of messages will the relationship begin to show signs of difficulties.

To combat the sleeper effect, couples must "wake up" to the precise ways that their communications go astray. They must have a sound understanding of what qualities about their own messages will have a negative impact on their partners and learn how filters alter the intent of their partners' messages. They must learn how to use communication to build and maintain a strong personal relationship with their partner. Your Predict quiz will already have given you some insight into the patterns of your communication that may need to be worked on to fight the sleeper effect in your own home.

FROM INTENTS TO ACTIONS

In order for us to help you wake up to the *precise* ways that communication is used to build and maintain intimacy in happy relationships or to tear down the walls of love in unhappy ones, we will need to go beyond the information in this one chapter. Here we have dealt with the relationship bank account and the importance of how positive or negative the listener finds each message. To enable you to determine exactly what causes your partner to receive a message as negative or positive, we must delve further into the nature of the communication process. This journey is undertaken in the next three chapters, which make up part 2 of this book.

Next, in chapter 5, we will explore what types of relationship talk lead to greater understanding and deposits to your relationship account and what types of talk lead to fights and withdrawals from your account. When your partner speaks to you, the words spoken and the manner in which they are uttered are the end result of many complex influences. These influences include: the beliefs that you and your partner have about each other and about being able to make progress with the topic (Do you believe you will resolve your disagreements or not?—chapter 6) and how *aroused* each of you are in the face of conflict (Are you calm and collected or frazzled and distraught?—chapter 7).

In these upcoming chapters, you will learn how to take charge of every message you offer as speaker and to give shape to every message you receive as listener. Your capacity to control your communication is one of the hidden reservoirs of hope for the future of your relationship.

PART II

Better Understanding

Chapter 5

MAKING SENSE OUT OF NONSENSE

WHEN THE dust settles from a relationship fight, battle-weary partners often conduct a conversation autopsy to figure out what went wrong: "If you loved me, you wouldn't walk away in the middle of a discussion"; "If you loved me, you wouldn't yell in my face and wave a finger at me." Most fights are triggered by some small issue, and exactly where all the misery comes from is not terribly clear to either partner. Faced with confusion, it is in our nature to try to explain the painful events in our lives. In the process we often spin some pretty complex explanations for relationship distress. Usually these explanations try to pin blame on someone or something, as if that would help. Common targets for the blame are a person's family ("He's just like his lazy father"), a partner's unconscious feelings ("She has lots of repressed anger"), or even ourselves ("I'm an enabler because my father was an alcoholic").

In this chapter, you will learn how to identify the specific conversation maneuvers that make a fight likely and that, over time, slowly erode the foundation of relationship well-being. You will be able to see firsthand what happens to couples when relationship talk turns to "nonsense" and talking becomes another word for arguing.

Like it or not, the way you say things can have a dramatic impact on your partner and cannot be dismissed as just "semantics." If your partner is not responding to you as you wish, perhaps your wishes are not being clearly stated. If your partner is not being sympathetic, perhaps you are not asking for sympathy. If your partner is hurling criticisms at you, is it any wonder that you return the fire or run for cover?

But who's to say what kinds of messages are helpful or harmful to relationships? You have a right to be skeptical when we or anyone else tells you that you must speak to your partner in a certain way. In fact, we can't and won't tell you the way partners *should or shouldn't* speak to each other. That remains your choice. Instead, we will share with you the real-life communication strategies that couples use and the inevitable consequences that these strategies have for relationships. These are the precise communication strategies that we found to distinguish between happy and unhappy couples and predict long-term happiness.

We believe these "reality tested" communication patterns are the essence of satisfaction or despair in a relationship. Practice the communication styles of happy couples and you are likely to feel happy. Practice the communication styles of unhappy couples and you are likely to be miserable. This is your choice to make every time you and your partner have a conversation.

Simple Truth #1 tells us most of the time communication begins with good intentions. So if the majority of couples have good intentions, but aren't necessarily happy, what's going wrong? It's the way good intentions are translated into talk. Let this chapter be your guidebook for turning good intentions into good talk and for turning good talk into relationship happiness.

A DICTIONARY OF RELATIONSHIP TALK

If you don't speak French and you visit Paris, it can be hard to get the taxi driver to take you to your hotel, order your dinner, or find the Musée d'Orsay. However, if you are armed with a simple phrase book for tourists, you can often make your wishes known and have your desires met. Understanding the real, underlying message in relationship talk can also be a bit like trying to understand a foreign language. "Pronounce" something slightly wrong, and you could be insulting the listener rather than asking for help.

Therefore, we are going to provide you with a couples' equivalent to the phrase book to a foreign language: a Dictionary of Relationship Talk. This "dictionary" will help you find your way through the often-unfamiliar terrain of couples' communication by teaching you how to identify, decipher, and unravel self-defeating patterns of discussion. After you learn our Dictionary of Relationship Talk, you will no longer be mystified by how a simple discussion can turn into an explosive argument.

Positive problem talk:

Any statement that gives information about the nature of a problem. Example: "I think the wall color of the living room clashes with the rest of the house. I'd like to discuss repainting it." It could appear in the form of a question seeking information, as in, "What do you think of the wall color in the living room?" (The statement cannot be yelled, whined, muttered, or blurted out.)

Negative problem talk:

Similar to positive problem talk, but the message is conveyed in a nasty tone of voice. It might be said sarcastically, or yelled, whined, muttered, or blurted out. Example: "I want you to paint the living room *now*. Do you think you could manage that?"

Excuses and explanations:

Any response to partner that tries to justify one's actions. Example: "I know I said I'd repaint the walls, but I've been too busy with other things to get to it."

Positive solution talk:

Any kind of statement that offers a reasonable solution to a problem. Example: "I'll paint the living room next weekend and would appreciate your help."

Negative solution talk:

Any kind of statement that offers an unreasonable, unrealistic, impractical solution to a problem. Example: "I'll get around to painting the walls sometime in the next year. Trust me."

Mind-reading talk:

Any statement that assumes knowledge about the partner. Example: "You haven't painted the walls because you don't want to do anything that I ask you to do." Often these statements start with "You always . . ." or "You never . . ."

Critical talk:

Any statement that criticizes oneself or one's partner. The criticism can be of the person, the person's behavior, or the person's communication. Example: "You're the laziest person I know. You can't even paint one lousy room."

Listening talk:

Any statement that serves to show a speaker that a message just spoken was in fact heard and received. Example: "I know you're really angry with me for not painting the walls when I said I would."

Agreement:

Any statement that shows agreement with what partner just said. Example: "Yes, that's right."

Disagreement:

Any statement that shows disagreement with what partner just said. Any statement that first agrees with partner but then offers some overriding qualification is still taken as a disagreement. Example: "Yes, I understand where you are coming from, but there are lots of reason why you are wrong."

Hopeless talk:

Any statement that expresses pessimism about the relationship, the problem, the discussion, or the partner. Example: "I can't take this anymore."

Now, let's apply the Dictionary of Relationship Talk to one couple whose communication processes are causing trouble. Gail is twenty-six years old and she is finishing up a Master's degree program at a large state university. Fred is twenty-eight and works for a big investment firm. They have known each other for about nine years, and they have been married for five. They met in college at a freshman mixer and discovered that they came from the same hometown. Neither had dated much before meeting the other. Gail broke off the relationship twice in the first two years, but they quickly got back together when Fred promised to make some changes in his behavior. They have no children.

They volunteered to participate in our study because Gail had read a story in the newspaper about our research and wanted to learn more about the project. Fred was not all that thrilled about coming into the laboratory and talking with strangers about his relationship, but he wanted to please Gail and thus agreed to participate. On their PPP (Personal Problem Plan), the couple concurred that household chores, money, and sex were the top three problem areas. They were asked to talk about household chores and to try to reach a mutually satisfactory solution to this issue.

Let's listen in on their conversation. Actually, we want you to listen in on this conversation *twice*. First, we want you to see how the conversation plays out without looking up the statements in the Dictionary of Relationship Talk. Just pay attention to how the conversation flows, whether Gail and Fred will feel good about the conversation when it ends, and less important, whether it seems as if they will reach a solution. In this first read through, *skip over our corresponding comments* that appear to the right of each person's statement. Remember, speech in a verbatim transcript is not as smooth as theater dialogue, but this is how real people talk to each other.

After you have read through the conversation once, and have had a chance to form your own thoughts as to what determined the outcome, we want you to reread the conversation. This time, pay careful attention to our comments and note how we apply the Dictionary of Relationship Talk to each person's statement. After your second read through, we will have more to say about Fred and Gail's conversation and relationship.

GAIL: "I think that you usually leave everything for me to do. You don't think you should have to do anything around the house because you work and I stay at home. So you think that I should just do all the housework."

COMMENT: This first statement is **mind-reading talk** because Gail is telling Fred what he thinks. Often, these types of statements make the other person defensive and therefore increase the likelihood of a defensive reply. These defensive replies often take the form of a disagreement or a justification. This is not what Gail is looking for; when speakers bring up a gripe, they want their feelings acknowledged. With Gail's opening, the likelihood of getting acknowledged is pretty small. Thus, this is not the best way to start a problem-solving conversation.

FRED: "Well, it's hard, I realize. I do things in spurts. You know, like I vacuum, I do the dishes, sometimes I try to keep the room neat. But it is true, I do come home really tired."

COMMENT: Fred is following the pattern we have observed in hundreds of couples. He responds to the mind reading with **excuses and explanations.** He doesn't pay attention to the essence of Gail's gripe but defends himself from what he perceives as an attack. After just two statements, this conversation is off on the wrong foot. Fred and Gail both have contributed to the misdirection. Gail might have had an easier time being heard if she had not mind-read; Fred might have brought the conversation back on track if he had showed **listening talk** instead of becoming defensive.

GAIL: "Except that even when I am busy and tired, I do it. You never do."

COMMENT: In essence, what Gail is saying here is that she tends the house even when she is tired but that Fred doesn't. She is criticizing him and so this statement is **critical talk.** Gail and Fred seem to be headed into an argument about the past. These types of arguments are rarely productive.

FRED: "Yeah, I know."

COMMENT: The most likely response to a criticism is another criticism, a disagreement, or an excuse. Here Fred does not offer one of these typical responses. Instead of a tit-for-tat exchange of criticisms or other negative behaviors, Fred **agrees** with Gail's point of view. This is a positive interactional maneuver. An agreement after a short message is often an invitation to the speaker to go on and elaborate on the point. That is what Gail does.

GAIL: "I think that men should help with the household chores. If I am going to school at night and become a professional, I can't be spending the days being superwoman, cleaning and taking care of the kids and everything all myself, while you come home and sit and read the newspaper or watch TV. I mean . . . I don't think that's fair."

COMMENT: Here Gail offers a combination of **criticism** and **negative problem talk.** In general it is better to say what you want and need through **positive problem talk** rather than try to make a case for what you want by building an argument for your point of view. The latter will often be critical, as it implies a flaw in your partner.

FRED: "I guess I feel like if I do my 35 or 40 percent, that should be enough even if it's not fifty-fifty."

COMMENT: In response to a criticism, Fred provides a **negative solution** as he resumes his personal defense. He does not show that he has heard Gail's gripe. **Listening talk** here would help the couple get this conversation back on sounder footing. Again both Gail and Fred are contributing to the troubling tone of this conversation.

GAIL: "You think you should do 35 because housework is woman's work. I'm not clear why you think you should do only 35. I'm not going to argue

COMMENT: One of the common characteristics of conversations that leave partners feeling angry and distant is that they seem to get in a rut and simply whether you do 35 or not—I don't think you do. I'm very skeptical of that figure."

spin their wheels without going anywhere. The content of the statements may change, but the Dictionary of Relationship Talk shows that the underlying messages remain the same. Here, Gail offers more **mind reading,** she **disagrees** with Fred's estimate of his contribution to household work, and she is **critical** of his efforts.

FRED: "You play down everything I do. I don't think I'm doing that horribly less than you are."

COMMENT: Fred returns the **criticism.** At this point the couple is getting more stuck and decreasing the likelihood of a satisfying conversation. They appear locked in an exchange of negative behaviors. Although the conversation sounds as though the partners are responding to each other, neither person makes the effort to show an *explicit* understanding of what the other is saying. The best way to show understanding is through **listening talk.**

GAIL: "Whenever we have company, who cleans the house? It gets to a point of panic—well, your father is coming or my mother is coming, or I am having people over for a meeting."

COMMENT: Since Gail does not feel she has been listened to, she continues to argue her point of view and support her argument. However, at this point in the conversation, no amount of **criticism** or **negative problem talk** is likely to get Fred to listen to her. A new tactic is needed.

FRED: "I've cleaned, like, the bathroom a couple of times already."

COMMENT: The pattern is well established. In response to **criticism** and **negative problem talk,** the most likely response is to offer **excuses and explanations.**

GAIL: "This notorious time you cleaned the bathroom! You did it after weeks of saying you were going to do it. Usually you go off and play racquetball or work out."

COMMENT: If the conversation sounds repetitious at this point, it is. This feeling of going around in circles is a direct result of the process of communication bouncing back and forth between **critical talk** and defensive reactions, and it takes two players to make it happen. If one starts playing a different game, the process of communication will change. As we have noted, **listening talk** and **positive problem talk** are good ways to break the destructive cycle that traps Gail and Fred.

FRED: "I went off that time because you were so depressed. You know, you kept the shades closed."

COMMENT: Here is an **explanation** for behavior that is also **critical** of Gail. It introduces another topic into the conversation and since earlier topics have not been dealt with well, this will likely lead both partners to feel more emotionally charged and distant from each other.

GAIL: "I don't see what that has to do with cleaning. There are certain times when I know you are really busy, yet I always rise to the occasion. I may do extra things for you. I get up and make your lunches and I only assume that when I am having problems you will do the same thing. And I don't see you doing that. I don't see you jumping in and helping me out like I do for you."

COMMENT: Gail directs the conversation back to the original topic and provides information from her point of view. This is good **problem talk.** Yet, the message ends with **criticism** of Fred. We'll see if Fred is attentive to the problem talk, to the criticism, or to both.

FRED: "Yeah. I know I feel guilty about it sometimes. I try to justify it in my mind that I'm doing enough to keep it, you know, so that I can say I help out. But it is not fifty-fifty."

COMMENT: Fred is somewhat attentive to Gail's concern and acknowledges it with **agreement.** However, he also offers **excuses and explanations** for why the problem stays as it is. It is not clear here where the conversation will go. There have been many negative exchanges, and both partners are likely to feel ignored and unappreciated. This will make a positive end unlikely. At the same time, this type of agreement after so much criticism is relatively rare and might signal that a change in tone is coming.

GAIL: "Yeah. I mean I hate household stuff—you know, cooking and cleaning, even though I've done them all my

COMMENT: Gail **agrees** with Fred. The conversation has taken on a softer tone here, and this usually creates more of an life. I have all the more resentment toward them because all the women in my family did all the cooking and all the cleaning and all that stuff and that's what I had to do until I left home. And now I find myself doing it again."

FRED: "Yeah, I know it really bugs you to do the stuff. And I can really see why. I think the solution is that you should, maybe, you know, ease up on yourself and let the house stay dirty. We don't need to vacuum more than once every other month. I work too hard during the week to clean house on weekends. That's what I feel, maybe not rightly, but I am due some additional grace."

opportunity for partners to share their thoughts and feelings. These thoughts and feelings are an important part of intimacy. Gail's **positive problem talk** gives Fred new information about the nature of the problem from her perspective.

COMMENT: Fred is attentive to Gail's feelings and shows that he has heard her message. He offers **agreement and listening talk.** Unfortunately he then goes on to offer a **negative solution** to what he sees as the problem. He doesn't show an understanding of the problem from Gail's perspective and this will make a positive outcome very unlikely. Fred also returns the focus to himself as he implicitly **criticizes** Gail for not giving him "grace" when it comes to the cleaning of the house. After an attempt at softening the conversation, this return to negative talk will be very difficult to sidestep.

GAIL: "Why should I give you grace?"

COMMENT: All the troubling feelings that Fred and Gail provoked in each other through their interactions at the start of the conversation are still present and constitute a definite risk that this talk will end with both partners feeling very distant from each other. Here Gail expresses **negative problem talk.** This conversation had some positive potential to turn itself around, but without the skills to recognize the underlying process and then to alter it constructively, Fred and Gail are left frustrated and distant.

FRED: "If you just stop worrying about how the house looks, all this stuff wouldn't bother you."

COMMENT: Again, not realizing that the process of their communication is more the issue now than the household tasks that started the conversation, Fred returns to the issue in another attempt to repair the relationship. Although his intent is likely to be to make things better, his strategy of using **mind reading** and **negative problem solution** is not going to work.

GAIL: "I can't talk about this any more now. I give up."

This is hopeless talk.

FRED: "Fine. If you can't, you can't."

This is critical talk.

DIAGNOSING GAIL AND FRED'S PROBLEM

If this was your first read through the conversation, please go back now and read it through again. This time pay special attention to each of our comments. We hope you will begin to see how the Dictionary of Relationship Talk is an important tool in making sense of Gail and Fred's disagreement.

You may have found it painful to listen in on Gail and Fred's dialogue. When a conversation is a Ping-Pong match of negative problem talk, negative problem solutions, mind reading, critical talk, excuses and explanations, and disagreements, there simply is no way that the conversation can feel good to either partner or lead to productive relationship outcomes. The adage that it is better to get your feelings out into the open needs qualification. There are helpful and harmful ways to accomplish the expression of gripes and anger. Fred and Gail are expressing negative feelings, but they are doing so in a destructive way. Despite positive intent, they are a couple trapped by their own communication style and illustrate what predictably happens when couples get swept into streams of negative communication, overwhelming any existing trends toward positive communication. Any couple will find it hard to recover from such negative exchanges. These negative exchanges graphically demonstrate one of our foremost simple truths: that it takes only one or two zingers to erase many acts of kindness.

In our comments on Gail and Fred's conversation we suggested that they were unknowingly caught up in seemingly irresistible negative patterns. Like many couples, they were weaving complicated explanations for their distress that led them to false conclusions and misdirected attempts to change. Using the Dictionary of Relationship Talk, we suggested that certain types of statements were more likely to elicit certain types of replies. The linkage between various types of messages is an extremely important concept.

If someone comes up to you and says "Knock knock," there is a very high likelihood that you will say "Who's there?" If you say in reply to "Knock knock," "I don't know where all that knocking is coming from," you will surprise the would-be joke teller. Predictable messages contain little information, and they are not at all surprising. Messages that contain new information are always somewhat surprising because we are learning something for the first time.

Communication much more complex than a knock-knock joke follows this same principle. One of the most striking features of an unhappy couple's conversation is that it is entirely predictable. Gail mind-reads Fred; Fred disagrees. Fred criticizes Gail; Gail criticizes Fred. Happy couples showed us that their communication was much more *unpredictable*. Each message in a happy relationship is a bit of a surprise. Sometimes criticism begets criticism, but sometimes criticism leads to listening talk. Sometimes mind reading begets excuses and explanations, but sometimes it elicits agreement and listening talk. Because the likelihood of any message is not so apt to be set in stone, happy partners pay more careful attention to each other and are constantly adjusting to what is being said. *Partners in a happy relationship seem to be writing their relationship script as they go along. Partners in an unhappy relationship seem to be reading from a well-worn and well-rehearsed script.*

Fred and Gail acted out their well-rehearsed script. We now want to introduce you to a contrasting couple, Marsha and Will. They will show us how they write their relationship script anew as they talk.

MARSHA AND WILL

Marsha, age thirty-nine, is an operating room nurse at a small private hospital. She met Will twelve years ago when he was visiting a friend at the hospital, and they started talking in an elevator. Will is forty-two and a career military officer. The couple takes joy in talking about their relationship, how lucky they feel to have met each other, and their current shared interests of running and gardening. They also have an easy time talking about the relationship difficulties that they've struggled with over the years and the challenges that currently confront them. The topic they chose for discussion was communication. Marsha and Will give the impression that they are continually crafting their relationship to meet the demands of their busy lives, their changing likes and dislikes, and their unique struggles and dreams. They have that rare ability to reaffirm the relationship at the same time that they help each other grow as individuals.

MARSHA: "Well, as far as communication goes, I think, we just come from totally different backgrounds and have different personalities. I think that you turn things off a lot more than I do. But things still bother you."

COMMENT: Marsha opens the conversation by defining the problem as she sees it **(positive problem talk).** She also tries to infer what is going on in Will and that is **mind reading.**

WILL: "A lot of times, part of that is, you know, when you were so sick that you said, 'Don't talk to me when I feel like this.' And it sort of got to where I couldn't afford to tell you anything that was bothering me 'cause I didn't think you wanted to hear it. And that was not the time to tell you."

COMMENT: At this point there is no telling where the conversation will head. Marsha is somewhat **critical** of Will's tendency to withdraw from conversation and Will is a defensive listener **(excuses and explanations),** explaining that Marsha is partly responsible for his withdrawal.

MARSHA: "I know what that was like, and I couldn't talk then. But I'm not sick now."

WILL: "I know. And we don't have as much of a communication problem now as we have had in the past."

COMMENT: Even though Marsha's message is short, it carries a lot of new information. Instead of continuing on with some form of negative talk, which is the most likely response to excuses and explanations, Marsha accepts responsibility for her role in past communication difficulties **(agreement)** and forces the couple back to the issue that exists in the present **(positive problem talk).** Will acknowledges the change in the relationship **(agreement)** and backs away from his defensive stance **(positive problem talk).**

MARSHA: "Yeah. I do think some things bother you, but you don't tell me about them. I think a lot bothers you. But you don't come forth and say anything unless I just fish it out of you. When I get really angry or something, you really feel a terrible sense of despair. You're totally discouraged and full of despair over the situation, but you still don't make any attempt to communicate anything about it. And I really see that as a big problem. Because I think that it ends up being on my back to go down and make the peace."

COMMENT: Here, Marsha clarifies the nature of the problem from her perspective through the use of **positive problem talk** and also mixes in some guesses as to what is going on with Will. This **mind reading** and **critical talk** is a risky strategy. Let's see how it works.

WILL: "Sounds like you feel bad that you always have to be the leader or the aggressor and the peacemaker?"

COMMENT: Will's **listening talk** is a surprise. It is a relatively rare response to mind reading and critical talk. This statement shows interest and caring about what the listener is thinking and feeling even though some of Marsha's previous message is critical. Listening talk at this particular time in the conversation greatly increases the likelihood that this conversation will move forward.

MARSHA: *"Umm-hmm, Umm-hmm.* That's right."

WILL: "Why?"

COMMENT: **Agreements** are often brief acknowledgments, but they make a mighty contribution to the positive tone of a conversation. Will follows Marsha's agreement with a request for information to help him better understand his wife's feelings **(positive problem talk).**

MARSHA: " 'Cause I feel like, well, that I've tried that one time when I was so terribly angry with you. And I just thought, I'm not going to go down there and be the peacemaker. But you never came forward and made any attempt to be the peacemaker."

COMMENT: Marsha and Will are doing a good job in creating a conducive interactional setting for sharing some powerful feelings. Will's listening allows Marsha further to explore her concerns and leaves her feeling that Will is genuinely interested in her and her views.

WILL: "You're right. You mean what you're saying is you would prefer that I would change and do that some more."

COMMENT: Will **agrees** with Marsha and goes on to offer a **positive solution** to the issue they are discussing.

MARSHA: "Yeah, that's what I'm saying. I think that it's going to have to be a very conscious effort on your part. To say, 'Oh, we've had a fight now or we've had a disagreement, I'm going to, I owe, this is against something I generally do, but I am going to try it this time.' I think that is something you are going to have to do."

COMMENT: Once partners have had an opportunity to express themselves and are certain that their feelings and thoughts have been heard and appreciated, the couple can continue to discuss **problem solutions.** Many couples make the mistake of trying to solve problems too early in the conversation before both people have had a chance to express their thoughts and feelings. Marsha and Will avoid this pitfall.

WILL: "Well, I, one of my rationales is that, you know, I think this thing will blow over. We love each other enough not to worry about it, and I'd rather not have a confrontation. There's a little bit of that involved. But for you, you can't live with that."

COMMENT: The difficulty with excuses and explanations is that they simply try to defend the status quo. Here, Will is providing some insight into his motivation for past behavior in a way that facilitates change **(positive problem talk)**. He ends with some supportive **mind reading** of Marsha.

MARSHA: *"Umm-hmm, Umm-hmm."*

COMMENT: Marsha **agrees**.

WILL: "I know when something does come up that forces us to communicate with each other, we do it very well. When we are prodded into communicating, we can communicate better than anybody in the whole world, I think."

COMMENT: Will reaffirms the relationship with this **positive problem talk.**

MARSHA: "Oh, I know. I know. I think you are right."

WILL: "I know I need to seek you out more. To talk, if something is bothering me, I will seek you out. I promise. We've been married long enough that I know, deep down, that it helps, just being able to talk. Or even time. Sometimes time heals . . ."

COMMENT: Sometimes couples have just as much difficulty handling positive sentiments as they do handling negative ones. Marsha avoids that problem. Here she is appropriately responsive to Will's statement **(agreement).**

MARSHA: "No. Time doesn't heal."

COMMENT: A simple **disagreement.**

WILL: "I guess . . . , I know. You accelerate the healing by communicating. I need to do that. I will do that."

COMMENT: Will is struggling to find common ground between his own tendencies to achieve peace by avoiding talk and Marsha's tendencies to talk to achieve peace. The communication process remains open so that each can explore his or her tendencies and realize what the problem feels like from the other side. The conversation serves not only as a problem-solving session regarding how to settle arguments but also as a reaffirmation of the entire relationship. This support of the relationship above all else is obvious in Marsha's final statement.

MARSHA: "I get more comfortable in our marriage, and with our communication, as the years go by. And I just think that it's being more secure in the relationship that I have with you and more secure maybe in myself. 'Cause I'm trying to become a better person, you know, a more unique and independent woman. And I think that makes a great deal of difference also, for me."

WILL: "*Umm-hmm.* I know."

MARSHA AND WILL'S TALK: UNPREDICTABLE . . . AND HEALTHY

Marsha and Will's discussion obviously has a very different feel than Gail and Fred's. You doubtless won't be surprised to learn that on our questionnaires Gail and Fred report a great deal of unhappiness in their marriage and that Marsha and Will report themselves to be very happily married. You can also tell from Marsha and Will's conversation that their relationship is not simply problem free or without the occasional argument that causes them grief. You can also observe that not *all* of Fred and Gail's messages are negative and destructive, just as not all of Marsha and Will's message are positive or constructive.

But the fact that Gail and Fred's conversation does contain some positive messages, and even approaches a more positive outcome, is the very reason that some couples get so frustrated with the conflict. Gail and Fred move closer to understanding each other, and then one statement pulls them back into hopelessness. As you learn new ways of talking about relationship problems, these new constructive strategies will start to mingle with old destructive habits that cause such despair.

Remember, as you can see from the couples' conversations in this chapter, no problem discussion between intimate partners will be *all* good or *all* bad. How you feel coming out of one of these talks will most likely be determined by the skillfulness with which you listen to your partner and the success each of you has in responding constructively to your partner's negative messages. The outcome will not be favorable if your strategy is simply to "be positive all the time" or if you are overcome by hopeless talk when the "be positive strategy" crumbles.

The conversations we've analyzed illustrate that you may only need to alter three or four exchanges to change the course of a two-hour conversation. Small plot turns can significantly modify the old script and force partners to rewrite the current, tired, and predictable relationship scene. Look back and see how Marsha and Will's conversation took a positive turn with one statement by Will. Marsha criticized Will by saying ". . . You don't come forth and say anything unless I just fish it out of you." If Will had responded with a disagreement, followed by an excuse that reciprocated Marsha's criticism (for example, "That's not true. I don't say anything because you're yelling too loud to hear it"), then a tiresome exchange of hostile jabs probably would have resulted. Instead, Will made a sincere effort to understand Marsha's perspective: "Sounds like you feel bad that you always have to be the leader or the aggressor and the peacemaker?"

With this one statement, Will has significantly rewritten this scene from their marriage. By engaging in listening talk he has created an opportunity for altering the rest of the script so that he and Marsha can further explore each other's thoughts and feelings. As we discuss in

chapter 8, such sharing is vital for setting the stage for effective problem solving—without it, solving relationship problems is nearly impossible. Yet, as most of us know, overcoming the urge to defend
oneself aggressively (and therefore destructively) in the face of criticism is never easy. We should not underestimate the measure of Will's
resourcefulness in offering constructive listening talk at this pivotal
juncture of their conversation. In chapters 6, 7, and 8, we will help you
master the thoughts and actions necessary to enable your problem discussions to look more like Marsha and Will's and less like Fred and
Gail's. In the rest of this chapter, we show you how to put the Dictionary of Relationship Talk to use in your relationship.

Keep in mind, as you read further, an implication from our simple
truth #1—that even though one *positive* move can alter the course of an
interaction for the better, it is still critical to minimize the number of
negative responses. Negative talk and the cross-complaining it often elicits is like the "knock knock" joke being repeated over and over again
in troubled relationships.

PUTTING THE DICTIONARY OF RELATIONSHIP TALK
TO PROPER USE

We have presented the Dictionary of Relationship Talk so that you can
begin to study your own communication—not to overanalyze your
partner's messages. Because the only communication that you have
complete control over is your own, try to pay more attention to your
own messages than to your partner's talk the next time an issue arises.
As you assess your own communication, you will be served well by
increasing the frequency of:

- Positive problem talk
- Listening talk

and decreasing the frequency of:

- Negative problem talk
- Negative solution talk

- Mind reading
- Critical talk

Don't try to vanquish these negative behaviors completely—that would be inhuman!

If the conversation demands that you make one of these potentially harmful statements, then it will usually be best to avoid making the statement *immediately after* a similar kind of statement from your partner. Instead, try as often as possible to respond in the first breath to your partner's negative statements with *listening talk*. Then and only then, go ahead with the negative talk if you feel that you must.

When you do your part to improve your relationship, your partner will follow your lead. In fact, if you are using this book to try to change your relationship and your partner is not actively involved in the process at this point, you can still do a lot to change the destructive sequences and the predictability in interaction. You can try to alter your role. You can try to deescalate. You can try to meet criticisms with listening. If your mate still persists in critical talk, you can at least avoid getting drawn into a string of negative exchanges that often leave you feeling hurt, lonely, and, perhaps, hopeless.

By paying attention to your own communication, you can take control of the communication process. If you focus on your partner's messages, the danger is that you will shift your argument away from whatever you are talking about to *how* you are discussing whatever topic is before you. This is not a good shift and is characteristic of unhappy relationships. If you tell your partner, "Hey, you are using negative problem talk and the Dictionary says that is not so good" or you say "Tell me what *you* feel, don't mind-read what I feel," your intentions may be good but your statements are really *critical talk*. They only will fuel the fires of conflict. That is why we want you to focus on the only person's talk you have control over—your own.

Sam and Ali, now a happily married couple, came to see us before deciding to marry because they were unsure about staying together and wanted some help seeing if the relationship was "worth salvaging." As with other couples who present this concern to us, we suggested that they suspend evaluation of the relationship for two months so that they could concentrate their efforts on learning more effective ways of discussing relationship issues with each other. Further, we suggested that they would then be able to use their new skills to responsibly answer their question about staying together.

During their sixth therapy session, Ali and Sam wanted help in understanding what had gone wrong the previous evening. They had met after work to have dinner at a new restaurant that they both wanted to try. We pick up their conversation somewhere between their first beer and the salad:

ALI: "I'm planning to go home for the holidays. What are you doing?"

This sounded like problem talk, but Sam was taken aback because he had assumed they would be spending the holidays together. At first, he didn't say anything. Then he said with some irritation:

SAM: "I guess I'll have to find something to do to keep myself busy."

His angry tone of voice and averted glance made this "negative problem talk." Ali knew something was wrong but made the mistake of trying to defend herself before she knew exactly what she was defending against:

ALI: *"You* went home without me last time. Don't ruin this evening."

This explanation for her desire to be with her family and implied criticism of Sam's response further ensnared them in a tit-for-tat negative exchange. Like a nail reacting to a powerful magnet, Sam automatically extended the cycle:

SAM: "Fine. Do what you want. Just don't expect me to sit home alone."

By offering "negative solutions," Sam rekindled an ongoing concern the couple had about managing their feelings of jealousy toward past lovers.

At this point we had heard enough. Sam and Ali had gone through only two floor switches, but, like a speeding train headed downhill without brakes, they showed no sign of being able to avoid derailing their conversation.

Because all couples enter into conflict in much the same way, we told Sam and Ali that it was essential to focus their energies on *exiting* from a disagreement once it starts. Accordingly, we asked Ali to start the conversation in the same way she had last evening and we would help them write a new script. We then also instructed Sam to respond as he did in the restaurant. We wanted to take them to this point in the conversation so they could get some practice halting an argument that was spiraling out of control. Also, we wanted to impress upon them that no matter how hard they tried, from time to time, marital fires will start and learning how to contain and douse them quickly is an essential skill for all couples. They both repeated their opening lines:

Sam and Ali: Take Two

ALI: "I'm planning to go home for the holidays. What are you doing?"
SAM: "I guess I'll have to find something to do to keep myself busy."

To help redo their conversation from this point, Ali and Sam consulted their Dictionary of Relationship Talk. Ali's first attempt at a more constructive response was better, but still problematic:

ALI: "You're angry because I want to go home alone."

We stopped Ali and suggested that "mind reading" is a risky strategy; it is usually better to let your partner speak for himself. She tried again, this time calling a "stop action":

ALI: "Sam, wait a minute. What is going on here?"

Stop actions are always a useful tool that can help you halt a destructive conversation. We describe the stop-action tool more fully in chapter 7. We told Ali that she made a terrific change in the script. After a short pause, Sam's new response focused on how he was feeling:

SAM: "I was thinking we would be together this year, and it seemed to me this wasn't important to you."

Ali recognized that this was a critical time for "listening talk":

ALI: "So, you were disappointed with me when I said I was going home for the holidays and asked you what you were doing."

SAM: "Yeah, when you asked me what I was doing, I felt you didn't want to spend the holidays with me."

Even though she felt Sam had misread her, Ali again turned to "listening talk" to make sure she understood Sam's disappointment:

ALI: "You felt I was telling you I didn't want you to come home with me."
SAM: "Right."

Ali then had an opportunity to continue the problem talk and clarify her side of the issue,

ALI: "It is important to me to be home this holiday so that I can spend time with my grandfather. I just assumed that you didn't want to travel to be with my family. I would love to have you there. It's not that I want to be away from you. I just want to be with my family."

Sam now could easily problem-solve this situation:

SAM: "I would like to be with you over the holidays. I know it is important for you to spend some time with your grandfather. I may leave early to see my brother, but it would be nice to be together for at least the first few days."
ALI (WARMLY): "That's fine. I'm sorry I didn't handle this as well as I could have."
SAM: "Me, too. It's hard for me to get over that initial sting and pull out something constructive to say."

With a little help, Sam and Ali were able to put to good use all they had learned working with us for the previous six weeks. As Sam and Ali discovered, the largest obstacle you will face in breaking free from an escalating argument is your own anger. During conflict, anger gives you a sense of purpose and minimizes the chance that you will come face to face with some very powerful feelings about yourself. Anger toward a loved one usually erupts when we feel threatened, unloved, or incompetent. Because these self-doubts are so aversive and so powerfully experienced, we rely on our anger to mask the discomfort. When we feel angry, we can't feel our pain. But although anger is self-protective in the short run, it can destroy a relationship in the long run. In chapter 6 we will provide you with greater insight into the source of your anger, and in chapter 10 we offer specific guidelines for transforming anger into useful energy for relationship growth and development.

APPLYING THE DICTIONARY TO THE FOUR STYLES OF CONFLICT INTERACTION

As noted in chapter 3, after studying the conversations of hundreds of couples, we have found that relationship conflict appears to come in *only* four major types. Now we want to acquaint you with the precise communications that go along with escalation, withdrawal, and the two pursuit ↔ withdrawal patterns. Once you know how these strategies operate, you will be one step closer to disrupting their destructive influences.

Explosive Boilers Are Fueled by Escalation

We all know the meaning of escalation: it's your basic knock-down, drag-out fight. However, as we've stated, the script for most fights is utterly predictable. The partners have an illusion of talking, but in reality there is preciously little information exchanged. Instead, the couple marches to the battlefield with steady determination, few detours, and little hope of anything but pyrrhic victories.

Patrick and Lindsay married late, when both were in their mid-thirties. Soon thereafter they had twin daughters, Helen and Hillary. They entered therapy due to constant battles that started soon after the birth of the twins and that had not improved with time as they had hoped. One of their worst fights started innocently enough. Patrick was stretched out in the living room watching Tom Brokaw deliver the evening news. He had the newspaper on his lap to occupy himself during the commercials. The twins were quietly playing in the adjacent family room. Lindsay walked in from a hard day at work, said hello to Patrick, kissed the children good evening, and then went upstairs to change into jeans and a flannel shirt. Ten minutes later, she came downstairs and approached Patrick with a sense of urgency. We pick up the conversation at this point:

LINDSAY: "We really need to talk."

PATRICK: "Not now."

LINDSAY: "Pat, I said we really need to talk" (more emphatically and somewhat more negatively).

PATRICK: "I said, 'not now.' "

LINDSAY: "Not now, not ever. That's all I hear."

PATRICK (WITH EXASPERATION): "That is not true, I love to talk, but you don't know how to talk. All you know how to do is fight. That's all we do. Like now."

LINDSAY: "There you go again, always blaming me for everything. I really can't stand this much longer."

PATRICK (VEINS PULSING IN HIS NECK): "Don't go and threaten me again. If you left that would be fine with me. I've just about had it with this relationship, with you, and with this mess of a house."

LINDSAY: "You son of a bitch. You can go to hell. . . ."

PATRICK: "Living with you *is* hell, you asshole . . ."

He picked up a lamp and threw it toward Lindsay. She ducked and then rushed to him and started punching him in the chest and shoulders. He angrily pushed her away, and she fell down—crying uncontrollably as he stormed out of the room.

Unfortunately, Lindsay and Patrick are typical explosive boilers whose arguments are routinely destructive. They are experts at critical talk and hopeless talk. Because the most likely response to each of these types of statements is more critical talk and more hopeless talk, after each person shows his or her commitment to the old pattern, the outcome may as well be set in stone.

The typical features of Patrick and Lindsay's fight that define escalation for most couples are:

• One person says something negative (critical talk, mind-reading talk, hopeless talk).

- The other partner immediately replies with more critical talk, mind-reading talk, or hopeless talk.
- The first person continues the critical talk, mind-reading talk, or hopeless talk, often using more dramatic nonverbal cues to emphasize the message (e.g., raised voice, angry face).
- The second person responds in kind . . . and so on.
- Neither person shows understanding of the partner through the use of listening talk.

Of course, not all Pat and Lindsay's fights end with physical aggression. However, as with close to 33 percent of American couples, some arguments will escalate to aggression or more serious acts of violence and battering (see box 5.1).

INVALIDATION LEADS TO ESCALATION

Invalidation is a pattern of interaction that often underlies escalation. It involves putting down the other person, attacking his/her personality or character, and criticizing him/her rather than his/her ideas and behavior. When couples escalate a fight, invalidation is usually the corrosive undercurrent causing so much mutual distress.

Box 5.1
Relationship Aggression: Escalation in the Extreme

Sociologist Murray Straus says that a marriage license is a hitting license. Rates of relationship aggression are at an all-time high, with over 20 percent of couples in America pushing, shoving, hitting, or slapping each other at least once a year. There is little doubt that we tend to hurt the ones we love and that the disturbingly high rates of relationship aggression and violence are, in part, symptomatic of the fact that couples cannot handle conflict very well. Whatever the exact cause of marital aggression, the most important consideration for partners in a violent relationship is *safety*. If you feel you are in danger, leave. Seek help and if you decide to continue the relationship, make sure that the aggressive partner is getting help. Professional help for the relationship will also be important.

When we started our research, we strongly believed that its opposite—*validation*—would be one of the major predictors of future success in a relationship. We validate our partner when we demonstrate respect, empathy, positive regard, and support for him or her. We were proven wrong. When we examined the amount of validation in the premarital discussions of the couples that went on to be happy with those who subsequently became distressed or divorced, there were no differences. Couples who were later divorced showed equally high levels of validation as the couples who remained happy.

However, one of our major predictors of future misery was the amount of invalidation present before marriage. Couples who were later divorced showed rates of invalidation about three times that of the couples who stayed happy over time. This is yet another example of the simple truth that one negative comment erases twenty positive acts of kindness. *Like an invading cancer cell,* invalidation *kills the positive feelings on which relationships are built.*

We recently discovered one of the reasons that invalidation is so costly. We asked men and women what they wanted the most out of marriage. The resounding answer: "a friend." When we interviewed couples who were divorcing and talked with them about their feelings of loss, many of them said that they felt they had lost their best friend. When we asked people what they meant by friendship, they said that it is a relationship with someone who will listen to them without judging them, someone who will be supportive and empathic. People were letting us know that they want their spouse to be a friend who provides validation.

Why, then, is validation *not* a strong predictor of relationship success? Although we expect friendship and validation to occur in a relationship, we found that partners can deal with not always getting validation for having done something positive. However, partners *cannot* cope well with active invalidation. In unhappy relationships, spouses are often experienced as enemies who periodically swoop down in a sneak attack on our self-esteem. Humiliation, dismissal, and assassination attempts on our character are very costly and harmful to our relationships.

Silent Steamers Are Powered by Withdrawal

The counterpoint to escalation is withdrawal. As we've seen, fleeing partners are frightened by conflict and do their best to avoid it at all costs. On the surface, particularly in the early years of the relationship, these couples appear to have a happy relationship. But these are the couples who suddenly get a divorce, leaving all their friends wondering what went wrong because "they always seemed so together."

Rick and Arlene were one of these couples. They came to therapy after twenty-five years of marriage, with Arlene complaining of loneliness and depression. Rick had serious low-back pains and high blood pressure. Their youngest son had just graduated from college and taken a job in another state. Now they were facing the rest of their lives together. Rick and Arlene's symptoms reflected a marriage devoid of both intimacy and conflict.

What went wrong with Rick and Arlene, like most of these couples, is that they were so afraid of conflict that they assiduously avoided making their own wishes and desires known. They glossed over the differences between them to make sure that confrontations would never, ever erupt.

A typical conversation between Rick and Arlene was, therefore, very short and usually went like this:

ARLENE: "What do you want to do tonight?"
RICK: "Whatever you want is fine."
ARLENE: "How about a movie?"
RICK: "Okay, but we could just stay home and watch TV."
ARLENE (CLENCHING HER FISTS): "I don't really care what we do. Let's just do something."
RICK (PICKING UP THE REMOTE CONTROL): "Uh-uh."
ARLENE: "So, I guess we'll just stay home alone again."

As was the case with Rick, when asked for an opinion, the silent steamer is most likely to say "Whatever you want to do is fine." This strategy might work well for a couple for a while, even for several years. However, the partners never learn how to accept and manage conflict, and because conflict is an inevitable part of all relationships, they will eventually have to confront their worst fears.

Silent steamers are usually filled with smoldering resentments. Although the silent steamer is reluctant to make his or her wishes known, they come to resent the fact that they are always trying to please their partner. They tend to gloss over the fact that they have responsibility to present their side of issues and express their feelings when choices have to be made.

When "Whatever you want to do" falls short of a solution, the silent steamer resorts to more obvious strategies of withdrawal—such as avoiding, denying, or stonewalling.

Silent steamers make a lot of use of negative problem solutions ("I don't care what we do"), they avoid listening talk, and they often resort to excuses and explanations in the hope of avoiding conflict. The latter doesn't work well to avoid conflict and when an inevitable argument erupts, the silent steamer physically withdraws from the conversation and perhaps from the relationship.

As Rick and Arlene continued in relationship therapy, both partners started to reveal negative feelings about past events that they'd never before have dared to express. This became a jumping-off point for them to discard their long-held pattern of avoiding conflicts and to begin to learn how to deal with conflict constructively.

When Pursuit Finds Withdrawal: The Vicious Cyclers

As we've discussed, there are two basic pursuit ↔ withdrawal patterns. The most common and most discussed is when males withdraw in the face of female pursuit, or when females pursue in the face of male withdrawal. We doubt that this is headline news for our women readers. Moreover, when the male withdraws *early* in the relationship, this signals the likelihood of *future* distress—unless this pattern is altered. When the female withdraws *later* in the relationship, this is a sign of serious *current* problems and a predictor of divorce in the near future—unless help is sought.

MALE WITHDRAWAL ↔ FEMALE PURSUIT

To exemplify the classic male withdrawal ↔ female pursuit pattern, consider the following actual interaction from one of our research couples:

MARK: "What are we talking about?"

LYN: "We're talking about communication."

MARK: "We don't have a problem with communication."

LYN: "Yes, we do. You never talk to me. When I talk to you, you get antsy and just shut down."

MARK: "Uh-huh." (Mark is actually getting antsy in this conversation, just as Lyn describes it.)

This interaction demonstrates the typical complaints of men and women in marriage. Women complain that men don't listen, won't open up. Men complain that women nag and attack.

In the face of tension and conflicts, women seek peace by pursuing talk while men seek peace by trying to contain conflict, often by withdrawing, appeasing, or stonewalling. *In relationships that are successful, men and women* learn from each other *to manage conflict and to cultivate intimacy.* In relationships that are not successful, these differences polarize the partners and neither is capable of seeing their own role in maintaining the vicious cycle.

What too often happens to couples like Lyn and Mark is that the wife's negative feelings become the focus of attention. This, of course, is a red herring. The real issue is whatever the wife is concerned about. Two major problems arise when the couple defines the wife's anger as a relationship issue. First, she often feels invalidated because she is being told that she can't express her feelings. Second, because the real issues are not being discussed and solved, they tend to fester and worsen over time.

Returning to Mark and Lyn's discussion, we see another important feature of the male withdraw↔female pursue pattern—in this case concerning *intimacy.*

LYN: "Why don't you talk to me? You talk to your brother. In fact, I learn more from what's going on in your life from your brother than I do from you. I just can't take that."

MARK: "You don't ask the right questions."

LYN: "I need to know about you."

MARK: "It's on a need-to-know basis."

LYN: "Let me tell you something, your wife needs to know."

As we listen in on this conversation, it appears that Mark has the *capacity for the type of intimate talk Lyn wants* (he's telling his brother the things she wants him to be telling her). So what's keeping him from actualizing this intimacy potential with his wife? For Mark and many men like him, what keeps them bottled up is their fear that confrontations will erupt in the course of opening up to their wives. Research shows that men *can be* as intimate as women when talking, but either don't choose to do so or are afraid to do so. The solution: creating *ground rules* for couples to ensure that destructive conflicts do not erupt when talking. We detail these ground rules in part 3 of this book. This will create circumstances in which partners feel safe to be as intimate as they can be. Using the Dictionary of Relationship Talk also allows intimacy to develop by forcing conversations into a noncritical format.

FEMALE WITHDRAWAL ↔ MALE PURSUIT

There is one point in the course of the development of relationship distress where we *typically* see females withdrawing and males pursuing. This point occurs after a relatively long history of distress, during which the female has been trying to get her husband to talk, to work on the relationship, and/or to seek help but has run up against a wall. The major result is her strong feelings of anger, hostility, and depression. Finally, she decides to end the pursuit and to focus on other areas where she has more control, rather than try to get her husband to talk, to understand her, or to work on the relationship. Of course, this does not happen in the case of all couples, but we are seeing it more often as wives in unhappy marriages come to understand the root of their anger and depression.

Often, once the wife starts channeling her energy toward other activities, her anger and depression lessen considerably, and she may start taking actions toward divorce. Thus, wives are significantly more likely than husbands to file for divorce. It is at this point, as the wives make moves to exit the relationship, that the husband starts pursuing. As one husband recently put it: "Once she filed for divorce, boom, it was a reality check for me. It got my attention." Often, men then become more attentive, romantic, and behave the way they did during the dating/courting stages of the relationship. When the threatening or filing for divorce and the subsequent pursuit by the husband starts a process of positive change for the couple, the wife is not as totally withdrawn as in other couples. The nationwide data on the number of divorces that are filed for but never completed (around 25 percent) suggest that filing for or seeking a divorce may indeed be the first stage of transformation for some couples.

For other couples, once a partner has reactively withdrawn from the relationship, repairing the relationship can be very difficult and will frequently require professional assistance. In these cases, the husband's pursuit comes too late. For example, sometimes the wife enters into an affair and decides that the alternative relationship is the one she wishes to continue. In other situations, the positive feelings that drew the couple together have eroded over time, particularly when the wife has experienced years of previously repressed anger, loneliness, and depression. As one wife succinctly put it: "When he came back to me, it was too late; my feelings for him had died."

How Role Change Can Be Healing

For a more detailed example of how pursuit↔withdrawal roles can change over time, let's examine the history of Scott and Jill, married for seven years when they first came in for therapy.

While they were living together, Jill and Scott were very happy with their relationship. They spent most of their weekends in the mountains, riding bikes, hiking, canoeing, and rafting. A weekend hardly passed when they weren't out doing something. The birth of their first child, Stacy, changed all that. Jill noted that Scott had become distant and withdrawn shortly afterwards, and despite constant attempts to get him to talk about it, he would say everything was fine. Stacy was a difficult child, keeping them up most nights during the first year. Not only did their recreational activities drop to almost nil, they never discussed what was happening between them and drifted further apart. The second child, Will, was born when Stacy was one and a half years old, and within two years after marriage they had settled into a routine that left Jill feeling lonely, isolated, and puzzled about what had transpired.

Jill continued to talk to Scott, but he maintained that everything was fine, refusing to respond to her concerns. Soon they were fighting once or twice a week and not really understanding why. At that time, Jill pressed for them to enter therapy, but Scott resisted. This pattern continued for three more years and worsened. Meanwhile Jill resumed her career in the Forest Service once Will entered day care, and she derived increasing satisfaction from her work. Her efforts to coax Scott to talk or enter therapy abated as her sense of loneliness and distance increased. More and more she met her needs through a friendship with workmate Alice, and through her time with the children. Nevertheless, she felt that the best years of her life were being lost because she was not getting her emotional or sexual needs met by Scott.

One evening after the children were in bed, she walked up to Scott, picked up the remote control, turned off the television, and beseeched him to talk with her. "I'm in the middle of a program. Can't it wait?" he replied. Jill then advised him to hire a lawyer because she was planning to file for divorce. Scott was shocked. Although he recognized some of their weak areas, he still thought they were happy together as a family. He had actually interpreted Jill's cessation of efforts to talk or enter therapy as a sign that she had been more contented, perhaps because she had resumed the work she enjoyed.

Scott's disbelief was consistent with the operation of the denial filter discussed in chapter 3, and typical of his tendency toward avoidance. A week later, Jill again asked if he had talked to a lawyer yet. She did not want to serve him with papers, but she would go ahead if they could not begin a dialogue. She expressed these feelings with such force that it cut right through Scott's defenses, and he panicked. He started crying and begging her not to leave. For the first time, he agreed to go to therapy and try to work things out, especially for the sake of the children. Jill still had some positive feelings left for Scott, not having forgotten their three good years together, and also feeling a strong sense of family and commitment to the institution of marriage. She was moved by

Scott's reaction and surprised by his agreement to enter therapy. Jill said she would think about it, and that night they held and comforted each other.

The next morning Jill made it clear to Scott that even though they had gotten closer the previous night, things were still problematic for her. If there was any chance for improvement, he would have to take seriously his suggestion about therapy. Scott, who had started to relax, once again panicked. Later that morning, he called to make an appointment.

In therapy, Jill finally had the opportunity to express her feelings about the relationship—feelings that had been stifled for years. With our help, Scott listened to her and began to understand the roots of her unhappiness. As his awareness increased, he was able to acknowledge that he shared many of the same concerns but feared that directly tackling the issues would make matters worse. As the healing process continued, Jill and Scott started to feel like teammates. Soon they began to work together to solve their most pressing problems.

The healing process often begins with the pursuit ↔ withdraw roles changing. For many couples, like Jill and Scott, the first stage of the healing process is when the previous reluctant partner comes around and actively takes responsibility for the future of the relationship, as Scott did by making arrangements for the couple's therapy. In our experience, even the most distressed couples can be rescued from the brink of divorce if they are willing to seek help.

Escalation, Withdrawal, and Invalidation Can Occur Together

Jan and Bob both work outside the home, and they have three children ranging in age from two to ten years. One Saturday morning over breakfast, they were talking about what they wanted to accomplish over the weekend. Both expressed a very strong need to finish work projects that had to be ready by Monday. Their discussion about how to handle this predicament was starting to escalate. Jan finally suggested that Bob go to his office, work as long as he needed to, and she would try to get the children situated with baby-sitters. Then she would go to their office at home and work on the computer. Not surprisingly, Bob was pleased with that suggestion. He put some coffee in a thermos and rushed off to his office.

Jan did everything she promised and even managed to get her proposal done as well. She was just printing it out when Bob walked in the door. He looked at the kitchen, which was an absolute mess with breakfast dishes still piled in the sink, and complained about what a disaster area the place was. Yet Jan had been feeling pleased with herself and had expected Bob to come in and show his appreciation for the juggling act she had pulled off. She had even fantasized about a romantic dinner for two.

Bob not only didn't show gratitude, he actively invalidated her by complaining about the state of the house. Responding to his surprise attack, Jan became infuriated and demanded to know how he dared to complain about her housekeeping skills, when they had had such a hectic day. She castigated him for being unappreciative and stormed off to take a nap, leaving Bob to handle the problems of the house and the children.

This example is important because it shows how invalidation gets the process of escalation under way and how withdrawal enters in as an escape from both the invalidation and the escalation. As noted, we've found that each of these interactional maneuvers—invalidation, escalation, and withdrawal—are predictors of future problems.

Interestingly, Jan and Bob usually do a good job handling conflict and as a couple do not fit the description of either explosive boilers, silent steamers, or vicious cyclers. Like all couples, they have some conflicts that simply get out of hand. This is very likely to happen when there are lots of demands being placed on both persons' resources. Remember, no one argument is going to make or break a relationship. It is the repeated patterns that ultimately come to cause damage.

The key is to learn how to recognize and prevent the destructive progression from invalidation to escalation and then withdrawal. You now should be able to use descriptions provided in this chapter to *recognize* the early signs of this process. As soon as you are aware of being dragged down into this destructive spiral, no matter where you find yourself—say to yourself and then to your partner: "If we continue talking in this way, we're going to hurt ourselves." This essentially calls a "stop action" or "cease-fire" and will help keep you from following a tried-and-true path toward a bad fight. At this point, many couples just stop talking and never return to the issue at hand. Don't fall into this pattern. Instead, after a cooling-off period, use the Dictionary of Relationship Talk in conjunction with the floor exercise, or one of the techniques from our Better Talk program, in order to talk about the issue without fighting.

Although Jan and Bob were not able to recognize the early signs of invalidation and escalation, they did follow these principles to work though their argument. After Jan's nap, Bob said to her: "I don't feel very good about what happened before. Can we talk?" Jan acknowledged Bob's concern and suggested: "Let's wait until the kids are asleep." They agreed to talk later that night and used their common language from the Dictionary of Relationship Talk and the structure provided by the floor exercise to talk about what happened earlier. Bob expressed his appreciation for what Jan had done earlier and accepted responsibility for his critical remark when he walked in the door. Jan finally felt validated. The next time a similar pattern started, they recognized what was happening and short-circuited the destructive process.

We have found that even the most ingrained negative patterns can change. When partners are no longer mystified by why they fight and have the tools required to talk about negative feelings without the fear of conflict erupting, relationship growth, repair, and development are all possible.

FROM TALK TO THOUGHTS

In this chapter we have provided you with a Dictionary of Relationship Talk to help you solve the mystery of why couples fight and how to prevent destructive arguments. From this point on, you should be trying to dam the flow of withdrawals from your relationship bank account by decreasing negative talk—the kind of behavior that comes across as zingers. However, destructive talk is only one of the major clues to relationship distress that we have pursued in our research. In

the next chapter we expand our search for the causes of marital problems by moving inward to examine how we think. We will show how
hot thoughts fuel relationship conflicts and destructive talk by linking
how you *think* about your partner to how you *feel* about your relationship. Moreover, a Dictionary of Self-Talk will be provided to help you
identify the differences between hot and cold thoughts thus allowing
you to begin the process of thinking about your relationship in a way
that promotes positive change.

Chapter 6

HOT THOUGHTS: THE FUEL OF DESTRUCTIVE RELATIONSHIP CONFLICTS

In the last chapter, we showed you how destructive talk hurts your relationship and how it leads to patterns of escalation, invalidation, pursuit, and withdrawal. In this chapter we will show you how destructive *talk* often stems from destructive *thoughts*. Certain types of thoughts increase the likelihood of lapsing into the destructive talk patterns we outlined in chapter 4. We call them *hot thoughts* because they fuel the fires of relationship conflict. We will help you to identify hot thoughts that originate in your own internal dialogues and then give you specific suggestions for turning these destructive thoughts into cooler ones that will enable you to handle conflict in your relationship with flexibility.

The familiar expression "He's such a hothead" is generally used to describe someone who shows a great deal of anger when upset. The expression can be taken literally—it accurately describes a person whose thoughts are so hot and provocative that they eventually erupt into visible rage. Because the world only sees the outer expression of rage and not the hot thoughts that fuel that rage, we typically fail to recognize that the hothead's anger is just as much a problem in *thinking* as it is a problem in *expression*.

Part of the reason we tend to overlook the power of our thinking in shaping our behavior is that thoughts happen so quickly and automatically. Every waking moment, we take in and analyze a huge amount of information from our world and from the interactions we have with people in it. If that process did not happen with speed and efficiency, we'd be immobilized by the task of sorting through all that was occurring externally and internally.

Even though thoughts are automatic, this does not mean that they are unconscious and beyond your inspection. With a little work, you can determine what your daily "self-talk" consists of: evaluations of yourself and others and the everyday situations that you find yourselves in. Examples of "self-talk" are:

- "Because he hasn't called, he must not want to be with me."
- "She knows how much I love her."
- "She is being very supportive of me."
- "He really does care."
- "I hate it when he just stares at me like that and doesn't say anything."
- "I can't stand her yelling. I can't talk to her anymore."
- "He's a sensitive lover."
- "He'll never understand how I really feel."
- "She doesn't appreciate all the things I do for her and the family."
- "I'll never be good enough for her."

In this chapter, we will ask you to begin the work of tuning into your self-talk channel. The reason is simple: *How you feel about yourself, your* *partner, and the relationship is largely determined by the nature of your self-talk.* Specific types of self-talk will leave you feeling angry, resentful, and hopeless about the future, while other self-statements will leave you feeling satisfied, understood, and optimistic.

FEELING WHAT YOU THINK

At first blush, most of us believe that our partner's actions cause us to feel happy or sad, angry or content, disgusted or pleased. In fact, we often order our world by thinking that other people are responsible for our feelings. From this point on, we want you to realize that nobody makes you feel any particular way. You do it all by yourself. And because you are responsible for your feelings, you have control over how you feel in response to whatever happens. Eleanor Roosevelt once said something to the effect that no one can make you feel incompetent without your consent. There is much wisdom in this saying, and it applies to feelings of anger as well.

Because feelings follow your thoughts and not your partner's actions, it is essential that you listen to your inner voice. Once aware of your private voice, you can take control over it and ultimately over your feelings. Your goal will be to translate destructive self-talk that leaves you feeling angry and hopeless into constructive self-talk that enables change and makes you feel optimistic about the future. Your capacity to control the destructive thoughts that block conflict resolution is one basis for the hidden reservoir of hope in your relationship described in simple truth #2.

Ann is at a restaurant drumming her fingers on the table waiting for Ted, who is now twenty minutes late. She had rushed out of her office to be on time for their seventh-anniversary dinner and is growing increasingly more uncomfortable as the waiter asks for the second time, "Can't I bring you a drink while you wait?" Ann wonders where Ted is and tries to explain his tardiness to herself. Ann might give silent voice to several different explanations for Ted's absence:

> **Explanation #1:** "Ted does not manage his time well. He cares more about his damn business meetings than he does about me. He's probably still at the office."
>
> **Explanation #2:** "Traffic was really bad coming across town today. I bet he is stuck on Eye Street and frustrated beyond belief that he's late for our anniversary dinner."
>
> **Explanation #3:** "Maybe he was in an accident and has been hurt."
>
> **Explanation #4:** "We talked about going Indian or Italian. Maybe he is sitting over at the Tandoor waiting for me."
>
> **Explanation #5:** "I bet he went to work out at the gym and lost track of the time."

The inner voice that captures Ann's attention is going to exert a powerful influence on how she *feels* as she sits at the table waiting for Ted to arrive. This inner voice is also going to determine what type of statement Ann will pluck out of the Dictionary of Relationship Talk when Ted finally arrives. The following examples may be familiar to you.

If Ann listens to the voice telling her that Ted cares more about his damn business than her, she'll say: "Where the hell have you been? Is closing another deal more important than our anniversary?"

If, on the other hand, Ann listens to the voice telling her that Ted may have been in an accident, she'll say: "I'm so glad you're here. I was really worried something terrible had happened to you."

Ann and Ted will play out very different scenes, depending on which inner voice captures Ann's attention and which of the consequent greetings she serves up to Ted. As we noted in chapter 5, no conversation is ever set in stone (although negative patterns are certainly predictable), so we can't know with certainty how it will play out. But we know that the odds of an argument are much greater if Ann says "Where the hell have you been?" than if she says "I'm so glad you're here."

TUNING IN TO YOUR INNER VOICE

In the last chapter, you learned to categorize the messages that you and your partner exchanged. You learned that some messages (for example, listening talk) promoted constructive discussions and helped the relationship. Other forms of talk (for example, critical talk) made constructive discussions less likely. Now we want you to gain a better understanding of the automatic self-talk that silently echoes in your heads whenever your partner does something that either troubles or pleases you. As with the categories of relationship talk, most of us lack a good language to describe the helpful and harmful characteristics of our self-statements. The Dictionary of Self-Talk is designed to help you understand what thoughts fuel the fires of relationship conflict and what thoughts promote relationship change and adaptation. Once you know how the Dictionary of Self-Talk works, we will have you examine your hot thought potential. We will then offer you specific help in cooling hot thoughts and thinking constructively.

As you read through the categories, keep in mind that the same self-talk statement may fit in more than one category.

DICTIONARY OF SELF-TALK

Character assassination

These are self-statements meant to explain your partner's behavior that you find annoying or disappointing by resorting to vague and general descriptions of his or her personality. For instance: "She's a neatness freak"; "He's being passive-aggressive"; "She's pathetic." When speakers use character assassination self-talk, they take one instance of behavior (for example, tracking mud onto a newly cleaned floor) and react as if that one instance represented something fundamental about the person (for example, "He is an inconsiderate, selfish person who thinks only of himself").

Character adoration

Any self-statement explanation using a global or general description of character to explain your partner's behavior that you found to be a pleasing demonstration of caring and affection. Examples: "He's wonderful"; "She's terrific"; "She's great with the kids."

Always-never self-talk

Any self-statement explanation that involves the words *never* or *always*. These words are used to intensify the impact of character assassination (for example, "You never stop to consider my feelings") or character adoration ("You're always so thoughtful"). When used to explain an unpleasant behavior, these modifiers can lead to feelings of hopelessness and despair. They will prevent you from recognizing exceptions to *always* and *never* that can become the basis for hope and change. When always-never self-talk is openly expressed to a partner, the escalation cycle is often fed. Always-never self-talk is constructive when it is used to explain or account for pleasant behavior. Example: "I'll always remember our first date."

Here-and-now self-talk

Any self-statement explanation for a partner's actions that is specific as to time, place, or situation. Example: "My partner forgot to stop by the store this evening because he was rushing to get home." These statements are constructive when used to explain annoying behavior, because they focus your attention on specific aspects of the situation that can be changed rather than on global character assassinations that leave you feeling angry and hopeless. When used to explain a behavior that pleased you, these statements are likely to be destructive because they minimize the impact of the positive behavior. Example: "My partner is being nice tonight because he wants something from me."

Situation self-talk

Any self-statement explanation of your partner's behavior that takes into account the circumstances he or she confronted, rather than focusing on his or her personality. Example: "He's late because of traffic." When used to explain a behavior that bothered you, these statements are usually helpful. They replace character assassination with a compassionate awareness of the aspects of life that neither you nor your partner can control. *Situation self-talk places blame for problems outside of the relationship.* However, as with here-and-now self talk, situational explanations to explain our partner's kind behavior can be destructive because they tend to diminish the authenticity of their actions. Example: "The only reason my partner cleaned the bathroom is because his parents are coming to visit."

Competent self-talk

These are self-statements that express a belief in your ability to resolve disagreements that come up between you and your partner in a mutually satisfying manner. These thoughts enhance your chances for re-solving disagreements and minimize the chances for discord. Example: "When my partner and I disagree about our budget, I know we will be able to resolve the disagreement to our mutual satisfaction."

Hopeless-helpless self-talk

These are self-statements that express a sense of hopelessness about the future of the relationship, your ability to resolve disagreements, or the likelihood of self- or partner-change. These beliefs are destructive be-cause they act like self-fulfilling prophecies, bringing about the very outcomes you fear most. Example: "We're always going to have these problems." A particularly destructive form of hopeless-helpless self-talk occurs when the status of the relationship is threatened. Example: "I think we should give the relationship another month and if things are not better, I'm calling it quits."

Should self-talk

Any time you tell yourself that your partner should or should not be doing this or that, you are engaging in should self-talk. Believing that your partner should or shouldn't be doing something is a destructive practice, because it either leads to critical talk or it directs your attention away from expressing what you want from your partner in a manner that leads to change. When you engage in should self-talk, you're ask-ing your partner to be a clairvoyant who can mind-read your thoughts, behaviors, motivations, or desires. The best example is that common form of request: "I shouldn't have to ask for a hug; you should know I need one." With should self-talk, you also set yourself up as an author-ity on what's *best* for your partner—a sure prescription for resentment. For instance, "You should have asked for a raise a long time ago." Read: "Why are you such a wimp?"

Use the following summary table of our Dictionary of Self-Talk to help you pinpoint which of your thoughts will leave you feeling hot under the collar, thus fanning the flames of relationship conflict, and which thoughts are likely to keep you cool in the face of disappointments, annoyances, and conflict.

Self-Talk That Douses the Fires of Relationship Conflict

- Character adoration
- Situation self-talk
- Here-and-now self-talk
- Competent self-talk

Self-Talk That Fuels the Fires of Relationship Conflict

- Character assassination
- Always-never self-talk
- Hopeless-helpless self-talk
- Should-shouldn't self-talk

YES, BUT YOU DON'T KNOW MY PARTNER

As you read through the Dictionary of Self-Talk, you may have found the examples for bothersome behavior more familiar than the examples for pleasing behavior. We all tend to take more notice of our partner's actions that bother us than we do of those that give us pleasure. Therefore, we have lots of practice self-talking about the annoyances in our lives. The classic film *It's a Wonderful Life* dramatizes our tendencies to overlook the joyous aspects of our lives while dwelling on our dissatisfactions. Just as Jimmy Stewart lost all perspective on the glories of his friendships, family life, and community, we tend to lose all perspective on the wonderful aspects of our partners. Stewart needed a guardian angel to regain his positive perspective; we may need a guardian angel, at times, to combat our own negativism and resentment.

At this point, many of you caught in a tenacious pattern with your partner may be saying "But *my* partner *is* the problem! What you say may be true for other people, but it doesn't apply to me." Think back to

Ann, who was waiting for a partner who was late to a dinner appointment. If you were in her position, you would have been saying to yourself "I *know* why he's not here. He hasn't been to something on time for the last ten years. Why should today be any different?"

Psychologists have discovered that this type of reasoning, although very common, is counterproductive when the goal is to work on the relationship. All too often we tend to think the worst about our partner rather than the best. We don't even give our mate the same benefit of the doubt that we afford colleagues, friends, and even total strangers. When you latch on to the worst possible explanations for your partner's behavior, you're going to make your partner *and* yourself feel miserable.

Bill and Susan, a busy two-career couple, were looking forward to a fun weekend. Bill got up early on Saturday and started doing some weekend chores. He had already raked the leaves and had just started a load of permanent-press clothes in the washer when Susan asked him to take their son, Tim, to a soccer game. Bill agreed and asked Susan to put the clothes into the dryer and hang them up. When he returned from dropping Tim off, Susan was on the phone with her sister and the clothes were still sitting in the washer.

Bill was peeved. He thought, "Susan is not doing her share around the house. It's incredible that she can talk on the phone all morning when I'm trying to get all the house stuff done." When Susan got off the phone, he said, "Thanks for remembering the clothes." Susan, ignoring the sarcasm, said pointedly, "I didn't forget the clothes. I just had to talk to my sister. She was really upset, and she called as soon as you walked out of the house."

Overcoming Your Biases

Bill and Susan's self-talk exemplifies a *fundamental bias* in thinking that psychologists have discovered. We want you to start recognizing and changing this bias in your own thinking. When we observe our partner's behavior—especially the negative kind—we tend to *blame our partner* and hold him or her responsible for his or her actions. Thus Bill thought: "She spoke on the phone; she didn't tend to the clothes. She made a choice." The other tendency we have, in the face of our own negative behavior, is to *blame the situation.* Thus, Sue's explanation for her not getting to the clothes was: "I got a phone call, I had to talk to my sister, who was upset. I didn't have any choice." When in the role of "actors," we hold the situation responsible; whereas as "observers," we hold the actor responsible. The solution isn't blame; it's taking responsibility for our choices—good and bad—without punishing ourselves or our partners. Furthermore, our research has shown that unlike unhappy couples, happy partners avoid blame altogether and consider multiple causes for distressing relationship events.

These biases are built into each of us, but their pervasiveness does not mean that we are powerless to do anything about them or that relationship partners are victims of their perceptions, doomed to see the world from opposite points of view. On the contrary, we can change these biases by changing our thoughts. Keep in mind that you control your thoughts—they do not control you.

Now that you are aware of these potent perceptual biases, you can consider situations from multiple perspectives, your partner's as well as your own, and accept the fact that neither of you has cornered the "truth market." As a consequence, you will be in a position to acknowledge the reasonableness of each other's perspective, avoiding a narrow and destructive focus on only one point of view.

For the sake of argument, let's say that your blaming hot thoughts are not the result of this pervasive bias. Rather, you are convinced, beyond the shadow of a doubt, that your partner is to blame for a relationship problem and you want the world to know this "fact." Where does this get you? Even if there are some circumstances where your views are somehow more valid than your partner's, if you resort to self-talk laden with hot thoughts you are destined for relationship conflict. In the end, you will distance yourself from your partner, and the relationship will fail to fulfill your needs. It's unlikely that you will feel vindicated. Why?

Hot thoughts lead to feelings of hopelessness ("He's never going to change"), anger and resentment ("I don't deserve to be treated like this"), and even depression ("All I want to do is stay in bed, watch TV, and eat"). Hot thoughts also lead directly to destructive patterns of re-lationship talk. If you feel angry and hopeless, you will say things that communicate these feelings. You are likely to criticize your partner, offer negative problem solutions, mind-read your partner's thoughts and feelings, and fail to utilize listening talk. Because these behaviors tend to elicit replies in kind from your partner, you find yourself in the middle of an argument that confirms your worst thoughts. But it's a vicious cycle. Your thoughts lead to actions that increase the chance of conflict, and the inevitable conflict provides energy for more hot thoughts. You will rapidly find yourself trapped in one or more of the now-familiar patterns of escalation and pursuit ↔ withdrawal.

The way out of this bind is to identify *your goal* in any particular situ-ation and to behave in a way that maximizes your opportunity to attain this goal. We develop this theme further in chapter 8. For now, as you encounter conflict-laden situations, begin to consider your specific goal. Take a step back and ask yourself "What do I want to accom-plish?" In general, one goal should be selected and all your behavior should be aimed at achieving that goal.

When Bill and Susan discussed their Saturday-morning quarrel with us, we asked Bill to tell us what his primary goal was when he came home and noticed the clothes had not been removed from the washer. As is typically the case when we first ask this question, Bill said he wasn't sure. We suggested several possible goals: to get his clothes into the dryer, to punish Susan for talking on the phone, to start a fight, or to work out a plan for the future so that this situation did not repeat itself.

With more prodding, Bill finally identified his primary goal: to work out a plan for the future regarding housework. He realized that his thoughts had led him to act as if he wanted to punish Susan. Because berating Susan had actually made him less likely to achieve his primary goal, we helped him see that his actions were clearly counterpro-ductive.

Using the problem-solving techniques that we present in chapter 9, Bill and Susan agreed on a plan to call people back in five minutes if they were in the middle of a home chore that they had promised to complete. They acknowledged that there surely would be times when the plan would fail. Whenever that happened, Bill and Susan pledged themselves to consider multiple causes for the lapse, rather than to be tricked into blaming each other again by an "actor-observer" bias.

So even if some of your hot thoughts are in some sense "accurate," they are unlikely to enhance your ability to get your needs met, or to solidify and improve your relationship. As we stated at the outset of this chapter, our goal in raising your awareness of hot thoughts and changing them is to bring about constructive relationship change and adaptation. By cooling your thoughts, you will be able to express your feelings, wants, and desires in such a manner that your partner pays attention to you rather than shuts you out. You can ask for changes in the relationship that bring you closer together and allow you to maintain the collaborative spirit that will preserve your relationship rather than threaten its future.

EXAMINING YOUR HOT THOUGHT POTENTIAL

When you completed the Predict questionnaire in chapter 3, you took a peek at an important part of your hot thought potential—the beliefs you hold about being able to resolve disagreements that arise between you and your partner. Take a look at how you answered questions 26 through 28. If you answered "true" to these questions, it is very likely that you are laboring under hopeless-helpless self-talk and that you need to work on increasing the presence of competent self-talk. We have found that partners who use it have happier relationships in the present and the future.

Reliance upon competent self-talk is a powerful predictor of what will happen between you and your partner in the face of conflict. If you expect a disagreement with your partner to turn into an argument, chances are good that an argument will in fact occur. On the other hand, if you have a sense of mastery over your ability to resolve disagreements, the chances are equally good that you will be able to contain destructive exchanges.

We have found that for most partners, the motivation to work on their relationship is high—especially at the beginning of the relationship—but they don't have the skills to translate their high hopes into reality. Lacking skills, partners trying to deal with conflict are often misdirected and garner few positive results. Over the years, couples become frustrated and are left having little confidence in their ability to resolve issues.

The Better Talk program that we outline in part 3 of this book is specifically designed to help you increase your confidence in being able to resolve disagreements that arise between you. At this time, we want you to examine additional characteristics of your self-talk. Are you speaking words of encouragement and hope to yourself ("We'll be able to work this issue out to our mutual satisfaction") or words of hopelessness and despair ("We can't talk about anything without fighting")? Are your self-talk explanations for events fueling or dousing the fires of relationship conflict? Are your thoughts moving you closer to or further away from the goals you have for the relationship?

READING YOUR SELF-TALK: AN EXERCISE

Because self-talk happens automatically and is often beyond awareness, we have designed an exercise to help you tune in to the type of self-talk you typically use to explain your partner's behavior. Think for a moment about a recent event involving your partner that you experienced as quite unpleasant. Take out a piece of paper and jot down the essential details of the event.

With the details before you, note all the things you might have said to yourself about this event. Now read over what you have written down. If it does not contain your beliefs about what caused the event to happen, take a few moments to add these explanations to your list of thoughts. Finally, refer back to the Dictionary of Self-Talk and assign the applicable categories of self-talk to each of your statements. Don't worry if some statements cannot be categorized, and feel free to apply more than one category to a single self-statement. An example of how this exercise works is provided in box 6.1. Let's take a look at your list of self-statements. If your thoughts tended to be warm or hot, you should take time now to write down as many alternative explanations for what

---

Box 6.1
Carla's Self-Statement Exercise

Essential Details of Situation

José said he would watch the children Saturday morning. On Friday night, Frank called and asked him to go shopping for skis. José didn't think twice about saying that he would go. He never checked with me. I got so angry, I didn't say anything to him.

Self-Talk Explanations

- José should be more considerate of me (**should self-talk**).
- José always thinks of everyone else first . . . then me (**always-never self-talk**).
- He should have told Frank he couldn't go (**should self-talk**).
- There was no point in discussing it. All our discussions end in fights (**hopeless self-talk**).
- José is like all his brothers, thoughtless (**character assassination**).

Alternative Explanations

- José is often considerate of my feelings, although today he wasn't (**here-and-now self-talk**).
- José may have felt pressure to go with Frank and felt uncomfortable saying no (**situation self-talk**).
- We need to discuss these issues, and I'm sure we can without fighting (**competent self-talk**).
- All our discussions do not end in fights (**competent self-talk, here-and-now self-talk**).
- José is different from his family, that's why I married him (**character adoration**).

---

happened as you can. Remember, partners in happy relationships tend to think of many cool explanations for their partners' troubling behavior.

Since you have had a lifetime of practice developing your self-talk explanations for events in your world, don't expect to be able to alter your hot thoughts overnight. For this reason, we recommend that you repeat this exercise every time you are bothered by something your partner does. With practice, cool thoughts will gradually push aside the hot thoughts and, in time, will become as second nature to you as the hot thoughts once were.

THE DICTIONARY OF SELF-TALK IN USE

Todd and Meg, a young couple attending graduate school, had been dating for eighteen months and had already survived two breakups. One morning they decided to get up early to enjoy a springtime walk along the Potomac to drink in the smells and colors of the season. The trees were just coming into bloom, and the red buds against the cloudless blue sky were a sight to behold. Their plans for the day were just to "hang out together" and enjoy each other's company. As they walked along the towpath beside the river, Meg and Todd pleasantly discussed a play they had enjoyed two nights earlier.

Unfortunately, the outward conversation about the play was not the only "conversation" that was in progress. Todd and Meg were each distracted by a loud internal dialogue that vied for their personal attention. Todd heard himself wondering about Meg's family: "I think her family really has some serious problems. Her brother is in a drug rehabilitation center, her mother is an alcoholic, and her father is never home. Meg is always complaining about something. More and more she scares me. Maybe she is not as different from her family as I once thought. I'm not sure this relationship is right for me."

Meg's internal dialogue was different but equally distracting: "Todd's really egocentric. He always thinks of himself first. I can't remember the last time we did what I want. I go out of my way to think about him first; he goes out of his way to ignore me. He wants to go to a play; we go to a play. He wants to take a walk by the canal; we take a walk by the canal. I want to go to Alexandria; he suddenly has to fix the car. I want to stay home and watch a movie; he has to get some work done. Why can't he treat me more like an equal and be interested in the things I want to do?"

Listening in to Meg and Todd's thoughts shows us how, at times, our internal dialogues will become engaged without the occurrence of a specific external event. Our minds are always working, and hot thoughts can appear as if by spontaneous combustion. But once Meg and Todd's destructive internal dialogues were set in motion and remained unchallenged, it was only a matter of time before the gentle springtime walk was transformed into a battle based on long-standing conflicts between them. As they reached the end of the canal, Todd suggested they go have some coffee.

Meg *thought*, "Here we go again. He knows I stopped drinking coffee two weeks ago. One more example of his thinking only about himself. Things will never change between us. This relationship is hopeless."

Meg *said*, with some irritation, "No, I don't want to."

Todd *thought*, "Here we go again. One minute things are fine between us; the next minute she's angry about something. She's too emotional."

Todd *said*, "Well, let's call it a day. I'll call you later."

Meg sensed Todd's anger but thought he was overreacting to her declining to go for coffee. And because she was so angry herself, she didn't particularly care to find out why he had so abruptly called it a day. So she simply said, "Fine," and they parted with a lifeless exchange of pecks on the cheek. Both of them knew things were not fine.

Since Meg and Todd had been working to put a halt to destructive thinking, they walked only a few feet away from each other before beginning to challenge their self-statements. Todd caught himself resorting to destructive self-statements about Meg's family and her character. He challenged himself to come up with alternatives, and in a few moments he was saying to himself:

Alternative self-statement #1: "Meg has been under a lot of pressure at work this week; that's probably why she's been so on edge" (**situation** and **here-and-now self-talk**).

Alternative self-statement #2: "Meg and I can resolve disagreements" (**competent self-talk**).

Alternative self-statement #3: "Maybe I did something to push Meg away" (consider multiple causes for problems; avoid the actor-observer bias).

Meg also challenged her old self-statements and, instead, said to herself:

Alternative self-statement #1: "Todd just forgot I gave up coffee. He remembers lots of other things I ask him to do" (**here-and-now self-talk**).

Alternative self-statement #2: "We're learning new ways to think and behave, so change is always possible" (**competent self-talk**).

Alternative self-statement #3: "I've been trying to beat deadlines all month. I know my nerves are a bit frayed, and it must show (consider multiple causes for problems; avoid the actor-observer bias).

Having successfully cooled his hot thoughts by considering alternative explanations, Todd said to Meg, "I guess I got a little carried away for a minute and made myself angry—then I realized you've been under a lot of pressure at work and I know I can be hard to be around sometimes, so let's work this out. I don't want to call it a day. I wanted to spend the day with you, and I still do."

Meg, having already cooled her hot thoughts, responded by saying: "The same thing happened to me; sometimes I give up on us too quickly, but then I realized that we're both working on our relationship and we can't fall back into our old patterns. And you're right—I am stressed out with work. I want to be with you, too. Let's talk about this some more after the TV special we planned to watch tonight. Now, I'd love to get some lunch at Harry's. How does that sound?"

Todd recalled a special date they enjoyed at Harry's, and they made their way to the pub.

Because Meg and Todd's mutual goal for the day was to spend some enjoyable time together, there was no need to launch into a detailed analysis of what had gone wrong a few moments before. They recognized that a problem had occurred, and they used their cool thoughts to communicate better. They briefly let each other know that their hot thoughts had gotten out of hand and acknowledged other reasons for the tension. Once they had worked individually and as a team to bring the problem under control, they agreed to a discussion at a convenient time later in the day so as not further to disturb their mutual plans for a fun time together.

Keep in mind that there is no one right explanation for most events. The more explanations that you give voice to and consider, the better. It is most important to challenge the destructive hot thoughts as you consider as many alternatives as possible. If you find that most of your alternatives are equally hot, then you will need to deal with your anger. That is the topic we cover in chapter 10.

THINKING AS A TEAM

Another strategy to help you think constructively is to view a relationship problem as a foreign enemy threatening your home front. The only way to beat the enemy is to team up with your partner to provide a united front. If the enemy divides you, you will lose. Some therapists like to talk about this process as "externalizing the problem."

The essence of this strategy was neatly captured by an original "Star Trek" episode that aired many years ago. In this episode, the crew encountered a foreign life form that drew its strength from the crew's anger. The life form was creative in subtly provoking the crew into personal tiffs so that more and more anger was available for its sustenance. Wise Captain Kirk was able to realize what was happening, and he instructed his crew to replace their anger with laughter. The foreign life form continued to create provocative encounters among crew members, but the crew took control over their responses and met the continued provocations with laughter. The strategy worked. As laughter replaced anger, the invading life form lost its source of nourishment, and it was forced to leave the *Enterprise*.

Many couples seem to be held hostage by their anger in the same way that the *Enterprise* crew was attacked by a foreign life form. Partners don't want to fight with each other, or to remain separate and distant, and yet they seem compelled to indulge the angry outbursts that guarantee continued discord. We tell partners in such couples to team up together to fight a *common enemy* that is robbing the relationship of vitality and intimacy.

Jason and Karen were both physicians at a large medical clinic. They had been married for ten years and had been in marital therapy on three separate occasions. They had a long history of bitter disappointment with each other, and neither could contain his or her anger for very long. Jason and Karen's most frequent fights revolved around their three primary problem areas from the PPP: money, communication, and sex. They also fought about parenting issues as well. Neither liked the way the other disciplined their two boys, and they blamed each other for any difficulties. Jason thought that Karen was too lenient, letting the children get away with murder and not teaching them personal responsibility. Karen thought that Jason directed so much anger toward the boys that they were scared of him.

Despite their multiple problem areas and many years of struggle, Karen and Jason were committed to their marriage and wanted more than anything to recapture the intimacy they had had in the early years. Yet they were both filled with such hot thoughts, it was no wonder they were always arguing. Jason attributed the cause of most of their problems to Karen's character, and he expressed his hopelessness about relationship repair: "I can't do anything to please her. She's such a negative person, always so critical and demanding. I want my marriage to work, but I can't live like this much longer." Karen had a parallel set of destructive beliefs: "He's not capable of meeting my needs. He's selfish, unfeeling, uncaring. If three tries at therapy haven't worked, we need to give up. He'll never change."

At home, Karen and Jason were locked into patterns of mutual withdrawal. Their thoughts were so hot, and their interactions so predictable, that they avoided each other as much as possible. They had not had sex for over a year and rarely spent free time together. Stuffing their anger, hurt, and profound disappointment back into the darkness of their private thoughts did little to make these feelings disappear. Frequently, their hot thoughts bubbled to the surface and an argument broke the distant calm that had come to characterize their relationship. These arguments emerged over issues that required them to act as a team, yet there was virtually no spirit of teamwork between them. Disciplining their children was a ceaseless battleground—one they could not avoid.

To combat their destructive blaming, we suggested to both Jason and Karen that their problems were due not to flaws in the other person, but rather to destructive relational processes. We offered them a personalized version of the "Star Trek" tale. Because they were physicians, we had them view their destructive behavior as if it were a virus attacking their relationship. The only way to contain this virus was by teaming up together to find a cure. Fighting with each other only allowed the virus to thrive and the relationship to wither. As a team, they agreed that they wanted the same goals for and from their relationship: increased closeness, less bickering, and better parenting.

As Jason and Karen began to feel and act like a team, we reviewed with them the basic elements of politeness (covered in chapter 4), and we taught them how to use the Dictionary of Relationship Talk (chapter 5) and the Dictionary of Self-Talk (presented in this chapter). Jason and Karen said they were greatly helped by learning to replace destructive self-talk explanations for everyday marital events with positive alternatives. They were astonished to realize how much individual control they had over their thoughts and actions—and how rapidly this enabled them to develop teamwork.

Within a week, the couple stopped the spread of the "disease"—they reported no fights and no need for defensive retreats from each other. As two more weeks passed without fighting, Karen and Jason's confidence in their capacity to manage their disagreements without fighting or bitterness soared.

Also, as their hot thoughts chilled, they found room to entertain more constructive forms of self-talk that heated up the relationship in more desirable ways. Karen reported that one day she was looking out of their kitchen window at Jason as he played with the children in the backyard and thought, "He's really terrific with the kids. He's so patient. I love to watch him with them." Jason shared that he had been thinking about how much he took for granted around the house and thought, "Karen is often so tired at night because she does so much for the family. It is not fair to her, and I know she is not happy about it. I want to spend more of the evenings with her." Their interactions reflected the changes in their thoughts. Approval, support, and validation replaced criticisms, disagreements, and invalidation. They were well on their way to recreating their remembered intimacy that had been lost in the swirl of conflict.

ALLOW CHANGE TO HAPPEN

Unhappy couples who desperately want so much for their partners to change often do everything in their power to prevent change. This is one of the great paradoxes we have experienced in our work with couples over the years. We have already reviewed some of the reasons for this sorry state of affairs. The most common self-sabotage occurs when you minimize a positive change in your partner's behavior by attributing it to a specific and here-and-now situation. Chances are you will undermine the change and it will not last.

Steve wanted Glenda to initiate sex more often. Like many couples, anxieties made it difficult for them to talk about their sex life, and Steve didn't know how to get Glenda to initiate sex more often. They awkwardly talked about it once or twice, but he didn't see any change. Glenda felt she had made many efforts, but Steve was never responsive. After three months of therapy, Steve brought the problem up in a session. Glenda acknowledged that some of the difficulty she had initiating sex went back to her family where she remembers being taught that "good girls do not show any interest in sex." She was working hard to overcome these feelings but still needed encouragement. Glenda also revealed that sex was not pleasurable for her. She felt Steve was only interested in intercourse and assumed that he was not willing to engage in sufficient foreplay to make sex mutually enjoyable. Steve said he was willing to experiment but didn't know what to do.

We had Steve and Glenda read a small paperback book written for couples to help make sex enjoyable and fun. We discussed the book in therapy and gave them explicit instructions to follow for the next six days. Glenda was to initiate sexual play on at least two occasions, and Steve was to follow at least two of Glenda's suggestions to have lovemaking be more pleasurable for her.

The following week the couple reported that the exercises had not accomplished their desired ends. Glenda carried out her agreement to initiate sexual play, but Steve was a reluctant partner. Steve admitted, "Glenda was only initiating sex because you asked her to. She wasn't interested herself. If she were really sexually interested in me, she would have been initiating sex all along."

Can you spot the change-inhibiting quality of Steve's thinking? He attributed Glenda's new behavior to an external, infrequent, specific source (the therapist's instruction), and he mind-read Glenda's "true" feelings. Steve now finds himself—and his relationship—in a precarious predicament. He wants change and yet, when it arrives, he cannot accept it.

In order to encourage the process of change, partners must applaud the small efforts that are taken in the new direction. You can only accomplish this if you commit yourself to defeating your destructive self-statement explanations for the change. Stop yourself from thinking: "If my partner really loved me, I wouldn't have to ask her to do this for me." "She's not changing because she wants to; she's changing because the therapist (this book, the minister, the TV show) told her to." "The change is not nearly good enough, it's too late, and besides, it will never last. She'll do it for a while and then go right back to the way it was." These self-statements are guaranteed to undermine the transformation you and your partner should be tenderly nurturing.

Think back to our simple truth #3, about how small changes in you can lead to big changes in your marriage. Begin a new script of self-statements to promote the changes you desire: "My partner is making a good-faith effort to address my gripe." "Change is a process, never a fait accompli. It begins in small steps and if the small steps are encouraged, they will be repeated and grow into big steps. If the small steps are challenged by critical talk, then the process of change will grind to a halt and I will not get my needs met."

In relationships that work, partners are able to ask directly for what they need and want. Yet, many partners think, "If my partner loved me and understood me, he/she'd know what I need and want." While it certainly is pleasing when partners anticipate each other's needs, it's an even more loving act for your partner to respond to your *request* for change.

With new principles and skills in mind, we sent Steve and Glenda away to repeat the same exercises. This time, Steve worked to defeat his destructive self-talk. The self-defeating statements were not totally absent, but he was able to push them aside in favor of change-promoting thoughts. When Glenda initiated sexual play, he acknowledged her new behavior and happily experimented with some of her suggestions for foreplay. Although we'd asked them to try the exercise one more time during the week, they tried it several more times—a rather sure sign of progress! Glenda and Steve were well on their way toward building intimacy in their relationship, as they had conquered a powerful source of conflict.

ADDING EMOTIONS TO TALK AND THOUGHT

In chapter 5, we suggested that one of our goals in writing this book was to help you feel more like a "native" and less like a "tourist" in making your way around your relationship. We trust that your understanding of your relationship has grown in many directions. You've had the chance to think over the six simple truths and, ideally, to see them in action. You've taken stock of your relationship with Predict and RIP, learned to care for your relationship bank account, and become keenly aware of how your spoken word contributes to a sense of well-being or distress.

In this chapter, you've learned how hot thoughts can operate behind the scenes to set the stage for the destructive talk patterns that we detailed in the last chapter. Using the Dictionary of Self-Talk, you had the opportunity to identify the specific hot thoughts that are active in your relationship. With awareness of the hot thoughts that leave you burning in anger comes the opportunity to transform these thoughts into cooler alternatives that promote relationship change and adaptation. We've suggested several exercises to help you with this important agenda.

Notice that everything we've discussed so far depends on only one person for change . . . you! Sure it'd be nice if your partner made the changes you want first, but what's stopping you from being the instigator of change? Often, the best way of getting our partners to change is to begin to change ourselves.

There is one more piece of the relationship puzzle we want to put in place for you. You know that relationships are much more than talk and thought . . . relationships are felt at a gut level. Our individual emotional lives are an important part of every relationship. The emotions we experience on a somatic level will have a very powerful effect on everything we say or do. A complete understanding of relationships requires that we understand the intricate interplay between thought, action, and somatic arousal. That is at the heart of the next chapter.

Chapter 7

SWEATY PALMS AND
RACING HEARTS

THINK BACK to the last blowout fight you had with your partner, friend, or lover. With all the good times that the two of you have had together, how is it that a raging battle breaks out? In chapter 5, we showed how destructive talk promotes conflict, and in the last chapter we traced the contribution of negative thoughts. By themselves, words and thoughts have little destructive power; it is the visceral emotional reactions they trigger that cause so much suffering.

As you remember that last fight, do you recall saying or thinking any of the following phrases to complete the sentence "I was so angry . . .":

   . . . I just saw red.
   . . . I thought I'd explode.
   . . . I couldn't see straight.
   . . . I couldn't catch my breath.
   . . . I thought I'd have a heart attack.
   . . . I felt faint.

These statements all pay tribute to the role of our bodily reactions in determining how we each experience relationship conflict. Researchers have just begun to explore this interesting frontier, and the results may surprise you. In this chapter, we will demonstrate that destructive conflicts are truly gut-wrenching experiences and help you identify factors that trigger your arousal, as well as behaviors that offset these triggers. You will learn how men and women differ in what causes arousal and in their reactions to it. Finally, we will offer guidelines for containing arousal and preventing the turbulence it causes between you and your partner.

BEYOND FIGHT OR FLIGHT

We have portrayed how marital fights often produce massive levels of heat but shed no light on the real source of relationship problems. In chapters 5 and 6 we presented the first two components of the formula for marital failure (destructive talk and hot thoughts); here we add the last and least understood part of the recipe for distress and divorce (high arousal). The equation now looks like this:

Destructive talk + hot thoughts + high arousal = relationship distress

In reality, serious relationship strife is a bit more complicated. The terms on the left side of the equation actually interact with each other. In other words, destructive talk can get hot thoughts boiling and high arousal cooking. In the heat of that mixture, more hot thoughts are fueled and physical tension boils over. This stimulates even more destructive talk, which keeps the process rolling along with talk, thought, and arousal each feeding off one another. Any way you look at it, you've got a recipe for a volatile relationship fight.

We need to alter our equation to reflect these interactive effects. We want a circular model in which destructive talk, hot thoughts, and high arousal are constantly feeding each other to create ever-increasing relationship turmoil. The final model then looks like:

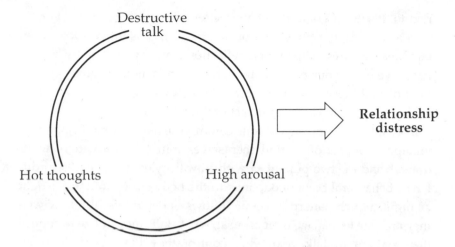

We can be even more specific about high arousal. When we perceive a physical threat to our well-being (for example, a mugger who jumps out from an alley in the dead of night), our body prepares for the emergency by getting us ready for flight or fight. The preparation includes an increase in sweating (leading to clammy hands), a decrease in saliva production (noticed as a dry mouth), and constriction of blood vessels near the skin's surface (experienced as cold feet and hands). Also we experience a dilation of the blood vessels in the muscles and brain, increased heart rate, and elevated blood pressure—all of which can result in a pounding sensation in the chest. These signs of activation of the sympathetic nervous system represent a coordinated and well-orchestrated effort by the body to protect itself from perceived threat. As a result of the arousal, you will either run faster or fight harder than you would have without the benefit of your somatic response (known as a successful "flight or fight" response).

All this arousal is put to good use when there is physical danger that requires generalized bodily activation to prepare for fight or flight. In relationships, the "danger" is not as likely to be a physical threat (except when the prospect of violence is real) as it is a psychological one. The psychological threat comes from our partner's destructive talk (i.e., "Just once, can't you do something right the first time without my having to beg you to do it?"), unless we construct it ourselves in the form of a hot thought (i.e., "What a pathetic baby I'm married to. It's never going to get any better. I've got to get out of here").

In any event, our physical arousal often leads us into trouble when the threat requires more rational reflection than physical action. In marriage, we expect our partners to be our friends, not our enemies. The fight or flight response, best reserved for a defense of our physical integrity, is rarely in the best interest of the relationship.

In chapter 3 we presented four common patterns of interaction that unhappy couples often find themselves mired in: escalation, withdrawal, and the two pursuit ↔ withdrawal styles. They represent different behavioral accommodations to the body's preparation for fight or flight. Which pattern a couple follows is determined by how well they are able to manage their arousal, what skills they utilize to control their pattern of talk, and what control they have over their hot thoughts.

Regardless of your typical style of reacting to arousal, you can benefit from understanding how arousal relates to thoughts, feelings, and behavior. When you discover how it can be harmful and learn specific techniques to help contain it, you will regain control over your mind-body interplay and the way it influences your relationship. Our purpose in the following sections is to give you these tools.

WHAT MAKES YOU SWEAT?

Perhaps your partner has told you that you are one in a million. He or she is undoubtedly right—you are unique, both on and below the surface. No one looks like you, no one thinks like you, no one acts like you, and no one feels exactly the way you do. The same can be said about the way your sympathetic nervous system prepares your body for flight or fight. Because the triggers of arousal in relationships are more likely to be psychological than physical, they are therefore more likely to be idiosyncratic and unique to the individual. The triggers that set you off are probably different from those that set off your partner.

We like to think of this fact as the true meaning behind the phrase "My partner really knows how to push my button." This phrase indicates that each of us has a unique vulnerability to specific relationship events and that our partners are often keenly aware of these areas of vulnerability. We become charged whenever our partner criticizes our parents; our partner becomes charged whenever we break a promise.

Our goal is to help you and your partner control the number of times you push each other's buttons. Remember that the two of you must team up together to defeat strong arousal from exacting a toll upon your relationship: Once arousal is present, you will find it difficult to deactivate hot thoughts, edit out destructive talk, and, in general, to work constructively on behalf of the relationship. Like it or not, you are dealing here with a basic law of psychology. In his famous experiment, Pavlov, the renowned Russian physiologist, observed that dogs he was studying would salivate to cues (such as the sound of a bell) that consistently occurred just before the dogs were fed. Pretty soon, every time the dogs heard the bell sound, they would start drooling for their food. Strange as it may seem, disagreements in marriage work the same way. Partners learn that disagreement leads to arousal and arousal leads to arguments. Soon you will find yourself responding physiologically to the initial disagreement as if you had been plopped right in the middle of a knock-down, drag-out fight.

Since an ounce of prevention is worth a pound of cure, we find that couples are richly rewarded for coming to understand the exact triggers of their arousal, and then working cooperatively to minimize the likelihood of these occurring.

There are three common triggers to physiological arousal in relationships: destructive patterns of relationship talk, hot thoughts, and lack of confidence in your ability to resolve disagreements. As an individual, you have the power to cool your hot thoughts and raise your expectancies for resolving disagreements. Control of relationship talk requires the cooperation of your partner. You've learned to dissect your communication into components in order to move conversations in the right direction and prevent arousal from getting out of hand. It won't do either of you any good if you are routinely saying things to your partner that leave him or her quaking with emotional reactivity. Let's look at each of the triggers.

Talk Can Trigger Arousal

Look back at the Dictionary of Relationship Talk presented in chapter 5. There are several types of talk that almost always ignite arousal in your partner. At the top of the list is critical talk, followed by disagreement. Because critical talk is usually perceived as a personal attack, it often triggers the physiological threat response we have described. Critical talk makes your partner feel unappreciated and thus is often a form of invalidation. It is also generally a form of disagreement. We prefer to have others agree with our view of things, and when they strongly disagree, our nervous system issues an alert for combat—even if only verbal—to resolve the disagreement via "force."

Other forms of talk can also lead to instant emotional reactions. When you mind-read your partner ("You don't care enough about us to tell your parents not to come this weekend"), when you express hopelessness ("I think we shouldn't spend time together for a while"), or when you offer up excuses and explanations about something bothering your partner ("I didn't say I'd be there at noon"), you are inciting him or her. We are not suggesting a blanket rule outlawing these types of statements. Rather, we want you to be fully informed about their consequences and then to act as consciously and responsibly as possible to bring about desired communication. If you want to poke your partner's nervous system and to push him or her away from you, the destructive forms of relationship talk will do the trick. If you want to draw your partner closer to you and gain comfort and support, then positive problem-talk and listening talk often succeed.

Thoughts Can Trigger Arousal

When your thoughts run hot with character assassinations, always-never self-talk, hopeless-helpless self-talk, and should-shouldn't self-talk (see chapter 6), your body will create the heat necessary to support the fires of relationship conflict. These thoughts set off the sympathetic nervous system, and your biological systems go into overdrive.

Because your thoughts are always on call, you can have them flash before you at any given time or circumstance. While standing on line to buy a loaf of sourdough, you think "Why the hell didn't Randy pick up the bread?" While stuck in traffic and the radio blares out a country-western tune, you think "She's probably out two-stepping with her buddies from work." These thoughts recreate a powerful scene in the theater of your memory, and your body helps to bring the scene to life with increased blood pressure, heart rate, and sweating.

This is one of the reasons why relationships often feel unsafe. At any time, you may find yourself subject to the intense physical feelings that accompany these hot thoughts. When it comes time actually to interact with your partner, you won't be starting from a neutral position. Your highly charged state sets you up for an immediate leap into conflict. Your "field" of arousal is like a dangerous storm, and when your partner comes near, both of you will soon be holding on for dear life.

This is yet another reason why simple truth #2—one zinger can erase twenty acts of kindness—is so powerful. Relationship zingers stay alive in memory, and so, too, does the potential to recreate the emotional charge that accompanied the original zinger when it first occurred.

Lack of Confidence Can Trigger Arousal

One type of thinking that triggers arousal deserves special attention. This is the type of thinking that we measured on Predict in questions 26 through 28. These questions determine whether you believe in your ability to resolve disagreements with your partner. Researchers have suggested that people who lack such confidence become more dangerously aroused than those who are confident in their skills.

Why is this so? We've found that couples lacking such confidence are far more likely to engage in the types of relationship talk that are highly arousing. These are partners who tend to tread in the waters of critical talk ("You know, it's much easier taking care of the two kids when you're our of town. When you're around, I've got three kids to take care of"), excuses and explanations ("I wouldn't stop talking to you if you didn't get so angry"), mind reading ("You were trying to irritate me"), disagreement ("I completely disagree with your reasoning"), hopeless talk ("It's been three years and not a thing has changed"), negative problem talk ("Don't tell me you never bounced a check"), and negative solutions ("From now on, you pay all the bills and balance our budget"). As we've stated, these forms of relationship talk simply add to the arousal that is brought into the start of a conversation by a person who lacks confidence in his or her ability to resolve conflict.

You may see this as a chicken-and-egg problem: which comes first, negative thoughts, lack of confidence, or arousal? This question brings us back to our cyclic model. How you choose to break the cycle maintaining your relationship despair does not matter. What matters is that, from this moment on, you commit yourself to breaking it, which means dealing with all *three* sources.

We have shown that arousal can be triggered by various words, deeds, or thoughts. In the next section, we will help you to understand precisely how physical arousal affects both members of a couple in a given interaction, and how change is initiated.

TRIGGERED AROUSAL DISRUPTS CONVERSATIONS

Under conditions of extremely high emotional arousal, you will find it very difficult to keep your conversation moving forward and preventing it from deteriorating into predictable conflict. All the new skills you are learning will be most difficult to apply. Picture a tightrope walker getting ready to perform on the high wire at a circus. The performer has practiced the skills needed to master the high wire over and over until she or he is comfortable carrying out the complex balancing act. But, rehearsing in private and performing in front of an audience in the Big Top are quite different. No matter how well the skills have been practiced, the performer may still be tense going before an audience. Because all human behavior is disrupted by high arousal, there is a chance that the tightrope walker may slip and fall. That's why most circus performers work with a net below.

Although you won't have a safety net below you when you try out the new skills we are teaching, you can take control over the arousal that disrupts your balance and threatens to send you crashing down. We have structured the program you are learning in recognition of the fact that all behavior is subject to the destructive influence of high arousal, which you must work to keep in check. That's why we've insisted that you start out discussing relatively minor problem areas first and major areas later. Your new skills could quickly be lost if you tackle highly charged areas prematurely. As you become more practiced in the new relationship skills and become more in control of your physiological reactions, you will be able to work through relationship issues—no matter how difficult or complex they may be.

Until then, you must accept the fact that arousal has a major impact on your interactions. When aroused, you are more likely to say things that you will come to regret, more likely to engage in conversational maneuvers that guarantee conflict, and more likely to see and hear your partner as part of the problem rather than a willing ally in search of a solution. Pay attention to the following consequences of arousal:

• *Miscommunication:* Each of you may intend to have a neutral or positive impact on the other, but arousal distorts the messages and causes them to be read as negative. Some couples have appreciated the following image to help them keep in mind the destructive potential for miscommunication. When the summer sun is intense enough, you can see the heat shimmering off the sidewalk or the roadway. Now if you imagine yourself on one side of the radiating heat wave, and your partner on the other, any talk that the two of you exchange must pass through the shimmering heat field. As it passes through this field, messages can become distorted and easily land on the listener, having a very different impact than intended. Arousal in the speaker, in the listener, or in both can easily act as the energy source distorting their messages.

• *Mind reading:* In the absence of clearly expressed verbal messages, both your own and your partner's arousal may be directly communicated through the body. You may notice that your partner's eyes are burning with anger and yet he or she claims that everything is "fine." These conditions provide a fertile ground for mind reading—and misreading—the cause of your partner's visible, though unexpressed, reactions. Because of your own arousal, you are likely to misinterpret badly what your partner is thinking and feeling.

• *Character assassination:* When aroused, we temporarily lose our ability to edit out the mean and nasty comments that really hurt our partners. For example, in the midst of a nasty fight, Victor was so keyed up and out of control that he said to Nina: "You're not capable of having a loving relationship. Even your therapist said you can't love anyone else until you learn to love yourself." Because the weapons we use in the heat of the moment often draw their power from intimate details of our partner's life, shared in moments of closeness, their use in the heat of battle can result in a loss of trust. If you were Nina, wouldn't

---

Box 7.1
Hold Your Tongue

When you are very aroused, you may say things that you will regret. Earlier in the text, we mentioned our position against those who would have you "get all your feelings off your chest and out into the open." Research has shown that this strategy is good neither for individuals nor for relationships. Now you are in a position to understand why. When you are a member of a couple, your arousal affects not only yourself but the relationship as well.

Nevertheless, many people believe that their arousal leads them to disclose their "true" feelings. A humorous example of this perspective is the story about a distressed wife who was describing to her therapist what had happened that morning during breakfast with her husband. She said to the therapist, "I made the worst Freudian slip this morning. I was looking at John, sitting there, reading his damn newspaper, and ignoring me as usual. I got so furious at that moment that instead of saying 'Please pass the Cheerios,' I said, 'You son of a bitch, you've ruined my life!' "

We'd like partners to consider first what they hope to accomplish through the expression of their feelings. Then we'd like them to communicate their feelings in such a way that they have the impact they desire. If the goal is to push the partner further away and increase conflict, then a character assassination would be a good tool. If the goal is to get your partner to change a behavior that has been bothering you, then positive problem talk would be much more likely to have the desired impact.

---

you think twice before sharing an important feeling or event with Victor?

• *Turning inward:* While at times high arousal will lead to outbursts of anger, arousal can just as easily turn you inward. In the face of relationship conflict, your partner may suddenly appear to have been cast into the role of a "brick wall"—as is often the case in pursuit ↔ withdrawal patterns of conflict interaction. You may interpret this as a sign that your partner is uninvolved, unemotional, or just doesn't give a damn. More often than not, the rock-solid exterior is a cover for intense feelings held in. The surface calm may be your partner's effort to control and contain his arousal so that it doesn't get the better of him.

In one study on the physiology of marital conflict, we found that when partners (particularly men) appear uninvolved and nonresponsive on the surface, they are actually quite stirred up. If you are married to such a "silent steamer," don't assume the worst about his or her behavior ("He doesn't care"; "She's selfish"). Instead, wait till the tension dies down, and then talk about what transpired.

• *Listening out:* No doubt you've heard the expression "Listen in" as in, "Let's listen in on their conversation." "Listening out" refers to those times when your partner is speaking to you, but you fail to take in the words or, more important, the sentiment behind those words. We tend to "listen out" because we are so provoked that words and meanings lose their proper effect. Arousal impedes our ability to attend to our loved ones and take in what they are saying. As noted above, when inflamed, we focus more on what's happening inside our bodies and less on what is happening around us.

Our work on the psychology of listening indicates that it is very hard to be a good listener, even under the best of conditions—such as those described in the next chapter. In order to be a good listener you *need to understand* what your partner is saying and you *must sincerely convince* your partner of your understanding. Taken together, these two skills combine to produce *empathy.* Our point is that the delicate skills of empathy require maximal attention to "outside" emotional information and are, therefore, almost impossible to learn and engage when your body is raging "inside."

One Sunday afternoon, Kyle and Anne, a two-career professional couple, were driving to a family picnic dinner at the home of the CEO of Anne's company. Their three-year-old son, Adam, was sleeping in the backseat. They were talking about plans for their upcoming vacation when Anne revealed that she had a special project for a new account and wanted to talk about the possibility of postponing their trip to Hawaii. As soon as Kyle heard Anne mention the new project, he thought, "I can't believe this is happening again. It's work over our relationship one more time. She doesn't care about me." Sparked by these hot thoughts and others that quickly followed, Kyle became very upset and noticeably aroused. His eyes glazed over with anger, he could feel his heart racing, and he "listened out" to the fact that Anne only wished to discuss the possibility of changing their vacation plans. He angrily responded to a mind read of what he *thought* Anne said: "I won't agree to that; I'll go to Hawaii alone before canceling another vacation. It's time you put me before your work." By combining three types of destructive talk (disagreement, critical talk, and hopeless talk) he sent a major salvo toward Anne. He scored a direct hit on her physiology—she felt attacked and threatened by his remarks and, as she described it later, "My heart started pounding so hard I thought I'd explode." Anne, too, was no longer listening, and she was unable to hear his hurt and his concern that her work always came first. Anne brought the car to a screeching halt on the side of the road, dropped her head over the steering wheel, and began sobbing.

The escalation process was derailed when Adam started screaming in the backseat and they both turned their attention to him. Unfortunately, Kyle and Anne were both so aroused that they had trouble calming Adam. They decided to forget about the picnic and go home. Anne and Kyle were sufficiently shaken by their argument that they made a commitment to each other to call a "stop action" before any conflict got either of them so excited that they could not see, speak, or listen straight. They used this technique as a first step in working out a ground rule for maintaining constructive engagement in any conflict discussion.

There is one more piece of this puzzle we want to put into place before you turn to our suggestions on managing arousal. It has to do with differences between men and women in how they experience and react to conflict. Given the obvious biological differences, it should not be surprising that men and women show very different patterns of excitation in the face of marital tension.

SHE SAID; HE STEAMED

One of the major complaints we hear from women about their husbands is: "He doesn't express his feelings." Many women go further and say, "He doesn't seem to feel anything." The men complain, just as strongly, "She's always out of control. I wish we could talk rationally without all this yelling." As common as these complaints are from men and women who have been married a few years, we are much less likely to hear them from newlyweds.

Then, as the inevitable conflicts of marriage are mishandled, some couples use these talks as a marker of current problems. Wives wonder how an expressive and loving partner during courtship became transformed into a silent and unfeeling partner after marriage. Husbands wonder how an interested and caring partner turned into a raging and inconsiderate one.

Warren and Louise were from a rural Colorado mountain community. They had been married for twenty-seven years and had one child in college. Louise's major complaint was that Warren never expressed his feelings. In the initial session, he sat pressed back as far as he could in the chair, stoically listening to his wife's story. When we asked him to respond to Louise, he said, "I don't know what to say." Rather than pressing him and replicating the pursuit ↔ withdraw pattern deeply rooted in their relationship, we said, "It seems like it's hard for you to express yourself at times like this. But if we hooked you up to a machine that reads your inside arousal, we'd bet on you showing all kinds of reactions." This got Warren's attention, and he acknowledged feeling very tense. We noted that when aroused it's sometimes hard to do or say things that come naturally at other times. We then asked the couple to recount what it was like when they first got to know each other. Louise recalled that one of things that really attracted her to Warren was that they talked all the time, and that he was very attentive. Louise was surprised to hear Warren say, "You know, that is exactly what attracted me to you as well. I loved those talks. I remember the time we sat on the swings in the schoolyard by your house and talked into the dawn."

Louise and Warren agreed that this level of communication had diminished. Although they found it impossible to date its departure, they both felt a change after some bitter battles over where they would reside. The topic came up frequently because Warren's employer repeatedly urged him to take a promotion that would have required a move to Sacramento. Each time his boss asked him to consider the move, he would come home, mention it to Louise, and a fight would break out. Neither was sure about what they wanted to do, but they never got too far because Warren wouldn't discuss the move. Louise felt that she had no idea what Warren's true feelings were about his job and moving.

More and more, the tone and tenor of their disagreements in other areas came to resemble their reactions over this particular issue. Louise thought that Warren didn't feel much of anything, and Warren believed that Louise was not interested in what he really felt.

Our research has helped couples like Louise and Warren to understand their differences. We have found that many men who appear out of touch actually experience very intense feelings. In the face of many of the triggers discussed above, men can be even more aroused than women—but are less likely to *display* their feelings, either verbally or nonverbally, than women. Why? It is as if men are paralyzed by their emotional arousal; the greater the excitation, the more pronounced the immobility. Recall our earlier comments that arousal makes the execution of skills very difficult. When men like Warren are highly affected by the eruption of conflict, they lose the ability to use the communication skills they already possess.

This was the case with Mark, whom you met in chapter 5. Recall that Lyn wondered why Mark could talk to his brother about all sorts of things but would not to talk to her about anything. An even more striking illustration of men's capacity to talk occurred when a caller to Den-

Box 7.2
A Couple's Guide to Feelings

For most partners, once conflict is managed, feelings will be easily expressed. However, for others, even when conflict is managed, it is a challenge to access and/or express emotions. We've identified three major types of patterns when it comes to difficulties in the area of feelings: 1) being out of touch with your feelings; 2) being aware of a great deal of upset, but having trouble putting labels on your inner experience; and 3) being able to express positive but not negative emotions or being able to express negative but not positive emotions. We have created the following Feeling Guide to help partners get in touch with and express both positive and negative emotions.

When using our guide, keep in mind three rules:

1. Your partner can't make you feel something—you are reacting to his or her behavior (see chapter 6). Thus we want you to preface an emotional expression with "I feel," rather than "You made me feel."

2. Feelings do not occur in a vacuum—thus, it is helpful to *set the stage* for the emotions you'll be sharing with each other. For example, "Last night while you were at work, I was thinking about our relationship and starting feeling very *sad* and *lonely*—I'm not sure why."

3. Talk from your perspective—don't mind-read. For example: "When we were at the party last night, I felt *jealous* because you seemed to be spending time with Marlene rather than with me." Note in this example the speaker said "You seemed," to indicate that this was her recall, and thus she avoided "mind reading" her partner's actual behavior or intent.

Using the Guide

As a preliminary step, read over the feeling chart and add any words that are your personal favorites to each emotion group. Now you're ready to put the guide to use, and there are two ways to do so. First,
continued

when you're alone, take out a piece of paper and this guide and write sentences expressing your feelings about the major current issues in your relationship. Start with a low-conflict issue on your RIP, and go from there. For example, if religion is a 2, due to conflicts over a mixed marriage and child rearing, you might write, "I feel sad that John won't be having the type of religious upbringing that I had."

The second way is to have the guide available during your relating discussions described in the next chapter and consult the guide as needed.

Love-Related Emotions

I feel: loving, caring, sexy, attracted, passionate, affectionate, moved, lovesick, excited, longing

Joy- and Efficacy-Related Emotions

I feel: happy, joyful, delighted, merry, satisfied, cheerful, optimistic, encouraged, hopeful, amused, confident

Surprise-Related Emotions

I feel: surprised, bewildered, amazed, shocked, astonished, stunned, thunderstruck

Anger-Related Emotions

I feel: angry, hostile, pissed off, furious, enraged, displeased, irritated, mad, bitter, bitchy, scornful, resentful, hostile, hateful, livid

Sadness-Related Emotions

I feel: sad, upset, hurt, glum, misused, wounded, abused, mistreated, disappointed, discouraged, remorseful, apathetic, low, miserable, depressed, hopeless, heartbroken

Fear- and Guilt-Related Emotions

I feel: afraid, alarmed, guilty, ashamed, horrified, scared, jealous, envious, nervous, anxious, panicked, overwhelmed ver radio psychologist Andrea Van Steinhouse disclosed, "My wife is threatening to leave me because she says I don't talk to her. I don't know why, but I can't. But I feel that I can talk to you."

An alternative explanation for the expressive differences between men and women in relationships is that men have an easy time talking when they feel they are in control, possess power, or are trying to manipulate a situation to achieve their goals. Men are able to handle conflict well in situations that provide clear rules for what to do. These situations usually involve some hierarchy of authority, as in sports, business, politics, or the military. In these arenas, conflict is handled by appeals to authority (for example, the CEO who has the final word on every decision) or to agreed-upon rules (for example, in baseball, three strikes and you're out). Similar kinds of rules exist in *traditional* relationships where male and female roles are clearly inculcated by the culture. If you know what men and women are "supposed" to do in the "typical" family, then there is much less to negotiate and much less opportunity for conflict.

Following the reasoning of this alternative explanation, men encounter difficulty managing conflict and communicating when the rules of authority are absent—as in the more *egalitarian relationship* of marriage, in which men and women must negotiate as equals. In these marriages, men who have been conditioned that it is good to be strong and confident in the world face a relationship reality that is uncharted and uncertain. Lacking both rules and skills, small day-to-day conflicts can seem overwhelming and are too quickly converted into fuel for emotional arousal.

Even more frustrating for many men is the discovery that trying hard to make the relationship work is not always enough. Men in particular have been brought up to believe that with effort, anything can be accomplished. Making relationships work takes not only effort but also *knowledge* of what makes relationships successful and the *tools* necessary for change.

Despite lots of experience with conflict in other areas of their lives, men have more trouble than women handling relationship conflict precisely because they *withdraw* from it, and then don't get the chance to master it. This is one of the great promises of marriage. Having a chance to work out intimate conflict with a person we love and trust is an accomplishment that facilitates our own individual growth and adaptation and allows us to realize the great hopes implied by our taking the pledge "for better or for worse."

Low Self-Esteem: A Common Trigger

Women tend to get aroused when they feel threatened or ignored—both of which lead to invalidation—whereas men tend to get aroused when they feel attacked. Yet for both men and women, a low level of self-esteem makes it easy for partners to perceive events as threatening or attacking.

Jake and Lindsay came for therapy after one of their frequent quarrels escalated into violence for the first time. They normally got along very well, but about once a week, they'd get into an argument that spiraled out of control. Lindsay had said, "The week was going pretty well until the weekend came around. We had some houseguests over and one of the women was flirting with Jake. I asked Jake to stop drinking for a moment and to talk to his friend about his girlfriend's behavior. At first, he didn't respond at all—I thought, 'He's ignoring me again.' I got so mad I was boiling. So I had to ask him again, then, zip boom bang, it was like I pushed one of his buttons—Jake flew off the handle. He rushed toward me and yelled that I was crazy. I became enraged and demanded he back off or else. When he didn't, I shoved him and tried to get away. He then pushed me against the wall and held me tight. I pulled his hair hard to get him to let me go and he screamed 'you ——— bitch' and stormed out of the room."

Jake's account was somewhat different. "I was talking to my friend Lionel, having a beer, and out of nowhere Lindsay roared in like a wounded lion and in a jealous rage accused me of coming on to Lionel's girlfriend. I thought, 'I can't believe she's going off again, this time embarrassing me in front of my friends.' I squeezed my fists so tight that they hurt as I tried to control myself and not make a bad situation worse. But did she stop? *No!!* She pushed me, and I finally lost it."

After having read chapter 6, you should be able to recognize some of Jake and Lindsay's destructive thoughts that led to an eruption of bodily arousal. She became aroused in the face of feeling *threatened* by the flirtatious houseguest and by Jake invalidating her concern. Jake became aroused in the face of feeling attacked by Lindsay. As therapy progressed, we learned that both were children of divorce and had grown up in high-conflict homes. Like some of these children, Jake and Lindsay had relatively low levels of self-esteem—in their cases, well hidden from each other and the world by a surface appearance of success and competence. However, they were extremely vulnerable to threats to their sense of well-being, and their arousal served quickly to erect defensive walls, as well as lead to mind reading and hot thoughts.

The mortar of such defensive walls are misperceptions of events as attacks or threats, intense reactions to accurate perceptions, and chronic revival of thoughts regarding past transgressions. Low self-esteem leads to these three arousal triggers, based upon a fear of being hurt. High levels of arousal and anger are characteristic defenses against feeling the hurt.

As we discuss in detail in chapter 10, we helped Jake and Lindsay recognize the importance of understanding and supporting each other as a method of repairing esteem issues. As they grew to become teammates, they were able to learn our approach to managing conflict so as to contain arousal. They discovered alternatives to violence and, as of our last contact, they never again repeated the aggression that had scared them into our program.

Given the importance of containing conflict and arousal, in the next section of this chapter we provide a set of clinically tested ground rules. Their purpose is to help partners to stay engaged through the first rounds of a conflict, during which time you need to work as a team to exchange thoughts and feelings and to do so in a way that contains, rather than inflames, your partner's emotional reactions—as well as your own.

TAKING CONTROL OF AROUSAL

In this section, we will teach you both how to diminish arousal once it is high and how to prevent high levels of arousal in the first place. We will highlight why preventative efforts pay off in the long run, given the costliness of conversational meltdowns. Even when you are finally able to contain a destructive reaction before a complete disaster unfolds, it may still take more effort cleaning up the remains than would have been required containing it in the first place.

Your Personal Arousal Quotient

Every partner has what we call a personal arousal quotient. Once this threshold is breached, there is likely to be an interactional disaster. You can get an approximation of which side of the threshold you often tread upon in the face of conflict by adding your scores on items 13 through 18 on the Predict questionnaire from chapter 3. If you answered true to most of these items, it suggests that your relationship is highly volatile, a veritable volcano ready to erupt at any time. If your partner also completed Predict, his or her score on these items is equally important.

All it takes for the relationship to have difficulty managing conflict is for one person to be highly aroused. Like a mixed-doubles team in tennis, if one person is not functioning well because he or she is so aroused, the team will not play well. Good mixed-doubles players find a way to manage their own arousal and avoid being a source of their partner's arousal (e.g., they don't criticize their partner for missing an easy shot at the net).

If you have determined that it is necessary to take some control over the arousal levels in your relationship, you will need to pay attention to the role that words, deeds, and thoughts play in determining the arousal levels you experience. Each of these areas offers an opportunity for change. Following are the ground rules to enable you to manage your arousal level.

Stop Action

We start here because we want you to realize that you can exert control even when you are so aroused that you cannot think straight and may say things that promote more marital heat than light. At these times, it is essential that you stop the eruption and begin a process of quieting down your mind and body. In so doing, you and your partner will take a step toward mastering your relationship conflicts instead of becoming slaves to them.

The single best way to halt the eruption is to call a *stop action*. The stop-action technique works best when the two of you have agreed *beforehand* on having a stop-action rule in your relationship. The stop-action ground rule states that when either person feels that conflict is escalating to the point of diminishing returns—when a run on the relationship bank account is imminent—either one of you can call a stop action or time out. When you feel that your arousal has made it impossible for you to continue a meaningful discussion, you might say to your partner: "We need to stop the action. I am very aroused, I am not thinking straight, and I need some time to regroup." Stopping the destructive process acts as a form of damage control. It does not repair the relationship so much as prevent the need for even more reconstruction. The stop action is one more tool you have at your disposal to control the hurling of a dangerous zinger. Remember simple truth # 2: One zinger will erase twenty acts of kindness.

After a stop action has been called, we recommend a cooling-off period sufficient for each person to feel personally available to the relationship. The person who calls the stop action must take responsibility for scheduling a Couple Meeting during which the speaker-listener tool will be used. The Couple Meeting is a time set aside for a discussion when both partners agree to use all the tools they've acquired and when distractions are unlikely. (The Couple Meeting and the speaker-listener tool are described in the next chapter.) Ideally, the Couple Meeting will take place within a few hours of or, at most, a day after the eruption. If you called the stop action and remain so aroused and angry that you are not ready for a Couple Meeting after twenty-four hours, then you will need to examine and take responsibility for your hot thoughts. You will also need to work through the material that we present in chapter 10.

On occasion, you will find yourself on the opposite end of a request for a stop action. If that is the case, you may be delving into an issue that you wish to pursue further, but your partner is so aroused that he or she has called a stop action. This may leave you standing on the threshold of a pursuit ↔ withdrawal argument—or, worse, mutual escalation. *Don't cross that threshold.* It may be frustrating to stop the discussion but it will be more frustrating if, as is likely to have been the case in the past, you simply plow ahead and confirm the inevitable . . . people cannot discuss an issue when they are aroused. Keep in mind that the stop action is a *relationship maneuver* to control arousal. It is not an individual maneuver to dodge conversation. Realize, too, that the stop action is a request for a *temporary* pause in the conversation and a *promise* to resume the conversation soon. This is the critical difference between times when a conversation stopped suddenly because one person simply walked away. The stop action gives you an opportunity to join together with your partner to combat "common enemies"—destructive talk, hot thoughts, and high arousal.

Regina and Ted packed their one-year-old son off to Regina's parents and packed themselves off to Vail, Colorado, for their first weekend away together in over a year. Ten inches of Colorado champagne powder had fallen the night before, and they were among the first skiers up on the lift—ready to make tracks together through the fresh snow. Then relationship lightning struck!

As they rode the high-speed quad lift up the mountain for their first run, Regina asked Ted why he was wearing his old ski jacket, which she felt looked "ratty and worn." Ted, who had always resented Regina's comments about the way he dressed, was primed for arousal and, upon its initial surge, he tried to change the subject: "Can I see the ski map?" Regina felt ignored and said, "Well, why didn't you wear the new jacket I got you?" Ted was full of hot thoughts and growing arousal, and before answering Regina, they were ready to take their first run down the mountain. Ted skied off leaving Regina to make her way down alone. Regina, a better skier than Ted, completed her run and, after several minutes, Ted finally skied past her covered with snow.

Regina skied up to Ted and said, "Why couldn't you wait for me?"

Ted answered, "Your comment about my jacket got me so upset I just fell and bruised my knee. Thanks a lot."

Regina kept the escalation going: "I can't help it if you can't ski as well as I can. Don't blame me for your falls."

Ted took a deep breath and realized that he was so aroused that he suddenly started to feel warm in the winter cold. He said: "Our conversation is going downhill. I'm so aroused that I can't really talk now."

Regina agreed: "I'm really charged up, too. I probably could talk about it now, but I respect your need to take a break."

Ted continued: "Can we discuss what happened when we break for lunch?"

Regina agreed, and the couple enjoyed skiing together for the rest of the morning. Their first vacation day in over a year was not ruined by marital conflict. When they stopped for lunch, Ted completed his side of the stop-action bargain. He took responsibility for bringing up the issue because he had called the stop action. They held a good Couple Meeting during which time they were both able to express their gripes. Each partner felt that the other understood what caused so much upset, and they made plans to avoid this type of conflict in the future. You will learn more about the techniques Regina and Ted applied as you work through chapters 8 through 10.

Cool the Arousal

You may not need to call a stop action if you and your partner are able to work as a team to keep the arousal level within manageable bounds. Keep in mind that if one of you is indulging in destructive talk (criticisms, negative problem talk, hopeless talk, etc.), then it is likely that the other will feel some degree of emotional and physical distress.

As we noted, everyone is different. There is no relationship rule book that can say with certainty that your partner *should* be able to withstand two criticisms, one mind read, and one negative solution before needing to call a stop action. And some arousal will be present in all relationships because it is not realistic to think that *all* negative talk can be avoided. Therefore, all we ask is that you do your best to avoid actions that inevitably keep the vicious cycle of arousal rolling. And that is all you can ask of your partner. As we showed in chapter 5, unpredictable departures from the cycle are a hallmark of the happy relationship.

Any time you take action to reduce your arousal or your partner's, you are contributing to the health of your relationship. There are two behaviors that you have control over that reduce your own and your partner's arousal:

- Accepting responsibility
- Editing

ACCEPTING RESPONSIBILITY

This means just what it says. You acknowledge a problem in the relationship and accept responsibility for your role in it. Nothing goes further toward repairing a painful rift than the simple acknowledgment of your role in the conflict.

LeRoy and Naomi were having some difficulty working out division of household chores. At one point in their discussion, LeRoy told Naomi: "I think you have gotten to a point where you take what I do for granted. You just assume I'll do it all, and you don't have to worry."

Naomi paused for a moment and said, "I *have* been taking what you do for granted. I can see you are doing a lot and I have not really appreciated it. I'm ready to change that." Naomi uttered one of those improbable statements that represent a telltale sign of a happy relationship.

After Naomi said this, LeRoy's body seemed visibly to relax. They were able to discuss household chores and made an agreement to try out some changes. When Naomi accepted responsibility for her part, the couple took control of their conflict.

The major obstacle to accepting responsibility is a partner's fear that giving in on one issue will signify some profound weakness of character and result in surrender on all matters that surface in the future. Did Naomi strike you as weak in the above example? On the contrary, it is a *measure of strength* to take responsibility for your role in a relationship problem. This strength helps alter the course of a conversation away from the predictable routine of conflict and toward the unpredictable novelty of solution and compromise. Neither you nor your partner can be expected to be perfect. Simply acknowledging those times when you can see your contribution to a problem will help your relationship thrive. Remember, accepting responsibility for today's problem does not mean that you must accept responsibility for tomorrow's. If a partner in fact were giving in on problem after problem, then such a predictable maneuver would be likely to be associated with relationship unhappiness—not success.

EDITING

Editing is a skill that we want all partners to master. Editing refers to a deliberate effort to hold back destructive talk in favor of something more polite. Whenever you are about to say something harsh to your partner ("This food you cooked is not fit for the dog") but instead decide on something more polite ("Thanks for taking the time to cook dinner"), you are engaging in what we call editing. Editing incorporates basic politeness: a quality sadly missing from too many relationships.

Try editing out comments when you see that your partner is getting aroused, especially when it is important to you to discuss an issue further. If you need to reach a decision about an important life event (e.g., changing a job, moving, selling some stock), it will be in your best interest to edit out a harsh criticism, no matter how well deserved you may feel it is, in favor of promoting teamwork to reach a fair consensus.

By recommending editing, we are not asking you to put a lid on your "true" feelings. Rather, we are recommending that you take control of the timing of your expression of these "truths." After all, if the feelings are important, and so true, then bringing them up in a context in which your partner is more likely to listen and understand them is far better than venting at a time when they are only likely to ignite further conflict or just be ignored.

Adrienne and Paul had been married for only two years and had spent the previous four months working with a marital therapist. They both expressed appreciation to their therapist and were sincere in their belief that they had learned a lot about their relationship and each other from their work. Their major goal in coming to us was to learn how to talk without fighting. They said they had gained enough insight into their families at this time and now needed some direct guidance to help them manage their conflicts.

It soon became clear that Paul was a nightmare of arousal and Adrienne an expressive demon. She would become so angry at him for not meeting her needs—primarily by withdrawing—that she would lash out at him. This, of course, had the effect of pushing him further and further away—and producing incredible arousal. After we had the couple keep track of their pattern for a week, we learned that Paul was so aroused, so often, that he found it impossible to talk to Adrienne.

It wouldn't have worked to tell Adrienne that she had to help Paul to control his arousal, any more than it would have worked to tell Paul he had to help Adrienne reel in her emotions. In fact, she was already devoting too much effort to trying to stifle his reactivity and he was working too hard to limit her expressivity. Due to this dynamic, Paul and Adrienne were so fearful of communication that they had made a major life change (Paul took a new job) with hardly any discussion at all.

Our treatment plan was deceptively simple. As discussed in chapter 6, we first helped them "team up" against the disease that was afflicting them. This enabled each of them to pay less attention to the other's major issue and freed them up to focus their energy on their own contributions to the relationship disease. Paul learned how to calm himself, following the guidelines set forth in chapter 6 and below. Adrienne learned how to edit out destructive messages so that she no longer overwhelmed Paul. When Paul came home complaining about his job one day, Adrienne edited out her first thought: "It serves you right for changing jobs without talking to me." Instead she said, "Sounds like you had a hard day. I'd like to talk more about your job. How about after dinner?" She became more confident that Paul would stay engaged and not retreat at the first sign of conflict, as had been his trademark behavior in the past. These changes set the stage for them to complete the Better Talk program—which enabled them to cement the initial changes as well as learn new skills. Learning the new skills would have been impossible without first lowering the level of arousal that came to characterize their relationship.

By the end of the program, Paul and Adrienne were no longer overreacting to the inevitable disagreements in their relationship. Neither was perfect, but because their words and actions did not follow a predictable pattern, more of their marital meltdowns were turning into marital discussions that left them feeling closer. Paul, for example, noted that he was engaging in less avoidance: "I'm more likely to say what's on my mind in a constructive way and not hold it *all* back out of fear that she will jump all over any comment or suggestion I might have. Like last week, we were talking about redecorating the house, a topic we avoided before. I always had opinions but was too gun-shy to express them for fear we'd just come to blows. She'd make all the decisions about the house, and I would just steam for weeks and finally explode and yell at her for spending too much money. It was all so predictable. This time I took a chance and said what I thought about a particular color for new drapes. I was surprised that she didn't criticize me."

Adrienne viewed the changes from her perspective: "It was so different for him not to be wound up so tightly but to be available to me that, even though I disagreed with his opinion, I was able to listen and eventually compromise. I'm more willing to compromise on issues now, because I feel I'm not compromising myself when I do. We were being a team as we made the decision concerning the color of the drapes."

Adrienne noted that much of her accumulated hostility and negative feelings were previously triggered whenever Paul expressed an opinion. She felt like a rubber band stretching and stretching. She always felt strung out, and the smallest thing could snap the band. Now she could feel how much the tension had decreased. *They were cutting each other more slack.* There was less predictability and more a sense of being themselves. Teamwork helps happy partners find their individuality; conflict makes unhappy partners appear disturbingly similar.

It is somewhat ironic that Paul and Adrienne actually started to have more disagreements (because they were confronting rather than avoiding issues). However, they were experiencing less conflict. As a result, they were making better decisions about problems that affected their lives because more information, resources, and opinions were brought to bear on the issues that they were facing (e.g., what to buy the children for the holidays, how to redecorate the house, what parties to go to, or how to deal with visits home to the relatives).

CALM YOURSELF

When we work with partners who become very aroused in the face of relationship issues, or even when they think about past events, we use specific calming techniques. As we have pointed out, arousal of this kind not only takes a toll on the relationship, it also exacts a toll on the individual. Being in a state of chronic arousal is likely to impair the functioning of the immune system, may increase the incidence of cardiovascular disease, and may also affect one's sense of mental well-being.

Your general level of arousal in response to relationship events is likely to be related to your overall level of fitness. If you get little exercise, then you are likely to get more aroused and stay aroused longer than a more physically fit individual. Certainly, working out by itself is not necessarily going to improve your relationship. However, the fitter you are, the faster you will recover from relationship arousal and the less likely you will be to reach a point of no return when confronted by conflict. (Of course, there are many health-related reasons for becoming fit that have nothing to do with relationships. Regular exercise is a no-lose proposition.)

Another strategy to lower your overall level of arousal is relaxation. If you walk in the door after a miserable commute with horrible memories of a day from hell, we're willing to bet that when your spouse says "I really need to talk to you about . . ." you are not going to be in the most receptive state. You need to take care of yourself first. You can do this by practicing any one of a number of proven relaxation exercises. There are audiotapes, videotapes, and paperback books available to guide you through these structured exercises. We recommend *The Relaxation Response*, by Herbert Benson.

The benefit of any effort you make is that you are likely to be far less aroused going into the conversation than if you had jumped right in before taking control of your own arousal. It is much better to say "I need twenty minutes to relax" than it is to plow ahead with conversation and hope that your arousal does not get the better of you. Remember, though, that you ought to use the twenty minutes for *structured relaxation*. We do not mean twenty minutes reading a book, watching

TV, or playing with the computer. The exercises we have in mind here require your active participation in order to be effective. In fact, studies have shown that watching television actually increases rather than decreases anxiety levels.

BREAKING THE CYCLE THROUGH BETTER TALK

In the first two parts of this book, we have provided a research-based understanding of the inner workings of a marriage. We have laid the groundwork for our actual communication program. Along the way, we have equipped you with a set of tools for putting into action these research-based insights. Now, building on this foundation, in the third part of the book we present our research and clinically tested Better Talk program. In the next chapter, the first part of Better Talk teaches you a set of communication skills and techniques for talking sense—our term for how to communicate clearly with your partner in a safe environment.

PART III

Better Talk

Chapter 8

A NO-NONSENSE GUIDE
TO TALKING SENSE

In PARTS 1 and 2 of this book, we presented our latest findings from twenty years of research on making sense of marital conflict. We have focused on what we have found to be the major sources of relationship distress; identified the sources of relationship happiness; provided the necessary diagnostic tools for pinpointing key trouble spots; offered specific suggestions on how to change the thoughts and bodily states that fuel destructive conflicts; and provided you with new models and opportunities to apply your increased understanding directly on behalf of your relationship. We have provided specific aids to help you untangle the web of marital conflict, such as the Dictionary of Relationship Talk and the Dictionary of Self-Talk, and taught skills that you can use to contain conflict, such as editing, stop actions, and personal relaxation techniques.

These are all vital elements of making your relationship work. Using these approaches, you may already have begun to handle conflict more effectively than in the past. Now, we are ready to guide you to the next level: to go from Better Understanding to becoming Better Understood. Couples working with us who are at the same point where you are now are generally better able to diminish conflict, but they are not quite sure what to do next. "We're not fighting as much, but we also are not talking much," these partners often say. Couples must have a way to discuss their gripes, concerns, wishes, desires, hopes, fears, and fantasies. Our goal is to lead you toward discussions that happen routinely and result in your feeling closer together rather than further apart. Conflict management without future discussion will only lead to an eventual eruption that will be very hard to control.

As we begin part 3 of this book, we will be adding the specific tools you need to enhance your ability to initiate a new level of relatedness and to resolve conflicts—to build a new structure to replace the old one you have been phasing out. We call this the Better Talk stage of our program, and the tools provided will enable you to realize your hopes for the one special relationship in your life. Issues that previously pushed the two of you into patterns of escalation, withdrawal, or pursuit ↔ withdrawal will yield to conversation that draws you closer together. We will also try to anticipate the barriers that can interfere with your new skills. Therefore, we devote chapter 10 to helping you rise above these temporary challenges and chapter 11 to maintaining and expanding the changes you have made. In sum, the purpose of part 3 is to empower you and your partner to handle confidently any issue that comes up, no matter how trivial or monumental it may be.

In this chapter, you will learn the first set of Better Talk tools to help you constructively discuss *any* issue or concern in your relationship. These tools have been carefully formulated to adhere to our six simple truths of marriage offered in chapter 2.

WHAT'S YOUR GOAL?

In previous chapters, we introduced the idea that certain types of communication were better suited to some goals than to others. Think a hot thought, offer a criticism, and turn up the arousal level in the relationship, and you'll be making a withdrawal from the relationship bank, no matter what your intent may have been. As a first step toward talking sense, it will help to become more conscious of your precise goals or intents.

Take a moment now to think back to the last time you and your partner had a fight or experienced a misunderstanding. It might have been a small annoyance, something your partner said, or just a desire to talk about something that ended in frustration. Whatever it was, think about how the scene played out and ask yourself the following questions: "What was my goal?"; "What did I wish to accomplish?" These deceptively easy questions are nevertheless worth serious consideration.

Most often, intimate partners will say that they had one of two goals in mind. They wanted to either resolve a problem or openly discuss their thoughts and feelings. Let's take a closer look at these two goals.

The first thing we want you to notice is that these are two entirely separate goals. Each is equally important, but each requires very different skills to achieve success. *Relationship riots* occur when one partner's goal is to *resolve* a problem and the other's goal is to *discuss* thoughts and feelings.

Ann and Roger, a middle-age couple who had just recently moved from the mid-west, came to their third therapy appointment and gave us this "play by play" account of a recent argument that had caught them by surprise.

ANN: "Last night, when we got home with dinner and the video and you asked me to dish out dinner while you went to change clothes, I was annoyed. That's when I said: 'Why can't *you* do it?' "

ROGER: "And I said, 'Fine, I'll go do it.' "

ANN: "You were angry."

ROGER: "No I wasn't."

ANN: "Yes you were. Be honest. You wouldn't talk to me all night. I wanted to tell you what bothered me about you asking me to serve the dinner, and you weren't interested."

ROGER: "It was no big deal. You didn't want to dish out dinner, so I said I would do it. Problem resolved, case closed."

ANN: "You're right. It wasn't a big deal . . . at first. But when you wouldn't talk to me, I felt shut out and got angrier and angrier."

ROGER: "There was nothing to talk about. I got the dinner. We could have watched the movie in peace. Instead, you wanted to talk . . . and there was nothing to talk about."

Ann: "My feelings are not nothing. If you had just listened to me, we could have settled this thing and had a nice night. But instead, we wound up yelling at each other and sleeping in separate rooms."

Roger: "I don't understand. You said you didn't want to dish out dinner. So I did it. What's the problem?"

You probably noticed in Ann and Roger's conversation many examples of destructive talk, and you may have also inferred the types of self-talk that fueled their rather predictable conversation. No doubt, Ann and Roger finished the conversation more aroused than they were when they began.

Ann and Roger's report of their recent riot is a good example of what can happen when one partner's intent is to have a *relating* conversation, in which the goal is to share private thoughts and feelings and be understood, and the other partner's intent is to *resolve* a problem and end the discussion. These two goals do not mix well, and the result is often an interactional riot that robs the relationship bank account. As with any destructive conflict, it is essential to interrupt a riot as quickly as possible.

SETTING THE PROPER GOAL

Because relating to your partner and resolving problems are both important goals, and because either one would end a riot, which goal should have priority? The answer is actually rather simple:

| Relate first, Resolve second |

This is the golden rule of Better Talk. It is impossible to resolve relationship concerns if either partner feels misunderstood, unappreciated, or ignored. Relating discussions foster understanding, appreciation, and validation, and they create a sense of being on the same team. Under these conditions, resolving problems is a relatively easy task.

Bob and Sue are an attractive and articulate couple caught in the web of marital unhappiness. When they sought help, they had been married for eight years and felt that the last four had been, more or less, a long-drawn-out fight. To Bob and Sue's credit, they were unwilling to accept these fights as an inevitable part of married life and were not ready to walk away from a relationship they both had worked hard to maintain. At the beginning of a particular session, Sue complained that Bob is withdrawn and unable to talk about his feelings. She angrily described his behavior from the night before:

SUE: "You got home from work, and there was this black cloud around you. You didn't help with dinner, you went around slamming doors, and then you went and disappeared into the basement."

Bob listened to this description of his behavior with no obvious expression on his face, his arms folded in front of his chest. He seemed removed from the session (although undoubtedly he was steaming inside with smoldering thoughts). He glanced at the therapist, glared at Sue, looked away from everybody, and didn't speak. Bob was a powder keg about to detonate. Not having gotten a reaction from Bob, Sue started to direct her comments to the therapist:

SUE: "I get the feeling that Bob is more interested in his work than in me, or his family. He may as well stay at work. Whenever I try to talk to him, he tunes me out. This is *hopeless*. We've been through this a few dozen times. Nothing is going to change."

Sue's mind reading and hopeless talk made it very likely that Bob would offer yet another round of his own negative relationship talk. Let's see if he broke the cycle or kept it rolling:

BOB: "You see what she's like? How can I talk to her? She's out of control. She's always angry. And if she isn't yelling at me or the kids, she's nagging me to do something around the house. I work my tail off for this family, and I'm sick and tired of hearing no thanks or appreciation for all I do.

"Most of the time when I'm home, I feel under attack. I don't know what to say or do to make things better and not cause more of a fight. I feel totally helpless. It's really frustrating, I can work out all sorts of difficulties with everybody at work. Why can't I do it with Sue?"

He kept it rolling with critical talk, negative problem talk, and help-less talk. The time had come for them to stop their respective mono-logues. We asked Bob and Sue to "stop action" and for each one to answer the following questions: "What am I trying to accomplish right now?" "What is my goal?" Like many couples, Bob and Sue felt that they were trying to *resolve* a relationship problem. Sue said: "I was try-ing to get Bob to open up more. I want him to show some interest in me." Bob's goal was similar: "I was trying to get Sue to stop yelling at me. If she would only stop being so angry, we could solve our prob-lems." Good goals . . . but in violation of the rule: Relate first, resolve second.

We have found that violations of the goal rule are one reason why couples have the destructive conversations that we charted in chapter 5. When you are trying to accomplish one goal, and your efforts do not bring you closer to that goal, your disappointment and frustration are likely to turn what should be a relating conversation into an escalating riot. This is especially so when partners are not adept at avoiding pre-dictable exchanges of negative relationship talk, engage freely in in-flammatory self-talk, and do not control their arousal.

Although Bob and Sue were quite puzzled about their own difficul-ties, we are confident you can make sense of their argument. Bob and Sue's fight did not stem from Sue's insecurity, Bob's insensitivity, or any other aspects of their personalities. *It came from their learned pattern of faulty communication, hot thoughts, and insufficient arousal management.* Like most of the couples we see, Bob and Sue were unaware of how their misdirection at the very start of a conversation interfered with talking sense. Off on the wrong foot and heading blindly down a dead-end street, Bob and Sue became ever more lost in the darkness of con-flict.

As you learn the Better Talk tools for talking sense, it's best if each partner take *equal responsibility* to follow the steps outlined below. However, positive change is possible even if only one person starts and pursues this process. For now, try to concentrate your efforts on your-self and worry less about what your partner is or is not doing. Often, when one partner has the courage to change, the other follows closely behind.

The Better Talk Tools for Talking Sense

THE CORNERSTONE OF RELATING: THE COMMUNICATION OF UNDERSTANDING

Nothing hurts partners more in an intimate relationship than feeling misunderstood. "Having a partner who understands me" and "having a friend" are, in fact, two of the major qualities both men and women look for in a partner in the first place. Nothing fuels a conflict more than the belief that our partner is missing our point of view. The more we feel ignored, the more we think to ourselves, "If only my partner could see the supreme reasonableness of my point of view, our problem would be solved!" Unfortunately, because there are usually **two** reasonable perspectives, trying to convince our partner that ours is best will get us nowhere.

Talking sense means that you and your partner listen carefully to each other's thoughts and feelings and show that you sincerely understand them. Communicating understanding to an intimate partner is not an easy task. Although you may be able to listen and demonstrate understanding to business associates and others with whom you have casual relationships, relating depends on your ability to use these skills when you're feeling hurt, unloved, angry, put down, and aroused.

A relating conversation begins with *dedicated listening*. You cannot hope to understand what your partner is saying, thinking, and feeling if you are: a) concentrating on what you will say next; b) desperately trying to get your partner to see your side of things; c) certain that you already know what your partner thinks and feels; or d) distracted by the TV or stereo. Dedicated listening means that you pay full attention to what your partner is saying but also that, immediately after your partner is done speaking, you *demonstrate* your sincere understanding by briefly restating in your own words what your partner has just said. Sound easy? Trust us, it's anything but easy. But it will be worth the effort.

In order to demonstrate understanding to your partner, you must try to crawl inside your partner's skin and see the world as he or she does. We are *not* asking you to agree with your partner's point of view. We are only asking that, during these isolated moments of critical conversation, you try to see the world as your partner does. Remember, the sooner that you, as the listener, are able to communicate a *sincere* understanding of your partner's thoughts and feelings from his or her perspective, the sooner you will be able to become the speaker and have your partner grant the same empathy to your side of the issue.

Here is another way of thinking about relating conversations that may help you achieve this most important phase of talking sense. Swimmers at the ocean are frequently warned about the dangers of undertow. Undertow is a strong current that can pull unsuspecting bathers away from the beach and out to sea. If caught in an undertow, you should not try to swim directly back to the shoreline; most swimmers do not have enough strength to fight the power of the ocean. Instead, it is best to follow a counterintuitive strategy and swim parallel to the beach. Then, once free of the forceful undertow, you will find it easy to turn toward the shore and swim to safety.

Many couples experience their initial attempts at having a relating conversation as if they were being dragged out to sea in an undertow: the calm surface at the start of a relating conversation is often disturbed by the powerful forces of conflict that seem to arise from nowhere. Unfortunately, despite their best efforts to swim to shore, nothing seems to lessen the grip of the "undertow" and bring the partners back to solid ground. The solution is to ride out the power of *each* person's hurt, anger, or disappointment through a relating conversation until the energy is spent and both partners can swim calmly to shore. Here's specifically what we mean.

When a relationship event happens that bothers either of you enough to provoke immediate comment, too often the listener's first response is to erect a defense against the criticism. Or when one of you expresses disappointment in the other's behavior, too often the first reaction from the one criticized consists of excellent reasons why the feeling of disappointment is somehow invalid.

Box 8.1
Pitfalls to the Communication of Understanding
and Their Solution

Having worked with hundreds of couples, we know the common pitfalls to the communication of understanding.

1. Listener just says: "I understand what you are saying."
The pitfall: After a speaker has tried hard to air thoughts and feelings, it will seem that the listener does not appreciate the full importance if the response simply is "I understand."
The solution: The listener takes everything the speaker said and tries to capture in his or her own words the ideas and the feelings just expressed by the speaker.

2. Listener parrots back what the speaker just said, as if the listener were a computer.
The pitfall: After expressing our thoughts and feelings, hearing the listener respond in a cold, distant way makes us feel that our perspective is not appreciated.
The solution: Live up to the spirit, not just the letter, of the new rules for having a relating discussion. The goal of communicating understanding is to show our interest in what is being said and our understanding of our partner's perspective. The best way to accomplish this is to take in our partner's message, try to sense our partner's feelings, and then communicate back a blended mix of those thoughts and feelings.

3. Listener apologizes for "making" the speaker feel bad.
The pitfall: When the listener apologizes to the speaker, it is an attempt to stop the conversation prematurely. It is as if the listener were saying "Okay, I apologized; let's move on to something else."
The solution: Even if the listener is feeling guilty, an apology focuses attention on the apologizer, when attention should be focused on the speaker. The listener should show respect for the speaker's feelings and not try to dilute them by waving an apology at them.

continued

4. Listener offers an explanation for his or her behavior that makes the speaker feel bad.

The pitfall: This maneuver also will shift the focus of understanding away from the speaker's thoughts and feelings and onto the listener, leaving the speaker feeling frustrated and misunderstood.

The solution: The listener must accept the possibility that he or she did something that the speaker did not like, even if it wasn't the listener's intention. The listener must develop a sense of confidence in taking turns, knowing that her or his position will be given equal "air time" as soon as the speaker and listener roles switch.

SPEAKER: "I'm disappointed you didn't remember our anniversary."
LISTENER: "You don't understand how much pressure I am under."

This type of reaction from a listener is counterproductive in the same way that it is counterproductive to swim directly to shore when caught in an undertow. When greeted with such strong feelings from your partner, the first step you should take is *actively* to "ride out the under-tow," *not* to fight against it by trying to lessen the intensity of your mate's feelings, by ignoring them, or by deciding that they are "irra-tional." One of the most serious mistakes partners make at this stage of discussion is *not* to allow the initial energy of a disappointment to play itself out.

The listener may need to stay afloat in the troubled waters for some time and not attempt a hasty swim away from the undertow. The es-sential resource here is listening talk, and it may need to be repeated several times. Only then will the speaker begin to feel sufficiently un-derstood (if not agreed with) to move forward in the discussion.

Kate and Don, a couple we treated who had a checkered history of past "riots," had just arrived at their hotel for a week-long vacation that they had been looking forward to for months. While unpacking, Don asked Kate for the camera to take a picture of the magnificent sunset outside their window and heard, "Camera? You said you were going to pack it. Damn it! We're on another vacation without the camera. I can't believe this."

Don clearly remembers telling Kate that the camera, lenses, and film were on the bureau and asking her to pack them in her suitcase. Just at that moment, Don realized it was time to ride the undertow. He knew in an instant that to argue his side would be to swim sharply against the current, and that he and Kate were as likely to drown as to safely reach the shore. Don was also confident that he'd have his opportunity to present his side—once Kate's energy had run its course.

Don said, "Sounds like you're pretty upset we don't have a camera." Kate's undertow continues: "You bet I'm angry. I really wanted to take pictures of this trip. How come you didn't pack the camera stuff?" Although Don and Kate's conversation here and throughout their encounter may seem a bit unnatural to your ear, it is because they are engaging the skills necessary to have a relating conversation when they need it most. The next time you're very upset and your partner is able to offer you good listening talk, you'll have a chance to see firsthand how these statements provide relief and comfort and, at that moment, do not seem strained at all. Let's see how Don and Kate continue their relating conversation.

"So you're really disappointed we won't have any pictures of the trip. It also sounds like you're mad at me because you expected me to pack the camera." Don has attentively listened to Kate without fighting the undertow.

"I'm disappointed. I am. We always forget something important. And I remember asking you take the camera and film." The tide of Kate's anger is ebbing and giving way to the safety of feeling understood.

Don stays with it: "So you're angry with me for forgetting to take the camera and film."

"Yeah, I am."

Don checks the energy left in the undertow, "I can see you're angry with me and disappointed about not having a camera. Is there anything else you want to tell me?" Kate thinks for a moment and says, "I guess not. Thanks for listening."

Don's opportunity for his side of things has now arrived. "Okay. I do see your disappointment, and I do feel your anger at me. From my side, I remember telling you that I got the camera stuff together for us, put it all on the bureau, and asked you to pack it. I didn't forget."

It is time now for Kate to ride out the undertow. "So you're saying you remember telling me to pack the camera and that I didn't do it." Don clarifies, "Well, I am not saying you intentionally didn't do it. Only that I did think about the camera, I did gather the stuff together, and I remember asking you to pack it all."

Kate summarizes: "You recall telling me to pack the camera after you took care to gather all the stuff together. I do hear that you thought about the camera, you didn't forget it, and got the stuff all together."

Don acknowledges Kate's summary: "That's right."

The couple had ridden out the undertow and can now practically wade to shore. Kate says, "Well, I guess we had a misunderstanding. Very human of us! Why don't we go into town and buy one of those cameras with film in it?" Don agrees: "That's a great idea; it's too bad we don't have ours, but at least we'll have some pictures."

Many couples in the same circumstance would be swallowed up by conflict if they had chosen to fight the undertow by relentlessly arguing their own points of view. However, once couples learn to "go with the flow," their confidence rises at being able to handle such simple disagreements or disappointments without drowning in them.

The greatest fear that most partners have when trying out our suggestions is that they are giving in to their partner's "irrational emotions." People are loathe to engage in any interaction they see as "admitting" they were "wrong" when they knew they were "right." As we have noted, the trouble is that in all disagreements, both partners believe that they are "right"! That is why there is disagreement. *The fight to prove oneself right challenges the healthy forces of nature and is a no-win proposition.* The more each person feels that his or her side is being dismissed or not clearly understood, the more he or she will argue. This is a couple battling against unseen undertow, destined to drift out to sea. Partners deserve to know that both of them can, *in turn,* express their thoughts and feelings—and be certain they are appreciated and understood by their partner.

The conditions under which you attempt to accomplish this understanding cannot be taken for granted. Too often we overlook how strongly our behavior is determined by the situational forces surrounding us. In chapter 6, we discussed how our tendency to overlook the situational factors of our partner's behavior represents a fundamental bias in our thinking.

Imagine that you've been in the kitchen all day preparing a gourmet feast for some dinner guests who are due at your house in five minutes. Your partner comes into the kitchen, and before you know it the two of you are in an argument about who misplaced the cutlery set. Although it would no doubt help to have the kind of conversation that Kate and Don had in their hotel room, in which they immediately moved to a relating discussion, your ability to engage all the skills necessary to achieve such results takes practice. When dinner guests are about to arrive and the meal preparation is unfinished, it is not the best time to stop everything and have a relating conversation. As you learn these skills for the first time, allow yourself the opportunity to have relating discussions under the best possible circumstances. It's better in such situations to edit out your immediate gripes and then to schedule a time for a Couple Meeting as soon as is convenient.

We have designed a structured approach to develop confidence in your ability to complete the kind of relating discussions we have just described. We call this a Couple Meeting, and in the next section we will explain how to structure these meetings to get the most from them. Not only is the Couple Meeting useful in learning how to master a relating discussion, you may also come back to this structure again and again to process the hot issues in your relationship—issues that must be worked through under conditions that maximize your chances of success.

THE COUPLE MEETING: STARTING OUT ON THE RIGHT FOOT

To get started with your first Couple Meeting, reserve at least *thirty minutes* a week when you will not be distracted by the TV, stereo, phone, children, or friends.

During your first Couple Meeting, look at your Personalized Problem Plan (PPP) from chapter 3. If it wasn't completed then, take a few minutes now to set up your own PPP. Because the Couple Meeting will

---

Box 8.2
How to Set Up a Couple Meeting

1. *Make a date.* Set up a regular weekly time for half an hour. This time should go on your calendar, on your refrigerator, wherever you make note of important appointments. Even if you get very busy, at least you know that a time has been set aside for the two of you and the relationship.

At times other than your regular meeting, when one partner wants to discuss an issue he/she should say: "I'd like to talk about ———. Is this a good time?" The other partner has the right to decline to talk at that moment, but it becomes that partner's responsibility to make sure the talk happens within twenty-four hours.

2. *Focus on the problem.* When you sit down to talk, it should be face-to-face, with no distractions—no newspaper, television, children, etc. Stay on one subject at a time, even though your thoughts may run to many related items.

3. *Use the speaker-listener tool.* Decide what you will talk about and who will be the speaker. To help keep the roles of speaker and listener straight, get a piece of paper and write the word *floor* on it. Trade the "floor" back and forth to each other, remembering to speak only when you have the floor. In the next section of this chapter, there are more details on the speaker-listener tool. The speaker should keep his or her statements short so the listener can follow them.

4. *Do not blame and/or attack.* Remember your problems are between *the two of you;* they are *relationship* problems. Focus on how you feel, not on your partner. Look at *your* role in the problem, not your partner's.

5. *Reserve the right to take a break.* When the discussion is not going well, i.e., when one of you starts to blame, attack, and/or escalate the conflict, either partner can call a stop action. At that point, agree to stop talking and pick up the conversation again at some point, but within twenty-four hours.

require you and your partner to relate in new ways, it is important that you choose one of the "cooler" issues surfacing in your PPP, thus avoiding major problem areas that may be too hot to handle right away. Keep in mind that learning any new skill takes a great deal of time and practice, and arousal will make the new skill difficult to both learn and use.

Whereas the flight-or-fight reactions we described in chapter 7 are biologically hard-wired into each of us, the Better Talk strategies for a relating talk must be learned. Use the Couple Meeting to practice the tools of Better Talk, and give yourself and your partner the freedom to make mistakes as you experiment and begin to revitalize your relationship. During the Couple Meeting, focus only on your own behavior as you try to communicate with your partner in a relating discussion.

Once you've had a satisfying Couple Meeting dealing with the first areas targeted by your PPP and have gained some confidence in your ability to have a relating conversation, you can continue through the tougher issues emerging on your PPP. With practice, you'll find that the hot relationship issues that may have been troubling you or your partner for some time can be discussed without winding up in a riot. But remember, for now, use your PPP to guide you to an appropriate "low-level" topic for your first Couple Meeting.

THE BANNING OF RESOLUTION: A NECESSARY STEP

You may have been surprised by our assertion that the initial step to solving a relationship problem is agreeing not to discuss its solution! We'll help you with the solution stage in the next chapter; but for now, you'll be amazed at how hard it is to have a relating discussion *without* trying to solve a problem.

No one likes to see a loved one upset, and we certainly don't want to be viewed as the cause of our partner's distress. So we mistakenly try to make the problem go away by proposing a solution, or by quickly accepting blame for our partner's feelings. In fact, this is the best time simply to listen *carefully* to what has upset our partner and communicate an understanding of it: Begin your Couple Meeting in this spirit, and you'll soon be talking sense.

Your efforts, at this point, should be spent on raising different sides of an issue as you work to understand each other's point of view. Remember, do not go for "the resolving jugular." Just listen and validate what you hear. Avoid trying to get your point across or insisting on changing the other person's mind. When partners are able to express

---

Box 8.3
Premature Resolving

Shawn complained to Patrice: "I'm really annoyed with how late you've been getting home." Patrice resolved: "I won't be late anymore this week."

Can you spot what is wrong with this "solution"?

At this point the "problem" is not that Patrice has been getting home late. The "problem" is the fact that Shawn is upset about it. In a relating discussion, the first order of business is to attend to the partner and not to the issue. Here, Shawn's concerns need to be recognized and appreciated, even if at times they do not seem to be "rational."

Here's another example of a partner who had been expending too much effort on resolving and not enough on relating: In therapy, Bill said, "I have tried everything I can think of to make this marriage work; I have nothing left to give." The therapist asked him what he had tried. He said he had made enormous efforts to please Martha. "I've given in on too many issues. I don't see my family or my friends anymore, and I've given up on moving to the country to raise cattle. Yet she's still not happy and keeps on being nasty to me."

Can you spot Bill's mistake? By giving in to Martha's demands he was *focusing on solutions*.

Giving in on issues is not the same as working on the relationship, even though it may seem to be. The therapist worked with Bill until he expressed to Martha his hopes, needs, and desires. Once these were on the table and Martha communicated a sincere understanding of them, the couple was ready to move into the resolving phase. But not before.

---

their feelings without the pressure of solving anything, many relationship problems actually seem to evaporate before your eyes.

THE SPEAKER-LISTENER TOOL

The speaker-listener tool is an extension of the floor exercise that we provided in chapter 4. From the floor exercise you learned and practiced the exchange of "speaker" and "listener" roles during a conversation. During a Couple Meeting, we want you to continue to be deliberate, alternating between the roles of speaker and listener. The speaker's goal is to state thoughts, feelings, wants, desires, hopes, disappointments, or ideas as succinctly as possible. The listener's goal is to communicate an understanding of the speaker's message. How well the listener demonstrates understanding is critical. When applied correctly, the speaker-listener tool will prevent any of the damaging, destructive forms of conflict (e.g., escalation and withdrawal) that we discussed earlier, the ones that lie at the core of marital distress.

PRACTICE BEING A RESPONSIBLE COMMUNICATOR

The speaker-listener tool can be a powerful exercise to help you have a meaningful Couple Meeting. But like all tools, there is a right way and a wrong way to use it. We call the right way *responsible communication* and the wrong way *foul fighting.* Let's look first at the right way to use the speaker-listener tool. In the *speaker role,* there are five skills to practice. These skills are another way to ensure that your messages are positive examples of relationship talk.

Better Talk Skills of the Responsible Speaker

Speaker skill #1: *Share your side of things.*

Use your time as a speaker to share your perspective, how you experienced the events. Don't use critical talk: "You came home and started yelling at the kids. Then you screamed at me and stormed out of the

---

Box 8.4
How to Use the Speaker-Listener Tool in a Couple Meeting

Step 1—One partner, as speaker, states his or her thoughts, feelings, or concerns about issue or event X and then asks politely for the other partner to show understanding.

Step 2—The listener tries to communicate a sincere understanding of the speaker's thoughts and feelings about X without being defensive, apologizing for any role he or she may have had in X, or dismissing what the speaker has to say by simply saying "I understand." The listener concludes by asking the speaker, "Is that how you're feeling?" giving the speaker a chance to clarify anything that the listener might have missed. The listener should not introduce his or her side of the matter until the roles switch and he or she is the speaker.

Step 3—If the speaker feels the listener has sincerely understood, this should be simply acknowledged: "Yes, that's how I'm feeling." Steps 1 and 2 continue until the speaker has finished and says "I'm now ready to be a listener. What are your feelings about X?" Partners then may switch speaker and listener roles and carry out the same steps. If the speaker feels the listener has missed something important in step 2, steps 1 and 2 are repeated with both partners staying in the same speaker and listener roles until the speaker feels that the issues have been clarified.

---

room." Instead, use positive problem talk: "I was feeling stressed out from dealing with the kids and just wanted some relief, and I was disappointed and angry that we weren't able to work that out."

Speaker skill #2: *Keep your statements short—don't deliver a monologue.*

Some people feel that once they have the floor, it's their chance to get out everything they've been storing up (perhaps the thought is "Finally, he may be listening"). Don't be fooled. A monologue produces interruptions, fading away, and defensiveness. The rule should be "Short and to the point." When the topic is emotional and full of conflict, we can only keep one or two points in our memories at any one time. So if you want your partner to hear the most important things you say, stop after one or two thoughts. Then, *ask for a summary of what you said*. For example, say: "The issue I'd like to talk about is money. I feel our situation is getting out of control." Then, politely, ask, "Please show me you understand?" This allows you to make sure that your partner understands your message and, if not, for you to clarify it.

Speaker skill #3: *Gripe in specific talk.*

Specific talk allows you to express gripes that involve your partner in the most constructive way possible. One of the most negative experiences in marriage is to have your partner complain about *you*. The most irritating of these complaints are global, negative comments about personality—character assassinations are big trouble. "You're a jerk, a slob, and an uncaring lout." In contrast, specific gripe-talk is a statement about behavior with clear implications that such behavior might change. The general form of specific talk is: "I didn't like when you did X." For example, "I didn't like when you came home and started reading the newspaper without talking to me."

Also say why you didn't like what your partner did. "I don't like it when you come home and don't say more than hello to me. It makes me feel hurt, ignored, and taken for granted." If you need some help with the feeling part of this type of statement, you can consult the feeling guide from chapter 7. Either of these forms of specific talk are much better than the destructive alternatives such as critical talk, "You're pathetic"; hopeless talk, "I guess we've fallen out of love"; or negative problem talk, "Why can't you be nice to me anymore?" No one likes to hear gripes, yet couples must have a way to express negative feelings without damaging the relationship. When you use specific talk while having a relating conversation, you enhance the chances that you will be heard about important, though potentially volatile, issues.

Speaker skill #4: *Use declarative sentences, not questions that entrap your partner.*

Focus on saying what is on your mind in a simple declarative sentence, rather than coaxing the idea out of your partner by asking a question.

For example, the partner who says "I found the stereo was left on and I'm annoyed because I want it shut off after it's used" is on firmer ground than the partner who begins "Did you leave the stereo on again?" These types of questions are like baited hooks to catch the partner in some misdeed and then reel him or her in when the bait is taken. Using a question when a statement would do fine makes a relating conversation more difficult. Better to say what is on your mind.

Speaker skill #5: *Be polite.*

Research shows that we tend to be ruder to our loved ones than to actual strangers. Why? Partners say that when at home they do not want to "role-play" the way they do at work; they want to be themselves. It's just as important to be polite to our loved ones. You can refer back to the rules of politeness that we discussed in chapter 4.

Better Talk Skills of the Dedicated Listener

The most important *listener skill* is the communication of understanding. This is a top priority of our No-Nonsense Guide to Talking Sense. Here we list a few additional listener skills that will help you become a dedicated listener.

Listener skill #1: *Edit out your typical response.*

Have you ever noticed that, when listening to your partner, you are not really listening but rather forming a rebuttal, or saying to yourself something like "That's not true"? Perhaps the most difficult skill to master when it comes to listening is learning to edit out your internal responses and focus instead on what your partner is saying. Try to quiet your self-talk activity while your partner is speaking.

Listener skill #2: *Do not confuse understanding with agreement.*

When we ask people to show that they understand what their partner has said, they often feel that by summarizing the message, they are agreeing with it. Keep in mind that, as a responsible listener, *understanding* does not mean agreeing or disagreeing.

Listener skill #3: *Realize that understanding only happens when your partner feels understood.*

The old question "If a tree falls and no ones hears it, does the tree make a noise?" applies to being a responsible listener. If you understand what your partner is saying, but he or she doesn't know it, then do you really understand your partner? The answer we give couples is *no.* Your partner's sense that you understand what he or she is saying produces feelings of validation and caring, which are the very goals of a relating discussion.

Make sure to communicate that understanding your partner is important to you: you must "be there emotionally." Don't hurry up the conversation or appear impatient. You show your partner that you are paying attention when you:

- Look at your partner
- Nod your head to acknowledge what's being said
- Sit facing your partner

Avoid all Foul-Fighting Ploys

No matter what your goal, if your communication is laced with any of the foul-fighting, destructive-talk strategies that we list below, then you will surely have a relationship riot on your hands. Each of these techniques is fairly destructive by itself, but when paired with other foul-fighting ploys, an innocent conversation can turn nasty in short order. These advanced strategies of destructive talk take up where the Dictionary of Relationship Talk leaves off. Here, then, are the pitfalls to avoid during the speaker-listener exercise and ideally at other times as well.

Foul-fighting ploy #1: *"Kitchen-sinking."*

Couples who are headed for distress and divorce often get into discussions in which one issue leads to another, which leads to yet another. It is a phenomenon that we call kitchen-sinking, in which anything and everything gets dragged into the discussion. When Clara told Peter as soon as he walked in the door after work that she needed some help, Peter said: "You have no idea how tired I am when I come home." Clara responded: "And you think I'm not tired, too? I do everything around here—I take care of the kids, cook dinner—and all you do is work." Peter replied: "You're just like your mother, always complaining. No wonder your father left . . ." Clara interrupted: "There you go again, threatening to leave again. Go ahead, make my day—leave. I'm so empty anyway—you're so selfishly preoccupied, we haven't even made love for six weeks." In a matter of minutes the topics of household chores, in-laws, communication, divorce, and sex all bubbled to the surface. As you can see, kitchen-sinking is an excellent foul-fighting ploy that can drag down a conversation in no time at all.

Foul-fighting ploy #2: *"Throw this book at your partner!"*

We have found that some partners begin to use our suggestions (or those of other therapists, or various "authorities") as part of their foul-fighting repertoire. "Don't talk to me like that . . . the book says you are supposed to validate my feelings." This type of criticism is quite destructive and can lead to a riot.

Foul-fighting ploy #3: *Make sure there are lots of distractions.*

When you decide to have a Couple Meeting and use the speaker-listener tool, the odds of having a riot will be increased enormously by first turning on the TV, radio, or stereo, reaching for a newspaper to read, or interrupting the Couple Meeting to have a chat on the phone with a friend or relative. Why would your partner believe that you are genuinely interested if your attention is so unfocused?

Foul-fighting ploy #4: *Distance yourself from the conversation.*

There are many ways to use this destructive ploy to promote a riot. You can distance yourself physically by walking away from the Couple Meeting, by staring out a window, or by ignoring your partner. You can also distance yourself psychologically by changing the topic or by giving your partner the "silent treatment," or by hurrying up the conversation (e.g., say "Are we done yet?").

Foul-fighting ploy #5: *Monitor your partner's attempts to change and not your own.*

When you focus on your partner's attempts to change, you are making a fundamental mistake that can lead to a riot. In truth, we only have control over our own behavior and very little say about what our partners choose to think, feel, and do. Concentrating on your partner's behavior instead of on your own leaves you feeling disempowered and your partner feeling criticized.

FROM RELATING TO RESOLVING

Recall that the major complaint women have about relationships is that "he doesn't understand me," whereas men complain that "we fight too much." In this chapter, and parts 1 and 2 of this book, we have tried to provide you with tools that are as potent a remedy for feeling misunderstood as they are for fighting too much. Now that you know how to have a relating discussion, you're ready to move on to the next chapter where we lift the ban on problem solving and provide the next step of the Better Talk program—how to resolve problems.

Keep in mind, however, the critical importance of practicing the speaker-listener tools in ongoing Couple Meetings. Think back to our simple truth #6—learning skills requires practice. Practice of the speaker-listener tools during Couple Meetings will make it that much easier to use them on the run when conflict catches you unaware.

We end this chapter with an example of how practice pays off, by returning to a couple who mastered the techniques outlined in this chapter and have learned to "talk sense" with each other.

TALKING SENSE WITH BOB AND SUE

Earlier, we told you about Bob and Sue's undesired and unplanned riot. After learning and practicing the No-Nonsense Guide to Talking Sense, each of them was able to share concerns and to feel understood—they were able to have a relating discussion. Let's look at how they use a Couple Meeting to transform the discussion of the same issue that originally ended in a riot, so that it now leads to mutual understanding. Once again, notice how engaging the Better Talk skills may seem a bit unnatural and forced. In fact, that is part of their usefulness. In order to counteract the negative talk you may be familiar with, you need to substitute alternatives that you are not used to speaking and hearing. With practice, using these skills will become more natural, but they will always be different from casual talk when conflict is not present.

Sue: "I would like to discuss something that has been bothering me. Is this a good time?"

Bob: "Yes, this is fine."

Sue: "When you got home from work on Monday night, you seemed very angry. I had no idea why. But I felt I couldn't talk to you and that I could get no help with the kids from you."

Bob: "You're saying that I seemed angry and unavailable to you on Monday night and that I was no help with the kids."

Sue: "Yes, that's right. On Monday, when you came home, you immediately started slamming doors and seemed to be saying to all of us 'stay away.' I felt I'd have to do everything myself."

Bob: "So, when I came in and appeared really angry, you felt I put a burden on you because it seemed I wouldn't help with anything you were doing."

Sue: "Yeah, that's right. But it's more than that. At times I feel that what's important to me just isn't important to you and that often I feel you don't even care about me anymore . . . and (starting to cry) that makes me very sad."

Bob: "So, sometimes things happen, like Monday, and you feel that I don't care about you."

Sue: ". . . and at those times, I start to feel so lonely and scared and then eventually angry. I guess you see the anger more than anything else."

Bob: "You feel alone; and it comes out as anger toward me."

Sue: "Yes, that's right."

BOB: "Okay, I think I understand better now. Can I talk now?"

SUE: "Sure, go ahead."

BOB: "I had a miserable day at work on Monday. I couldn't even think straight when I came home, and it seemed that all you wanted to do was to dump the kids on me as soon as I walked in the door."

SUE: "You felt I wasn't sympathetic to you since you'd had a bad day and that all I wanted to do was have you take care of the kids."

BOB: "That's part of it. I guess I also feel like you just want me to be a helper and do things your way. Whenever I am taking care of the kids or working around the house, you usually criticize the way I'm acting."

SUE: "So you feel I don't value you and the things you do. You feel criticized by me."

BOB: "Yes, that's right."

Sue and Bob were able to continue this relating conversation during which they learned a great deal about each other's thoughts and feelings that they hadn't known before. They steered away from trying to solve their problems prematurely by proposing solutions, and they avoided having a riot by not resorting to foul-fighting ploys. At the end of the relating conversation, they were more in tune with each other, and they understood how they were turning minor events into gargantuan issues.

When we asked them about how the conversation felt to them, Bob said that he felt that Sue had finally opened up to him regarding issues she'd long held back. Sue saw it somewhat differently. She turned to Bob and said in a supportive tone, "I feel that you finally heard something I've been saying for a very long time."

Six months later: Bob and Sue had participated in twelve sessions of therapy, learning to follow the Talking Sense rules and skills. After several relating discussions, they were able to unravel some of the bad habits they'd brought with them into the relationship, habits that had blocked them from settling conflicts and experiencing the intimacy they deserve. In the last therapy session, Bob observed that if they had been able to learn these skills earlier, they might have *prevented* many of their most distressing marital and family problems. Before therapy, he had avoided talking because it always led to a riot, he said. Now he's confident that he and Sue can have relating discussions that don't deteriorate into riots.

Soon after they left this session, the therapist received the following note: "We went to our accountant's office yesterday and heard some bad news. When we left there, Bob was so angry about what the CPA told him that we started to riot. The good news: Four to five minutes into the riot I said, "This is our old pattern of arguing. I don't want to continue this in the car. Let's continue this tonight after Bill [their son] is in bed.' We did. Using the speaker-listener tool, we managed to understand each other's position and feelings. We quickly reached a compromise once we understood where we were each coming from! There is hope."

Chapter 9

A NO-NONSENSE GUIDE
TO RESOLVING
PROBLEMS

PROBLEM SOLVING IN CONTEXT

In the last chapter, we had you ban problem solving in order to experience mutual understanding in a relating discussion. If this cornerstone of successful relating has not been laid, it will be nearly impossible to have a successful problem-solving discussion. In this chapter we lift the ban on resolution. You will have the opportunity to apply the Better Talk tools you've mastered thus far to solving specific relationship problems. You will also pick up a few more tools that are specially designed for problem solving. Finally, you'll have the chance to use all the tools in tandem systematically to discuss and resolve issues from your Personal Problem Plan (PPP).

Our first goal in this chapter is to be certain that you've established understanding *before* you begin problem solving. Remember, *most of the time what seems to you like a problem in search of a solution is in fact a powerful feeling in search of understanding.* You and your partner can take turns summarizing the core of each other's point of view, practicing the skills from the last chapter. When each of you feels *understood* in regard to the issue being discussed, you are ready to move on.

Now you're ready to cross a second threshold into problem solving.

217

To start the journey, ask each other whether, among the various topics you discussed, there are any particular thorny or significant specific problems either one or both of you wish to solve. If the answer is *yes*, then problem solving is order.

THE BETTER TALK TOOLS FOR PROBLEM SOLVING

After a successful relating discussion, problem solving proceeds when you schedule a Couple Meeting to discuss and answer four questions:

- What is the problem?
- What are solutions to the problem?
- What solutions will we try?
- How will we evaluate our success?

You will deal with these questions as you proceed through six stages of problem solving:

- Relating—understanding and validating each other
- Focusing—narrowing a specific problem to solve
- Brainstorming—creatively generating potential solutions
- Selecting—choosing one or two solutions to try out
- Formalizing—committing to carry out agreement
- Recycling—integrating successful solutions into your relationship

In the rest of this chapter we will be detailing these stages, except for relating, which we took up in the last chapter. If you follow these steps, you will find that problem solving can actually put deposits into your relationship bank account.

Focusing Your Problem-Solving Discussion

By the end of a successful relating discussion, it is possible that you and your partner will have brought up several aspects of a single problem or several different problems. In either case, the first task of problem solving is to *focus in* on one aspect of the problem that will receive your

Box 9.1
Acceptance versus Solution

Some problems cannot be solved. Let's say your partner is five feet tall and you wish to be married to someone who is six feet tall. No matter what steps you follow in talking about this "problem," nothing will change that basic reality. Behavior change is simply not possible in some circumstances. This does not mean you can't talk about such issues. In fact, it can be useful to have a relating discussion in which you have an opportunity to express thoughts and feelings about aspects of the relationship that you cannot change. Such discussions can be effective as long as you don't threaten your partner with something he or she cannot change. For example, a message like "I'm never going to be happy until you grow another twelve inches" can only generate fuel for conflict.

At times, it is also useful to work toward acceptance of characteristics of your partner that could, in an ideal world, be changed, but in the reality of your relationship are unlikely to. Consider Kyle and Anne, the two-career couple you met in chapter 7. You may remember that we left them buried in an avalanche of arousal triggered by a fight over a forthcoming vacation in the tropics, a trip that was in jeopardy due to Anne's work schedule. They used their Better Talk tools to dig themselves out of the drifts of destructive quarrels and had a satisfying relating discussion about work issues. By the end of several discussions, each finally understood an important piece of the other's feelings.

Kyle had said, "I hear that you're feeling unappreciated for all the hard work you do that benefits the family. When I complain about your work schedule, you get upset because you feel you deserve praise, but what you get from me is disapproval." Anne, expressing both surprise and relief proclaimed: "So you're feeling that on the totem pole of my life, you're a faceless person at the bottom, and you care for me so much, you'd like to be at the top some of the time."

In this supportive climate, Kyle realized that he loved Anne for who she was. Even though he wished that she would work less, he felt no need to pursue the issue further. He was able to accept Anne's choices and give her the support she sought. As acceptance replaced the disquieting and urgent need for change, the topic of work no longer thrust the couple into instant conflict.

attention in the current problem-solving meeting. In the last chapter we encouraged you to think about your goal going into any conversation with your partner. In problem solving, the same principle holds true. What do you want to accomplish during the problem-solving stage?

Answering this question accurately is crucial to problem solving. Let's say you want to learn to play a better game of tennis. You've played the game for years but never with any instruction. You decide to take some lessons, and your instructor asks you, "What do you want to accomplish?" If you say, "I want to become a better player," you've handed over all responsibility for the lesson to the pro. You've also *framed* the question in the most general of terms. Only you know whether you need to focus on your backhand, forehand, serve, or volley. The pro might spend hours teaching you forehand strokes when you'd profit more by concentrating on your backhand—unless you tell her what you need. When it comes to a relationship problem, it is very important that you focus in on the specific problem area, avoid generalizing, and frame your discussion of the problem and its solutions in such a way that your needs (and the relationship's) have the greatest chance of *eventually* being met.

Here's how to accomplish this:

- State the problem in terms of positive desires rather than negative gripes about your partner's behavior (for example, "I would like us to come up with better ways of managing our finances," rather than "I don't want you spending our money without talking to me").

- Break down the problem into small, manageable components, so you can tackle each with efficiency. Use who, what, where, and how questions to help you home in, and add a time frame to help provide structure (for example, "I want to discuss how we'll pay the mortgage next month" rather than "I want to discuss *how* we're going to pay our bills for the next year").

Sometimes the problem will concern both partners equally, while at other times the problem will be of primary importance only to one partner. In either event, during your first problem-solving meetings, keep in mind that you are a team with common goals. If something concerns one of you enough to bring it up in a Couple Meeting, then it is worth the attention of both of you. Until you are *very* comfortable with problem solving with these guidelines, we advise you to keep all problem-solving sessions as a part of a Couple Meeting. You'll have a better chance of success than if you try to deal with these same issues spontaneously, when your spouse may not be prepared, focused, or engaged.

Sylvia and Craig had a tendency to frame their problem more in terms of behavior that they wanted the other partner to stop exhibiting than in terms of positive desires. With some reflection, Sylvia said: "Okay. What's the problem? For me, I want to spend time together on the weekends, just the two of us, doing fun things."

We told Sylvia that she was right on track, but we wanted her to be a bit more specific about the time frame—*all* weekends from now on? Sylvia caught on and said, "I want to spend time with you *this* weekend, just the two of us, doing fun things."

Craig's answer to the question "What's the problem" was: "I want this weekend to spend some time alone with my friends, and I don't want you to get angry."

Craig managed to be quite specific about the time frame, but he slipped in a request that Sylvia *not* do something. These types of indirect statements are usually interpreted as a criticism, and therefore Sylvia would likely defend herself, to explain why her anger is justified. That is an issue to be worked through in a relating conversation, not a problem-solving one. Craig edited his reply to: "I want to go out with Bill sometime this weekend to play squash."

Craig and Sylvia were now ready to move to the next stage of problem solving. Let's take a look at how another couple negotiated the transition from a relating discussion to the first stage of problem solving. Marc and Fern scheduled a Couple Meeting for Sunday at 7 P.M., right after their favorite television show, "60 Minutes." Fern asked for the Couple Meeting to talk about school plans for their five-year-old daughter, Jessica. City budget cuts had raised Fern's concerns about the public schools, and so she wondered about sending Jessica to a private school for kindergarten and beyond. After twenty minutes of a relating talk, Marc summarized his understanding of Fern's point of view: "You like the idea of public schools but are very concerned about the quality of education and think Jessica may do better in one of the private schools." After Fern acknowledged that this was correct, she demonstrated her understanding of Marc's position: "You're also concerned about the changes in the public schools, especially class size, but you're very nervous about our ability to afford a private school." With mutual understanding shown, Marc and Fern were ready to home in on a resolution.

Notice, however, the difference between Sylvia and Craig's disagreement and Marc and Fern's. Sylvia and Craig's issue was tightly focused at the end of relating, whereas Marc and Fern's issue is still quite global. Just as you can raise the power on a microscope to focus in more tightly on your subject, you can also intensify your focus in this stage of problem solving to define the immediate problem better. We asked Fern and Marc to zero in on a smaller aspect of the bigger issue. They decided to focus on what steps they could take in the coming week to help them reach a decision about schooling for Jessica. This allowed them to move on to the next step of problem solving—brainstorming, when they decided on the specific actions they each would take (e.g., getting information on the costs of three private schools).

Marc and Fern had defined the problem in such a way that they could attain short-term goals and move one step closer to reaching long-term ones. Notice how their plan allows them to achieve some small success and experience progress toward greater goals. Our hope is that the couple will continue to work together to reach the best possible solution, and not devote all their attention to the question that awaits them at the end of the trail (e.g., "Where will Jessica go to kindergarten?"). The importance of being able to master problem solving one piece at a time lies in a larger truth: *How* you as a couple make decisions reveals more about the health of your relationship than the decisions themselves.

Brainstorming Solutions

Once you've defined your problem, the stage is set for developing as many alternative solutions as possible. Even if you are a grand master at brainstorming solutions to professional problems with colleagues at work, it doesn't mean that you will be a wizard at brainstorming solutions to relationship problems with your partner. Making sure such skills work in your relationship requires a somewhat different knack, and a whole lot more sensitivity than competitiveness.

Derrick and Carmen were a brilliant couple. He was a rocket scientist at NASA and she was a federal judge. On their jobs, they could each research a work-related problem and come up with creative lists of possible solutions from which they were able to develop a good game plan to remedy whatever issue they were attacking. These *complex* work problems seldom involved other people, and that made these difficulties far different from their *"simple"* relationship concerns.

One such "simple" relationship problem that had them stymied was their five-year-old daughter's refusal to go to bed when asked. Before entering our program, they had defined this problem in a destructive manner. Carmen considered it one more burden of child care that Derrick let fall upon her shoulders without a second thought. Derrick considered it one more aspect of child care that he could not take care of without being hit with criticism from Carmen.

Neither of them had thought to define the problem as a mutual one: "We want Tina in bed by nine P.M." Once the problem was framed as a shared concern, they were able to launch into brainstorming solutions to the bedtime problem, applying the skills developed at work, but widely ignored at home. From their list of solutions, Carmen agreed to go to the bookstore in the next three days to get a recommended book on overcoming a child's sleep problems and Derrick agreed to read the book along with Carmen within the next four days. Carmen and Derrick were then ready to move along to the next stage of problem solving.

There are two basic ground rules to follow during brainstorming. One, don't evaluate either your own or your partner's solutions. Brainstorming involves a creative process that flourishes in the absence of evaluation. Two, try to be as creative as possible; there is no such thing as a potential solution that is too dumb, too stupid, or too far out. In fact, it is a good idea to propose some "wild" solutions that are just for fun. They may be impractical, impossible, or just plain silly. These fanciful brainstorms can bring a lightened emotional tone to the problem-solving meeting. Creative solutions are much more likely to occur in this atmosphere than if tension fills the air.

During brainstorming, it will be very helpful for one of you to act as the "idea scribe." The scribe simply jots down a word or two to keep track of all solutions that are suggested, even those made in the spirit of fantasy. This list will come in handy during the next phase of the problem-solving meeting.

Here's how brainstorming worked for Fern and Marc. Marc volunteered to be the idea scribe, and the two of them came up with the following list of possible solutions to the issue of what to do during the next week about Jessica's school:

- Talk to neighbors about the local public school.
- Visit the local public school.
- Call to get information on the costs of three private schools.
- Visit each of the private schools.
- Plan a budget.
- Get the name of a couples'-oriented financial counselor.
- Meet with the financial counselor.
- Talk with parents who have children in all the private schools.

Once you have worked together as a team to produce a list of possible solutions, you are ready for the third stage of problem resolution—selecting a solution.

Selecting the Solutions

In this stage of problem solving, you will review the written list of solutions generated during brainstorming and pick those solutions that you wish to try out in the next week. We suggest that you adopt an experimental mind-set about the solutions. Keep in mind that no solution commits you to a course of action for the rest of your life. You can try it out for a week before deciding whether or not to keep doing it or change directions. But once you decide to try out a solution, give it every chance to work. You do so by specifying exactly what you are going to do and when, within reasonable limits.

Making a Commitment

After you select your solutions, the next stage of problem solving is to formalize your choice with some agreed-upon ritual. This ritual might simply involve shaking hands, or it might involve a toast to each other with a favorite wine. Whatever it is, the ritual signifies your acknowledgment of the teamwork put forth on behalf of the relationship to complete a problem-solving discussion. It reaffirms your commitment to working out problems and expresses confidence in your ability to arrive at mutually satisfactory solutions.

Often couples come up with some creative solutions but stop short of a complete plan to turn them into reality. Confusion over responsibility may ensue, or the couple may simply forget to act on the agreed-upon solutions. This often leads to fights in which one person accuses the other of not living up to his or her agreement, while the other person denies that an agreement was ever made. Completing a ritual to acknowledge formally the selected solutions will maximize your chance of positive outcomes from the problem-solving stage of the Better Talk program.

Recycling Solutions That Work

All too often, couples are successful in carrying out a plan once or twice, but then they quickly revert to old habits. Unless you make an extra effort, the fruits of success are short-lived. Why doesn't one victory automatically produce a winning streak? Because old habits die hard and are stronger than new ones if new ones aren't practiced. Thus, the last stage of finding a solution is to integrate the solutions that work into your relationship, by trying them again and again, until they become an integral part of your relationship.

The Step-Wise Approach to Problem Solving

Let's return to Marc and Fern to see what solutions they selected and how they sealed their agreement with a ritual. They reviewed the list of possible solutions, and Marc suggested they visit three private schools closest to their house to find out what the tuition was at each one. Fern suggested that they go to each school during the morning so that they could observe a typical class in session, and Marc agreed. Fern volunteered to call the schools and make the appointments. Marc said he could visit any morning before eleven. They summarized what they had agreed to, wrote it down, and shook on it.

Often in the middle of brainstorming or selecting solutions to try out, couples drift out of the problem-solving mode. The conversation may wind its way back to a different aspect of the problem under discussion, or a new problem area may become the focus of attention. Departures from the problem-solving plan that we've laid out are not likely to be helpful, because different skills are called for at each stage of problem solving.

Also, it can be very frustrating for some partners who work hard to reach the problem-solving stage only to find themselves back dealing with a new problem and no solution to the original one. This can lead you to feel a loss of control over the course of your conversation. Make any movement back through a problem-solving conversation explicit and agree on a return to an earlier stage, if necessary. If this is too difficult, it is better to stop the Couple Meeting and reschedule it than to plow ahead and experience failure. We want your confidence to increase at being able to resolve relationship issues. If you need to walk through the six-step process several times before reaching a solution, that's fine and far preferable to forcing a solution that doesn't feel right.

Evaluating Your Progress

Don't fall into the trap of believing that the solutions you adopt to relationship problems must be a *fait accompli*. They are best viewed as a process to be revisited, evaluated, revised, and restored. Therefore, it's best to place your solutions into some time frame. After the time for implementing the agreement has passed, set up a meeting to evaluate how things went. Discuss what worked and what didn't, and appropriately revise your solutions.

When you evaluate your progress, be sure to keep your sights focused on the specific problem and solutions that were the targets of your efforts. Here's what happened when Jason and Katie failed to do this. Jason's problem was: "I want you to help me clean the basement this week." Katie said she would help from nine to twelve on Saturday, and this plan pleased Jason. They agreed to evaluate the plan on Sunday night. When Saturday rolled around, Katie got a call at 8:30 in the morning from a friend who pleaded with her to take her shift at the hospital. She owed her friend this favor and thus felt she had little choice but to respond. Jason was annoyed but said he understood. When Sunday rolled around, they held their evaluation meeting as planned. Jason started: "You obviously care more about your obligations to Catherine than your promise to me. How are we going to get anywhere when you break our first problem-solving plan?" Katie disagreed and they tried to talk about it further, but Jason was too upset to continue.

In their next therapy hour, we reviewed the week and pointed out to Jason that his evaluation of the problem-solving plan was divorced from the specifics of the plan he and Katie had worked out. We reminded him that his problem involved procuring some help to clean the basement. Because the solution to this problem did not occur as planned, they needed to recycle themselves through another problem-solving session. They completed this quickly, choosing the same solution, and reported the following week that all had worked out well. Now they were ready to tackle yet another problem, this time with greater confidence and a spirit of teamwork.

HOW TO USE THE BETTER TALK TOOLS IN TANDEM

King's Quest is a popular computer adventure game. The heroine learns about her mystifying situation and acquires a set of tools to keep in her inventory. In your quest for a better relationship, you have acquired a new set of tools that you now have in your relationship inventory. Let's take a moment and survey that inventory.

Better Understanding has increased your insight into the nature of relationship distress, and Better Talk has given you tools to put this heightened understanding to use in your relationship. To reach a successful resolution to a relationship problem, you will need to avoid the destructive relationship talk patterns outlined in chapter 5, give voice to the helpful and silence the inflammatory categories of self-talk detailed in chapter 6, manage your emotional arousal through the techniques described in chapter 7, and share a mutual understanding of the problem with your partner through a relating conversation following the guidelines in chapter 8. As your accomplishments in all these areas grow, so, too, will your success and ease at problem solving.

As you move along to problem solving, it will not be enough to have read along with us and say "I know what you mean"—you will have to put all your understanding and newly acquired tools to their proper use.

Start with a low-conflict problem area, use your tools for effective talk in a Couple Meeting, discuss the problem without escalation or withdrawal, and then move to specific solutions. At your next meeting, evaluate how the solutions you agreed upon are working and select the next problem on your list to discuss, and solve, if necessary. As you move up your list, you will gain the experience and confidence to address even your most difficult current issues (even number 1 on your PPP!). You will also be able to anticipate issues you are bound to encounter in the future (more on anticipation in the last chapter).

Try to distinguish those global, general issues, which most likely will require only a relating discussion, from those specific difficulties that cry out for problem solving. For example, take the issue of sex. When the topic is "What turns each other on and why?" you're not likely to require the final four steps of problem solving. A relating discussion will do. However, when the topic is "How can we increase the frequency of sex?" solutions are in order. Similarly, consider the issue of chores. When the topic is "How are we affected by societal gender roles?" a relating discussion may fill the bill. On the other hand, when the topic is "Who does what around our house?" solutions are clearly indicated, after a relating conversation.

Nevertheless, always keep in mind that all issues that arise, be they global ones that require relating or specific ones that require problem solving, call for validation, understanding, and the basic Better Talk skills that we've presented.

DON'T RUN AWAY FROM SUCCESS

The Better Talk tools can produce some fast results. You might have been struggling with an issue for several years, and in a few short weeks, you'll find a lasting resolution. Don't be lulled into complacency by this initial success. Relationship change will be maintained only by a commitment to continue working with the program. One success will not be enough. Not unlike dieting, unless you make a long-term life-style change, bad relationship habits will creep back over time just like unwanted pounds.

Emmett and Olivia were both in their early thirties, with twins in diapers at home. With these new additions to the family, the couple spent very little time together having fun. On a week-to-week basis, this recreation issue robbed their relationship bank account more than any other factor. Problem resolution was desperately needed to stop the run on the account.

Like many couples, Emmett and Olivia had little time to spend together during the week, so they looked forward to weekends as their opportunity for family recreation. However, they frequently ran into difficulty implementing a plan of action they could both accept. They wanted to spend time together as a couple alone, pay attention to the children individually, have some recreation time together as a family, see friends, finish chores around the house, and catch up on any incomplete work.

They set up a Couple Meeting on the topic of recreation so that each could air his and her views of the problem. Although they had recently talked about this problem at another meeting, they took the opportunity to review their thoughts and feelings and to express new ones. After about fifteen minutes of discussion, each acknowledged to the other feeling understood, and thus they were ready to move on to problem solving. Emmett and Olivia agreed on the need to use weekends better, but they had different priorities regarding how to accomplish this goal. Emmett was concerned that Olivia always had a list of tasks for him to do, and he never knew when one would be sprung on him. Olivia's main concern was that, although it seemed as if they had a lot of time to spend as a couple and as a family, once they got up on Saturday time seemed to slip away—particularly the time they wanted to spend alone as a couple. In the *focusing* stage of problem solving, they decided to discuss how they would spend their next weekend. They did *not* try to decide how they would spend all their future weekends, or how to meet *all* their recreational needs. Rather, they focused on a specific and solvable aspect of their larger issue.

Emmett and Olivia continued with a brainstorming session and came up with the following list of possible solutions:

- Rent a movie
- Get a baby-sitter and go out
- Go to the mall
- Go out to breakfast
- He gets to work out on Nordic Track
- She gets to work out at the health club
- Play racket ball together (as couple)
- Pay bills together
- Go see "Sesame Street" being taped
- He takes kids to outdoor playground if weather good
- He takes kids to indoor playground if weather bad
- Meet at mall and have lunch together as family
- Watch football game together
- Go out to dinner and movie

This was a fun stage for them, and after about ten minutes of brainstorming, they could sense their team spirit growing. Emmett then suggested that they answer the next question: What solutions should we try?

Based on the list, they created the following schedule for the next Saturday and Sunday:

The next week, Emmett and Olivia reported that they had followed their plan successfully. He noted that the reservoir of goodwill built up between them made the process rewarding and fun. In the past, when they had no clear agreement, the "default option" for the weekends—what would happen unless a plan was formed and followed—was to do nothing. Sadly, in the past, they all too often did nothing on the

---

Box 9.2

Emmett and Olivia's Schedule for Saturday and Sunday

Saturday, 7–10 A.M.: Unstructured

10–12:30 P.M.: Emmett takes the children to a neighborhood park, giving Olivia some time to herself at home.

12:30–2 P.M.: All meet at mall for lunch.

2–5 P.M.: Children's naps, unstructured time for Olivia and Emmett, kids play with friends, after naps.

5–6 P.M.: Baby-sitter arrives, Emmett and Olivia get ready for evening out.

6–11 P.M.: Go to a favorite restaurant and to a movie that their friends had been raving about.

Sunday, 7–9 A.M.: Unstructured

9–11 A.M.: Go to church.

11–12 P.M.: Lunch

12–2 P.M.: Go to the zoo or the Natural History Museum, depending on the weather.

2–5 P.M.: Naps (for all, including Emmett and Olivia), unstructured family time.

---

weekends except fight over the fact they were wasting another weekend.

We continued to work on other issues with Olivia and Emmett. Two weeks later, they came into a session discouraged that the past weekend had marked a return to their old pattern. It was as if they'd never learned the Better Talk tools. Olivia and Emmett were well versed in these tools but simply had not used them. They made the common mistake of assuming that patterns established over years of interaction would be permanently altered by a few weeks of success. We reminded Olivia and Emmett that the last stage of problem solving is to recycle the plan, and in our session together, we had them plan yet another weekend. The next weekend was again filled with pleasurable times together. The couple's renewed commitment to continue down this path was the key to their successful therapy.

PROBLEM-SOLVING PITFALLS TO AVOID

At this point in the book, you're close to having a full toolbox of skills to use to work out differences, disagreements, and problems in your relationship. You're also well versed in the common pitfalls that can destroy conversations, weaken communication, and create alienation between you and your partner. It is essential that you learn to recognize four additional maneuvers that cause communication breakdown so that you can cope with them. Here we provide you with a description of these maneuvers that guarantee problem-solving *failure* and their antidotes.

Bully Your Partner to Change

Using the destructive forms of conflict discussed throughout the book, we often try to bully our partners to change. Bullying can come in two different forms. In version 1, you whine on and on until your partner finally does what you want, and then you promptly stop whining. They get the idea that the only way to appease you is to comply with your wishes. This is a very costly way to bring about change in any relationship. In version 2, you do something sharply negative whenever your partner behaves in a manner that disturbs you. For example, if your partner comes home late from work, you might stop talking to him for an hour. Years of psychological research have clearly indicated that bullying versions 1 and 2 are very costly to relationships, even if they bring about short-term changes.

The solution: Catch your partner doing something you've hoped he or she would do and then notice the change with kindness—give a hug, say thanks.

Devise and Implement Unilateral Solutions

One of the best ways to push an arousal button in your partner is unilaterally to assert a solution to an issue. Any time you tell your partner that this is the way it's going to be ("We will go to my parents for the holidays!"), you are sure to cause inner rage, if not unleash outer hostility. Often, the person with the most power in the relationship is the one who feels entitled to assert unilateral solutions. The perceived power base may stem from being the primary income earner ("I work hard; I deserve to get my way"). At other times, the person with the most power is the one with the "least interest" in the relationship at that point. In any event, trying to muscle a unilateral solution will rarely, if ever, result in constructive relationship change.

The solution: Work as a team to come up with solutions that please both of you.

Plan to Change Only If Your Partner Changes First

One way to guarantee that a solution will fail is to withhold self-change until you have proof of partner change. This attitude will enter you into the game of "You go first" and, while you are both waiting for the other person to change, your relationship will often sink into a sea of conflict.

The solution: Decide that you will work on change no matter what your partner does or does not do. Keep in mind the adage that the best way to change your partner's behavior is to change your own first.

Punish the First Sign of Change You See

A curious thing happens in relationships when one person finally starts to accommodate to the wishes of the partner—the partner tries extra-hard to prevent the long-sought-after change.

Willa had been trying to get Tad to clean up after himself in the kitchen and bathroom ever since they had lived together. His messiness infuriated her, and she was guilty of all of the above pitfalls in trying to get him to change. Finally, after completing a weekend version of our program, Tad got the message and, fueled by a burst of team spirit, he made a special effort to clean the kitchen and bathroom Monday morning. Willa came into the kitchen to get her morning coffee, saw Tad cleaning, and—under the influence of intense arousal and hot thoughts—blurted out: "Great, now you're cleaning up—well, this is too little too late. You're just doing this because our therapist told you to. I don't understand why you couldn't do it because it was important to me." Tad glared at Willa but didn't say anything as he violently threw the sponge against the kitchen wall and left the room in a huff.

Spouses who pursue a similar maneuver when their partners finally start to comply with a request are moving themselves further away from maintaining the changes they had sought for so long.

The solution: Show your appreciation of small changes (even if the changes are not perfect)—especially in areas of long-standing conflict.

COMPROMISE IS NOT A DIRTY WORD

In any relationship that works, partners need to be looking out just as much for their partner's best interests as they are for their own. In fact, a sign of impending marital turmoil is when one or both partners feel a need strongly to protect their own interests. Therefore, when you feel yourself caught in an impasse, ask yourself what you can do to serve the best interests of the relationship—not what your partner can do for *you.* Open yourself up to compromise. Of course, the danger is that only one person will be doing the compromising. Over time, such inequality is sure to lead to problems.

Rose and Tony had been married three years and were deciding when to have their first child. Tony clearly wanted a baby but wished to delay getting pregnant for a while. Rose, however, was ready now. They had been coming to monthly therapy sessions for seven months. (Because she was out of town regularly, more frequent visits were precluded). They came to the November session at an impasse over where to spend the holidays—a chronic annual issue for them. He wanted to stay home; she wanted both of them to visit her folks in Toledo. Rose and Tony had several successful relating discussions about the issue and had tried problem solving, but they still couldn't reach a mutually satisfying decision. Each partner would not compromise his/her position an inch. They directly said to us: "Help us out of this impasse; tell us what to do!!"

We suggested that they try a radical (for them) plan. We told them that in a relationship that works, each partner—at some time or another—will make the ultimate sacrifice, giving up his or her position and actively advocating what the other partner wants. We asked them to put themselves into their partner's shoes, not only for the sake of understanding but also for the sake of resolution. Rose and Tony finally decided to give the plan a try, focusing on the holiday issue. While we'd used this approach before, we were still amazed to see the constructive transformation as Rose actually started advocating staying home, and Tony argued for going to Toledo. They reentered problem solving and generated a much more creative list of solutions. Under these new conditions, they ultimately decided to stay at home this year and put the time and effort into their relationship—recognizing that their needs as a couple had for too long taken a backseat to work and other concerns. They also began to talk about having a child in the near future—perhaps even trying to get pregnant during the holidays. Finally, they decided to take a short trip to Toledo to see Rose's parents during Easter and then to invite them to Denver for a visit the following December, when they could perhaps see their first grandchild.

PROBLEM IS NOT A DIRTY WORD, EITHER

Research indicates that one measure of a healthy relationship is the ability to adapt to new stages of the family life cycle. The person you are living with today is not the same individual you married ten years ago. Relationships that fly apart in the face of change are those with partners who have never implemented a plan to deal with the change-related disagreements that are inevitable—unless the relationship lasts less than a week.

Developmentally, our first response to the increased disagreements and tensions that occur once the honeymoon ends is to make heroic efforts to solve problems immediately rather than following the Better Talk plan. Many people think that this is particularly a male trait. However, our studies have shown that when understanding is required, both males and females tend to respond by trying to smooth over the distress and search for a solution, rather than listening and understanding what their partner has to say.

Thus, when you internalize simple truth # 4, that disagreements are inevitable and that all couples must develop strategies for resolution, you will be one step closer to meeting the challenge. Use the Better Talk tools to help you bridge differences and discover confidence in your ability to work with your partner to master whatever difficulties life casts your way.

WHEN BETTER TALK IS NOT ENOUGH

Throughout this book, we have shown that the inability to solve problems and handle differences constructively are among the major causes of relationship difficulties. At the same time, problem solving is one of the easiest skills to master—if you know when and how to apply the skills. You are now equipped with most of the tools needed to craft a successful marriage.

Sometimes, however, partners are absolutely unable to exert sufficient control over destructive talk patterns, hot thoughts, and their own arousal level, to the extent that it is impossible to have a relating conversation and therefore impossible to conduct a problem-solving meeting.

The next chapter is designed to help you gain more understanding and control over the barriers in your way to better talk between you and your partner.

Chapter 10

BLINDED BY A BLIZZARD: OVERCOMING ANGER ON THE PATH TO CHANGE

As YOU travel on the path toward better ways of relating, you may encounter the relationship equivalent of a fierce blizzard that temporarily blinds your progress. In this chapter, we will show you how buried doubts about yourself and underlying but powerful anger act together to keep you from achieving your goal of a warm, loving relationship with one partner. You will also discover how your relationship can be a shelter from even the most intense storm that life throws your way.

Many couples' progress is impeded by simmering resentments—a chronic and deep-seated anger that gnaws away at you throughout most hours of the day and keeps you company while you lie awake at night tossing and turning. One litmus test of this problem is whether or not your efforts to use the Better Talk tools we've presented thus far have only worked up to a point, and you find your path to change temporarily blocked. The block may appear as:

- An inability to complete even ten minutes of a speaker-listener discussion without a fight breaking out or one of you having the urge to run away

- A lack of resolve to stay with solutions worked out under the rules of Better Talk
- A reluctance to use the Better Talk tools even though they make sense to you, or
- A belief that your partner needs to change more than you, including a conviction that your partner has personality problems that must be conquered before happiness can be achieved

If you are so angry with your partner that your overriding concern is for him or her to see the error in his or her ways, to acknowledge that you are right and he or she is wrong, then it will be nearly impossible for you to apply the Better Talk skills successfully. It's very difficult to function as a team when all your actions involve pushing your mate away.

This chapter is also based on the premise that each of us, from time to time, experiences strong feelings of self-doubt. When these feelings occur, it is most comforting to have a loving partner available to share them with and to provide succor. When our partners cannot listen and give us needed support, we are likely to feel hurt and angry. At times, they can't provide the support we crave because their own needs are equally pressing. At other times, we *assume* that our partners cannot possibly be supportive, and consequently we don't even try to get our desires met. When both partners feel as if they are running on empty, the conditions are set for a substantial run on the relationship bank account. Again, it will be very challenging to use the Better Talk tools and difficult to maintain a loving relationship.

Rather than exploring the psychological dynamics of these emotional states, we want to focus your attention specifically on the nature of anger in your close personal relationships. As you'll recall from chapter 5, in distressed relationships the interactions between partners have a depressing predictability. In chapters 6 and 7 you learned techniques to overcome hot thoughts and to quiet destructive emotional arousal. In this chapter we will explore how anger, including unexpressed anger, is partly responsible for the repetitious behavior surrounding unresolved conflict.

Whether a couple is fighting over paying bills, leaving the cap off the toothpaste tube, or disciplining a child, anger below the surface is often the driving force. And, despite the variations in how conflict is played out on the surface of our intimate relationships, below the surface there are just a few themes related to anger that produce much of the turmoil. You will benefit by exploring, understanding, and using that anger on behalf of your relationship, and by not allowing it to rob you of intimacy.

Box 10.1
Are You Weighted Down with Hidden Anger?

The best clue to the presence of covert anger is noticing that simple little events frequently turn into *major* relationship battles. Here are some of the opening moves that signal an impending fight. Do you recognize yourself in any of these situations?

• He asks you for a Couple Meeting to talk about how much money is being spent on groceries and you feel so attacked, threatened, and enraged that you drop whatever you're doing, walk in the bedroom, and lock the door.

• She asks you to clean up the kitchen and, without a word, you start doing it but with a vengeance that scares the family dog—pots smash together, cabinets slam shut, and forks and knives get hurled into the drawer.

• While driving home from work, you dread walking in the front door because you don't know what battle will rage, but you're sure that one will break out.

Covert anger is also likely to be present if you would answer "yes" to any of the following questions:

• Do you feel that your partner is smothering you or is too distant from you?

• Do you feel controlled or dominated by your partner, or that you don't have sufficient influence in the relationship?

continued

- Do you feel that your partner pays more attention to other people than to you?

If the answer is "yes" to any of these questions, then it is likely that you will have had difficulty putting the Better Talk tools to their proper use because you are doubting your partner's intentions. Read on, and remember, the only person's behavior you have control over is your own.

PAY ATTENTION TO WHAT YOUR ANGER IS TELLING YOU

As we noted earlier, we do not subscribe to the school of thought that you should express your angry feelings whenever or wherever you want to. We also don't believe that you should stuff your anger into a hole in the hope that it will simply fade away. It won't. We think it is vitally important that you pay attention to your anger and learn to manage it appropriately.

If you shouldn't vent your anger, and you also shouldn't stuff your anger away, what are you to do with it? We believe anger should first be acknowledged and understood, and then transformed.

Acknowledging and understanding your anger means accepting it as a signal that something significant has happened and understanding that your reactions are probably fueled by more than what has just transpired in the immediate situation. *Transforming* your anger means that you find an appropriate way to express your reactions to immediate events in such a way that your relationship is preserved and nurtured. Because anger often pushes other people away, including your mate, when either of you is angry it will take teamwork to manage it properly. An important challenge for all relationships is to find a way to use anger to bring you closer to your underlying goals, including togetherness and independence, rather than to propel you into hot escalations or icy withdrawals.

Box 10.2
Monitor Your Goals, Actions, and Outcomes

In order to think more specifically about your goals in any interaction with your partner, you might consider two broad categories of personal goals—to pull your partner closer to you or to push him or her further away (in the sense that you need time alone). When you ask your partner out on a date, your goal is to pull together. When you tell your partner you want to read alone, your goal is to push apart. As you can see, both goals are "legitimate," and there will be some period of alternation between pulling together and pushing apart in all relationships. And because there are two of you, there is no reason to expect that your goals and your partner's goals will always be in sync. In a healthy relationship, you continually find ways to meet and balance individual and relationship goals.

Anger often leads partners to act in a manner that is inconsistent with their underlying goals. For example, over dinner, Jack asked Lorraine: "How was your day?" This message, a request for sharing the events of the day, is most often an invitation to pull together. However, Jack's mind was a million miles away from the dinner and what kind of day Lorraine had had because he was preoccupied with a pressing personnel problem that he was managing at work. As Lorraine started telling Jack about her day and the compliments she received on a proposal she had just completed, Jack appeared to be uninterested and distant. Lorraine got quite angry and challenged Jack: "Did you hear a word I said?" Jack and Lorraine's tendency at one time would have been to escalate the quarrel. Instead, in this instance, he assumed that Lorraine's anger was telling them something important. He realized at that moment that his behavior (not listening) was inconsistent with his desire to have an enjoyable evening out together (a goal of pulling together). Jack asked Lorraine what got her so angry and heard "I felt you were ignoring me, like you didn't want to be here with me." He acknowledged her hurt: "You're right. I wasn't listening. I've got this big problem with two people at work that is distracting me. I do want to be here with you, and I am interested in what happened during your day. Tell me again." Jack

continued

then was a good listener, and Lorraine felt that they had a good relating conversation. Jack and Lorraine had aligned their goals with actions necessary to accomplish them.

After Lorraine told Jack about her day, Jack shared what was happening at his office, and the couple was able to pull together and not let their initial false start ruin their evening.

HOW TO ACKNOWLEDGE, UNDERSTAND, AND TRANSFORM YOUR ANGER

There are three types of anger that frequently surface in relationships. We will elaborate upon each type to help you identify your anger's origin and the message it carries, as well as how to transform it to better your relationship. One warning: Dealing with anger—your own or your partner's—is not an easy agenda. You will have to use all your Better Understanding of relationships and all the Better Talk skills that you have learned.

TYPE I: ANGER FOR PERSONAL GAIN

Acknowledging and Understanding Your Anger for Personal Gain

When our path to something we want is blocked, anger can help us to break through whatever or whomever is in our way. We learn this form of anger very early in life. When a child does not get his way, he will often become angry and attempt to exert his will by force. If a friend swipes a favorite toy, an anger-fueled "search and retrieve" mission will usually result in a quick return of the prized possession.

For adults, anger for personal gain can be a constructive force. If you strongly desire something, your anger may be the driving energy that helps you obtain it. If your partner has been told that he has high blood pressure and you watch him ignore his medication and diet, it is entirely possible that you will get angry: your anger may be motivated by the desire to have a spouse by your side to share your later years together. Thus, your anger might be able to save a life. But your anger could also destroy a relationship. It all depends on how you manage and transform it—as you'll see below.

Transforming Your Anger for Personal Gain

Anger for personal gain will draw you closer to your goals when you transform it into an assertive, but polite, verbal request for action. Once you recognize what you want, your task is to translate your desire into words (for example, "I'd like you to take care of the kids on Saturday morning") and not into hostile actions because others are not automatically doing what you silently wish (for example, "Do you realize you've been out every Saturday morning for a month? It's not fair!"). Clinical research on assertion suggests that directly and politely asking for what you need yields the best chance of getting your needs met. You cannot expect your partner to mind-read your desires or to infer from your actions exactly what it is you want.

Consider the case of Stuart and Diane. Stuart liked to wake up in the morning to a clean kitchen and was bothered whenever Diane left dirty dishes in the sink or on the counter. The pair frequently argued about this problem, and their arguments played like a well-worn tape. Stuart would complain, "Why can't you just put the dishes in the dishwasher? You're not doing your share of the housework." Diane would reply, "You're a neatness freak. Life's too short to worry about dirty dishes in the kitchen." And so it went. On some occasions when Stuart greeted the day with dirty dishes in the kitchen, he simply cleaned up without saying anything, and they had a pleasant breakfast. On other days, he saw red and started to bang around the kitchen letting Diane know in unmistakable terms that he was furious about the mess. Frequently when this happened, Diane immediately pitched in to help Stuart clean up the dishes, and with both of them working the chore was completed rather quickly. Although it seemed that both partners were trying to pull together, their unspoken irritation and distance served to push them apart (see box 10.2). Stuart's visible but silent anger prodded Diane into helping him clean the kitchen, but Diane felt quietly chastised. Despite progress in other areas of their relationship, they were unable to put the Better Talk tools to full use to address the "kitchen problem."

We suggested to Stuart and Diane that they follow a new rule in their relationship: Express complaints and gripes with words, *not* actions. Express compliments and appreciation with actions *and* words. Stuart came to see that his angry cleaning of the kitchen was a strong action message to Diane of both his displeasure and his demand that Diane change. Following the rule, and being careful to use specific talk, Stuart politely presented his request:

"Diane, I don't like waking up to dirty dishes in the kitchen, and I would appreciate your help in making sure the kitchen is clean when we go to bed."

Diane heard the request and summarized it well:

"You'd like me to make sure I clean up after myself in the evening."

At this point, Diane challenged Stuart with her side of the issue:

"I'd like the freedom not to have to worry about dishes when I've had a bad day or when I have a lot on my mind."

As soon as Diane said this, Stuart looked angry. We encouraged him to continue to transform his anger into words designed to attain his goals rather than push Diane away.

"I hear you saying that you don't want to worry about keeping the kitchen clean."
DIANE: "Right."

Suddenly, Stuart was stuck, and he turned to us for help. We suggested that it was a mistake to try to convince Diane that his position had more merit than hers. Instead, we encouraged him to "own" this particular quirk of his. With some guidance, Stuart said:

"I don't really understand why it's so important to me that the kitchen be clean in the morning. I just like it. It means a lot to me. And I know it's a little excessive and I recognize I'm asking a favor of you. It would mean something to me to get your help."

Diane said, without prompting:

"I never knew this carried so much weight for you. I will certainly try to do my share to keep the kitchen clean. If I miss a night, please don't think I'm doing this to annoy you. I may just forget or I may be too tired. I will try, however, not to let it happen very often."

Stuart acknowledged Diane's offer:

"I would really appreciate that. I promise not to get upset when a night is missed."

In this way, Stuart took responsibility for getting his goals met and was able to ask a favor of Diane. Once he had transformed his anger, he was able to continue with a relating conversation that brought the couple closer together. Problem solving occurred naturally, and all that remained was for them to acknowledge their accomplishment.

"Diane, you know how long this issue has bothered me. I really feel so much better that we were able to talk about it and agree on a plan." DIANE (AGREEING): "Me, too."

When partners are able to own up to their "quirky" requests, transforming their anger, they create an opportunity for making deposits in the relationship bank account. If Stuart simply expected that Diane *should* share his need to wake up to a clean kitchen, then when it happened there would be nothing exceptional to acknowledge. However, when Stuart and Diane recognized that this was a special want of Stuart's, they created an opportunity for Diane to make a unilateral deposit in their relationship bank account. Such deposits set the stage for Stuart to offer a similar unilateral deposit to meet some request of Diane's that was also somewhat idiosyncratic. Looked at in this way, partners will find that they have plenty of individual desires and needs, the mutual recognition and acceptance of which can be opportunities for deposits in the relationship bank account.

Remember, these opportunities for building your account reserves are created when speakers transform their anger into words and take responsibility for politely verbalizing what they desire. You may have to exert some effort to overcome any reluctance you have to asking for what you want. This reluctance is tied to the realization that not all requests can be met and the power of imagining that you're being "rejected" whenever your stated needs are not satisfied. Too often the solution we come up with is to avoid rejection and fall back on an infantile wish for magical fulfillment of personal wants and desires. Our excuse for not asking is "Well, if I have to ask, it's not worth as much." That's not a helpful position for either yourself as an individual or for the relationship as a whole. In fact, if you don't ask for what you want, your needs are more likely to go unanswered.

As we've just suggested, even when you ask your partner to fulfill your personal wants and desires, all issues are not resolved as smoothly as in the case of Diane and Stuart. Because two individuals cannot be expected to agree on everything, there is a place for acceptance of some things that cannot change. That was true of Kevin and Paula.

Kevin and Paula were high-school sweethearts who had been married for about ten years. Neither had had much experience dating, and in the early years of their marriage they wondered if they had gotten married too soon. Now they were stuck on a problem. Kevin was somewhat more adventuresome in sexual play than Paula, although both partners enjoyed their sexual pleasures and were personally satisfied. However, Kevin wished that Paula showed more interest in dressing in sexy clothes when they went out to parties. Recently, Kevin became angry because Paula refused to wear any of the clothes that he had bought for her over the past few months. She felt they were too revealing, and she was not comfortable in them. Kevin's anger over Paula's refusal to try out different clothes was getting in the way of having any fun together when they went out.

The couple followed the Better Talk plan and ended a good relating discussion with Paula saying:

"I understand how much you enjoy seeing me in sexy clothes and how much you wish that I would show more willingness to wear the clothes you've gotten me. I'm just not comfortable in them, and that gets in the way of my feeling relaxed and having a good time."

Kevin and Paula's conversation took them right up to the point of behavior change or acceptance. Now a choice must be made. Kevin can accept that his current desires will not be met on this issue and that his anger is not going to bring him any closer to his goals. He can place this issue in perspective by focusing on the other aspects of the relationship that are working, thus finding his way toward acceptance. As he reaches a genuine understanding of his and Paula's differences on this one issue, his anger will lessen. He can let Paula know that this is a disappointment to him, but one that he can accept. He can also request that the couple discuss this topic again at some point in the future or whenever Paula wished to reconsider the issue.

If Kevin cannot or will not accept Paula's position, then he is faced with another alternative. He can decide that this issue is so important to him that he cannot remain in the relationship. Although this last choice may seem drastic, it may nevertheless be seen as preferable to the final alternative—remaining chronically angry with each other.

Had chronic anger taken over, Kevin could have become continually annoyed with Paula for being inflexible and would suddenly construe many of her actions as proof of her inflexibility. Paula might find herself chronically irritated at Kevin for having to have "everything" his way. When specific angers become global, total deterioration becomes an all-too-real possibility. When anger for personal gain fails to lead to change and acceptance, the status of the relationship must be reexamined lest the partners remain locked into the trap of chronic conflict.

Couples who enjoy large reserves in their relationship bank account can often reexamine issues and experiment with change that only one person wants. Unfortunately, couples with the least reserves are frequently the ones that push the hardest for asymmetrical changes. For such couples, it is better to begin relationship repair by working on issues that don't polarize the partners. Once deposits are flowing into the relationship bank, then the couple can return to thornier issues. It is a mistake to think that you can get the deposits flowing by immediately tackling the most explosive issues.

Using the Better Talk skills, Paula and Kevin continued to discuss the issue and were able to do so with less and less anger. They came deeply to appreciate each other's perspective, and Kevin had a clear view of how his anger was moving him further from his overall goals. It was critically important that Paula clearly state her preferences without blaming Kevin for his desires. On several occasions over the next two years, Paula and Kevin discussed many aspects of their sexual preferences and found their way out of this particular blizzard. Although Paula's preferences did not change, once the relationship conflict surrounding this issue abated, Paula decided to experiment with wearing some of the outfits that Kevin had bought for her. Paula found that she remained uncomfortable wearing certain clothes outside of their home but that she enjoyed wearing sexy outfits as part of the couple's lovemaking. "Dressing up for sex" became a special night for the couple and led them to discover a way that respected each other's preferences while allowing their relationship to grow.

TYPE II: ANGER FOR INDEPENDENCE

Acknowledging and Understanding Your Anger for Independence

Although most of us are social beings who yearn for closeness and intimacy that only relationships can provide, at the same time we are fiercely protective of our independence. When we feel that independence threatened, we often reassert our individuality with anger. Trivial matters can often become a flashpoint for such issues. When Beth asked Sam to take out the garbage, an action that would require little time or energy, Sam felt he had to assert his independence: "I'll do it later." Important issues can also be a battleground, such as when Lois decided to return to work after many years at home and Peter did not like the change in family life triggered by Lois's decision. The more Peter pleaded with Lois to stay at home, the angrier and more committed Lois became to break free and accomplish her goals.

Conflicts involving anger for independence often come up around changes in the relationship life cycle, when one partner begins to express new desires or interests. It may surface when a husband hits forty and begins to lobby for a new red sports car. Or it may arise when one partner wants to change jobs after many years of doing the same thing. Or it may come to light when a couple adjusts to becoming a family. In responding to changes in the family life cycle, couples can do a lot to anticipate these changes and take steps to prevent relationship difficulties surrounding these important transitions.

Transforming Your Anger for Independence

The best strategy for dealing with anger for independence is to legitimize your desire for change and then make these desires known without attacking your partner.

Valerie and Tyrone were in their late forties, and the last of their three children had just left for college. Their once-busy home was now quiet, and the couple was learning how to adjust to the "empty nest."

Tyrone was an investment analyst, and his career was settled and successful. Valerie had been an aspiring artist when the couple married, and she had continued to paint as a hobby while being busy as a parent and homemaker. With the children away from home, Valerie wanted to spend more time painting and was eager to take some classes in the fine arts department at the community college. As she became more excited about returning to school for professional training, Tyrone showed less and less enthusiasm and support for her decision.

Tyrone wondered if she would feel comfortable being back in school among younger students. He questioned if she and they would not be better off if she pursued some other interest that would bring more money into the household to offset the cost of the children's college tuition. Valerie and Tyrone discussed their respective sides of the issue but were having great difficulty. Many of the conversations ended with Valerie furious and Tyrone feeling mystified about their inability to work through the problem.

As Valerie considered her anger, she came to understand that her decision to pursue formal art training was something that was very important to her and that she wanted to do everything possible to accomplish her goal. She felt that she had given a lot to the family, and that this was her time to place her interests first. Once she saw her anger as a source of motivation propelling her toward achieving something that was very important to her, she was able both to stand up for herself and to understand how scared Tyrone was of further changes in the family.

Tyrone and Valerie then completed a relating conversation that had previously been beyond their grasp. Valerie concentrated, not on her anger, but on her desires to return to school for art lessons. She made a clear request to return to school and was, at the same time, able to understand Tyrone's fears and concerns. Tyrone was also able to move beyond his anger to disclose his own fears and uncertainty about all the changes occurring within his family and to show a keen understanding of how important it was for Valerie to pursue her career. Without Tyrone's understanding, the couple would have been faced with the same alternatives that Kevin and Paula confronted in dealing with anger regarding personal gain—either compromise, end the relationship, or lock horns in chronic anger. The last alternative is invariably the most costly to each partner's well-being.

TYPE III: ANGER FOR PROTECTION

Acknowledging and Understanding Your Anger for Protection

Anger for protection occurs to shield you from feeling something far more disturbing than anger. When you're angry and filled with all the hot thoughts and bodily reactions that we discussed in chapters 6 and 7, it is very difficult to feel any other emotion . . . such as hurt and loneliness. The hurt is often associated with a sense of incompetence and imagining that the entire world will see just how worthless we are. The loneliness is tied to a deep sense of isolation that is almost too unbearable to contemplate. It is rooted in our childhood fears of being abandoned and uncared for. When these feelings are triggered by something or someone in our world, anger rises up as an external defense against all those who might hurt us, and an internal defense against the pain of feeling worthless or abandoned. Although anger is not pleasant, it is experienced as a better alternative to the underlying feelings of emptiness that it replaces.

Partners struggling in a relationship in which anger for protection is a factor often describe their mates as having a Dr. Jekyll/Mr. Hyde personality. Everything is going along well and then, all of a sudden, it seems as though you're living with a different partner altogether. Partners often find themselves confused as to how one event can release a new "personality." These triggering events evoke such powerful waves of psychological pain that the person's anger rises in measure to overcome the pain. Once the pain is gone, the anger recedes.

Cora and Alan got into frequent arguments in which anger for protection played an important role. They recently reported to us the following fight: During the day at work, Cora had an argument with her employer over her yearly evaluation. Although generally pleased with her work, Cora's boss pointed out several areas that he felt could be improved upon. In this meeting, Cora learned that she would not receive as large a raise as last year's. Cora felt that she had been working very hard and was incensed at receiving what she considered a very unfair evaluation. After arguing her point of view without success, Cora stormed out of her boss's office and left work two hours early to try to calm down.

When she returned home to find Alan on the couch, she did not know that Alan had had a similarly awful day. On his way home from work, a car came out of a blind alley and he barely missed causing a serious accident. He slammed on his brakes and his briefcase went flying off the seat, scattering papers everywhere. The car behind him could not stop in time, and both his rear taillights were broken. With his hands still shaking from the experience, he had arrived home a few minutes before Cora, and he was sitting on the couch trying to collect himself. When Cora walked in, she began to tell Alan about what had happened in her evaluation meeting. Alan listened for a few minutes and then said, "Listen, it's no big deal. At least you have a job. Let me tell you what happened to me today." Alan didn't get far before Cora interrupted and said: "I know I have a job. And it's just as important as yours. Why can't you ever just listen to me?"

Alan, also bruised by his near miss with a serious accident, jumped into the fray. "I listen to you. You're the one who never listens to me. You want to know what happened to me today? I had one of the worst days in recent memory, and you're bitching about your evaluation. I almost got killed."

Why couldn't Cora and Alan comfort each other? From our position on the outside of the relationship, each of their perspectives is completely understandable. Cora and Alan are both in a desperate *but veiled* search for support and comfort from the other. They are peripherally aware of their own sore points but centrally aware of the other's shortcomings. It is as if they are both saying: "My needs are more important than yours. If you loved me, you would be there for me with open arms and without conditions." These core vulnerabilities are operating in both partners simultaneously. There isn't enough loving kindness to go around when both partners need to be taken care of and neither feels that he/she has anything left to give.

The solution to this dilemma is for each partner to acknowledge, express, and accept responsibility for his or her vulnerability while blocking the temptation to convert it all into simmering anger and blame. All that *either* Alan or Cora would have to say is: "Wait a minute. I see we're both getting angry really quickly here. I bet it has to do with each of us feeling pretty bad and in need of support from the other. You go first, and I'll be there for you. I care about you as much as I care about myself. Then we'll switch roles." Such a statement would enable both partners to weather the storm.

Acknowledging and understanding anger for protection requires that you and your partner act as a team with mutual goals. It also requires that you accept as a given that there will be powerful forces operating to make the above words (that we suggested to Cora or Alan) among the hardest ones you will ever speak. If anger for protection were easy to overcome, we would have dealt with it earlier in this book. We know from clinical experience how challenging it is. We also know that great rewards lie on the other side of the mountain once this climb to the top has been achieved.

Transforming Your Anger for Protection

The key is to transform anger for protection into requests for supportive caring. At those times when you are so angry that you are unaware of how bad you feel about yourself, you will need to take a step back and learn to transform the anger into expressions that convey just how much *you* are hurting. When you feel the sting of your partner's criticism as a loss of love, this is a signal for you to disclose how you feel about yourself—not to take the easy path and criticize your partner in retaliation. You can express your feelings in such a way that you do not *blame* your partner for making you feel as you do. Remember our discussion in chapter 6; no one *makes* you feel anything; you do that all by yourself as you interpret each other's actions.

Words do little justice to the power of underlying feelings of being unloved. One image (not for the squeamish) that we use to emphasize this point is to imagine yourself being physically knifed by your partner's criticism. You are on the floor bleeding. What do you do?

A destructive option is to act like a wounded dog who bites at any hand that tries to offer comfort. This type of fierce self-protection serves to drive away both friend and foe. It is very isolating and can be self-destructive; no one is allowed to be close enough to provide comfort. The other option is to call for help.

Even among the most distressed couples, when we ask a partner to imagine how his or her spouse would respond if he or she were discovered bleeding from fresh wounds, with very rare exceptions, all partners answer that their spouse would take care of them in the best way possible. We believe this to be true and it is another example of the reservoir of hope available to couples, as expressed in our first simple truth about relationships.

We want you to see the corollary when you are psychologically wounded by your partner. If you allow yourself to "bleed" *and* to be comforted, more often than not your partner will come to your assistance. Most of us are conditioned to respond with compassionate caring to expressions of vulnerability (sadness, pain, hurt; for example, "I felt really worthless when I was ignored") and to respond aggressively to expressions of anger that threaten our well-being ("Leave me alone— you never want to spend time with me, anyway").

Robert and Nancy could not get through a relating discussion. On the surface, they seemed to be listening to each other, but whenever they tried to move on to problem solving, there was rapid escalation of tensions and a return to griping.

Robert was silently furious with Nancy for what he perceived to be an endless stream of criticisms. The most recent round concerned Nancy's feeling that Robert was not fun to be with in social situations. She was annoyed that he tended to be quiet and felt that he had made too little effort to relate to her friends. They tried to process this issue, but it quickly ended with Robert complaining that Nancy was more concerned about her friends than him. Nancy denied this was true and criticized Robert for failing to follow the rules for a Couple Meeting.

Robert failed to transform his anger directly into a message that Nancy could hear. He had been profoundly hurt by Nancy's comments but never disclosed the impact her words had upon him. We encouraged him to "bleed." Robert told Nancy, "When you tell me I'm too quiet at parties, I feel worthless and embarrassed. I know I'm not very outgoing, and so your comments rub salt in a wound that is raw and open for me."

For perhaps the first time, Nancy grasped how deeply Robert was hurt by her comments. She wondered aloud why he had never told her this before. When Robert shrugged his answer, however, we clarified that his anger helped protect him from having to disclose such painful feelings. Nancy then asked: "So does this mean I should not say anything to Robert about how quiet he is at parties?"

Robert answered before we could: "My behavior at parties bothers me, too. It is something I have to work on. What I need is your support and understanding, not your critical evaluation of my problem or progress." Nancy showed that she heard and understood Robert's concern and promised to be more sensitive to the issue. This stubborn problem had bothered the couple for years, but before this discussion, they didn't even understand why it was so difficult an issue. Robert worked hard to transform his anger to direct expressions of hurt, and suddenly new doorways opened for the couple that enabled them to draw closer together.

A FINAL WORD

Because dealing with simmering anger is not an easy task for anyone, it is useful to have rules to guide you out from under its influence. Here are a few simple summary statements that can cue your recall of this chapter when you need it most—when you're so sure that you're right, he or she is wrong, and nothing else matters.

• As a general rule, find ways to express your anger in words that do not simply blame another for your feelings.

• If you have anger for personal gain, make a request to have your wishes, wants, and desires fulfilled. Remember, when you ask your partner to accommodate your admittedly individual requests, you give him or her the opportunity to make deposits in the relationship bank account.

• If you have anger for independence, express your yearnings for personal growth and work to meet these strivings with determination, not rageful assaults.

• If you have anger for protection, share your wounds and allow your partner to provide some comfort. Don't push your partner away by resorting to any of the destructive patterns of relationship talk that we uncovered in chapter 5. In return, find a way to soothe your partner's wounds because in nearly all cases of anger for protection, both members of the couple are expending energy blaming each other for how miserable they feel.

FROM REPAIR TO REVIVAL

In this chapter, we have endeavored to provide you with insights and skills to transform anger from a destructive into a constructive force in your relationship. For many of you, Better Understanding and Better

Talk will depend on your ability to make this vital conversion, day in and day out. The more you practice transforming anger, the more this learned skill becomes an ingrained habit based on the automatic recognition that your own and your partner's anger has more to do with unspoken needs and hurts than with any genuine wish to cause suffering.

In the next chapter, From Repair to Revival, we build upon your new foundation of Better Understanding and Better Talk by offering creative approaches that foster fun, friendship, and intimacy: the "good stuff" that your previous patterns kept you from achieving.

Chapter 11

FROM REPAIR TO
REVIVAL

THROUGHOUT THIS book we've focused on the importance of controlling destructive fights that rob your relationship bank account of precious resources and reserves. You've learned many strategies to take control of your conversations, your thoughts, and your body so that you and your partner can relate to each other as intimate partners and reach satisfying resolutions to current concerns. However, we're certain that you did not get married thinking about managing conflict constructively. When you exchanged wedding vows, you didn't say "We pledge to use the speaker-listener tool until death do us part."

Conflict is merely the inevitable by-product of marriage, and it must be dealt with in an effective manner so that it doesn't pollute the LIFE-blood of a happy relationship—*love, intimacy, friendship,* and *emotional* caring. As we noted earlier, these positive aspects of a relationship often emerge naturally once partners take hold of the reins of conflict. Nevertheless, we've found that some couples who complete our program are in need of a refresher course in returning joy to their relationships. They have lived so long with conflict or distance, they appear to be lost without one of these. Such couples react the way we might when we've gotten stuck with long-term work projects of little interest, leaving us longing for release. Often, when that day finally comes, we feel ambivalent because we don't know what to do with all the free time!

This chapter is designed to help you rebuild your relationship after the overriding difficulties of conflict resolution are "out of the way." During this rebuilding, you can make substantial deposits in your relationship bank account. Remember how important it is to have good reserves on hand to weather the periods of necessary withdrawals. Accordingly, this chapter will be helpful not only to couples who have worked hard to improve their relationship, but also to those who are currently happy and want to invest in their future happiness.

Relationship Revival

In our work with couples, we have developed a three-step approach to reviving relationships. Not everyone needs to go through all three steps, but the points covered are relevant to all couples.

- Find creative ways out of relationship ruts that cause stagnation.
- Enrich the friendship between the two of you.
- Enhance the fun in your relationship.

JUMP STARTING A STALLED RELATIONSHIP

In the case of couples for whom the easing of tensions and the resolution of problems do not yield a noticeable increase in closeness, connection, and playful good times, attention and energy must be devoted toward jump starting the relationship. Once revived, these relationships usually remain vital and dynamic.

One case in point involves Sherry and Alex. Married for six years, Sherry and Alex divided their relationship into two stages: the good part and the bad part. The good part—which took place before the arrival of their children—was a time when they felt very much in love and had fun times together. Even though they occasionally engaged in destructive talk, they were generally satisfied with their relationship. Over time, as they became a family and career pressures increased, their early difficulties in conflict resolution intensified and became big problems. They turned into "silent steamers," and an unremitting level of tension crept into their relationship until that became its defining feature.

Sherry and Alex completed our Better Talk program, and their level of tension and anger substantially subsided. However, they were still feeling distant and made no special efforts to restore the love and fun that had characterized their early years together. When asked why they thought this was the case, they both responded that it was a puzzle to them.

In the "good" part of their marriage they had looked forward to being together, but during the "bad" time they had avoided each other. Now, the mere thought of being alone together made them both feel anxious. In addition, their children, their work, and their friends and family demanded so much of their time that they had little in which to be alone as a couple. What once had come easily and required little thought was now fraught with difficulty and anxiety.

Alex and Sherry needed the relationship equivalent of "shock therapy" to reawaken the warmth and intimacy they had once enjoyed. The seeds of relationship happiness were buried deep in their past, lying dormant, but they remained viable and ready to emerge under proper care. We helped Sherry and Alex develop a systematic game plan to nourish these seeds—first through planning weekend dates, then overnight stays at local inns, and finally through a series of weekends at various entertaining places.

For couples like Sherry and Alex, the initial return to fun and friendship-promoting activities is rather difficult because the positive and loving feelings seem so distant. In a typical "Catch-22" scenario, some couples wait for warm, positive feelings to reawaken before they commit themselves to participate in enjoyable activities. Unfortunately, the wait can last a very long time—if not forever, if you don't take action. Sherry and Alex put this principle into practice and "forced" themselves to plan fun times together. Soon the couple felt that these enriching activities were happening more naturally and were evoking memories of the early years of their marriage.

At the same time, they realized that the relationship was no longer the same one that they nostalgically remembered. After one particularly nice weekend, Alex remarked that the basis of their newfound connections was rooted less in the past than in the present—as they got to know and like the person each had become over the years.

BECOMING BETTER FRIENDS

A second approach to relationship revival is to increase interactions that make partners feel they are each other's best friend. One way that partners who are best friends interact is to have conversations about issues that are personally important to each individual. There are two major types of friendship talk:

- Talk about individual experiences and interests (e.g., reactions to a news story, books you're reading, thoughts you have during the day about life)
- Talk about personal—not relationship—problems (e.g., conflict with parents, problems at work, concerns about death and dying)

As in the case of Sherry and Alex, couples often learn to have conversations dealing with problem issues, but they do not naturally evolve into "friendly" conversations about other topics. To start the process rolling for Alex and Sherry, we asked them to begin discussing topics they had been thinking about during the previous week. In one meeting, Alex began by discussing the pressure he felt at work to make a political contribution to a candidate he did not want to support. Sherry assumed a listener role, although she did not summarize and paraphrase to the degree called for in the speaker-listener process. The listener role here is much more that of a friend. As in any natural conversation, the speaker/listener roles tend to switch flexibly and easily. Couples who have mastered these skills find themselves automatically taking turns, paying attention, and periodically summarizing.

Once Sherry and Alex started engaging in these friendly discussions, they were amazed how rich their conversations became. Many important and interesting topics came up, and their discussions meandered leisurely into new issues, experiences, and ideas. For example, one recent talk started when Sherry shared thoughts she'd been having about her parents, both of whom were sick at the time. She aired her fears about sending them to a nursing home and expressed anxiety about what that would mean, both emotionally and financially for her parents and for herself. Alex empathized with her feelings and avoided making generalizations such as, "Oh, well, it will all work out," which would probably have ended the conversation abruptly.

Listening to Sherry spurred Alex to talk about concerns he was having about his mother, with whom he'd been engaged in a running battle over religious practices. Alex's mother was a devout Jew who, more than anything else, wanted her sons to be as orthodox in their practices as she. Alex revealed to Sherry how much he disliked deceiving his mother by pretending to practice his Judaism more seriously than he actually did. In the midst of their conversation, the following issues emerged: their own children's religious upbringing; visits to their parents; their feelings about growing older; their heretofore unstated beliefs about religion and God; Alex's relationships with his brothers; Sherry's relationships with her sisters; what is important in life; and the meaning of money, work, and family. Needless to say, once Alex and Sherry got going, a new level of intimacy and joy in the relationship was generated.

Occasionally, problems will emerge during intimacy-enhancing conversations that require use of the Better Talk plan for relating discussions (see chapters 8 and 9). Such topics can be jotted down on a notepad and scheduled for a Couple Meeting. It is generally not a good idea to let an intimacy-enhancing conversation drift into problem solving. Whereas intimacy-enhancing conversations benefit from being unstructured and spontaneous, problem-relating and resolution discussion are best when structured and planned.

HAVING MORE FUN TOGETHER

The third step toward relationship revival is to bring fun back into your relationship. Even for couples who are not coming out of years of conflict, the need to maintain a sense of fun often doesn't get as much attention as it deserves. Fun has been widely ignored by researchers, therapists, and couples alike. When we interview couples we often ask: Out of all the people in the world, why did the two of you decide to marry each other? Invariably, having fun together was one of the factors that attracted partners to each other. For example, many couples report:

- "We just hit it off and had a great time on our first date."
- "We laughed a lot together."
- "She was fun to be with."
- "We did a lot of things together that we both enjoyed."
- "He had a great sense of humor."

One of the reasons that couples have difficulty maintaining fun in their relationship is boredom. We easily fall into patterns in which our efforts to have fun and engage in recreation are repeated again and again. Eventually, we become satiated with these activities, and they become routine and dull.

When your goal is to have fun, several strategies are useful to break the dull routine. In our workshops, we give couples what we call a fun deck—a set of fun activities that couples have told us about over the years. We will give you examples of some of the best activities we've come across (see box 11.1) and then give you the chance to create your own, personalized fun deck.

How to Use the Fun Deck: "Let's Make a Date"

Here's an exercise using the fun deck that will lead to more enjoyment in your relationship. The goal is to plan a set of fun activities to be enjoyed in an agreed-upon time period. Each of you should make a list of

Box 11.1
Best of the Fun Deck

Here are some of our favorite fun activities that couples have told us about. You can create your own fun deck, using these examples as well as those presented throughout the book:

• Planning a surprise weekend in which one person plans a weekend or a date and the other person does not know where he/she is going. Partners can take turns planning these for each other.

• Sending electronic mail messages to each other as if you did not know each other well and were trying to pursue each other romantically

• Going house hunting together when you have no intention of buying a house

• Spending an overnight in a local bed-and-breakfast and pretending you are tourists in the city you live in

• Taking country-and-western dance lessons together (This can be generalized to tennis lessons, golf lessons, singing lessons.)

• Going to the store and buying a board game to play together

• Staging a murder mystery and having friends over to act out the roles

• Going to the tallest building in the area in the evening and riding up to a high floor to watch the sunset

• Reading a novel or a play to each other in front of a roaring fire in the fireplace, with a favorite drink

• Going to a minor- or major-league baseball game

continued

- Going on a horse-and-buggy ride together

- Browsing through antique shops

- Rummaging at garage sales to look for inexpensive but special items for your house

- Deciding not to watch television for a week. Tape your favorite shows and watch them all at one sitting, thus saving the extra time for fun activities.

---

three fun activities that *you* would like to do. Many couples do the fun exercise on a Friday night and plan for the upcoming weekend. When we hold weekend seminars, we have people do this exercise at the end of the first day, so that they can set aside time for the activity that evening.

When writing down the three activities, you may want to consult our fun deck to come up with ideas that break old patterns. Once you've made your list of three activities, exchange lists with your partner. Then choose one of the activities from your partner's list that you would also like to do and take *responsibility* for making sure the activity takes place. You now have two fun activities (one you've each selected from your partner's list) to enjoy in the agreed-upon time frame. Here's how this exercise worked for one couple.

Tony and Lydia were the parents of two delightful boys, aged two and five. Since they started therapy, they'd made a commitment to have a one night getaway at least once a month. The first two getaways went smoothly enough, but Tony and Lydia decided that they were not taking full advantage of the potential that these outings held for them. To enlarge their range of options for fun activities, they sat down and completed the fun deck exercise. They made a concerted effort to be creative and include one or two completely novel activities on the list. Lydia came up with the following list:

1. Getting a massage together
2. Renting a bicycle built for two and taking a scenic bike ride to Mt. Vernon
3. Packing a picnic lunch and taking a walk along the Potomac

Tony's list included the following:

1. Going to see the Orioles play a night game
2. Having a luxurious romantic evening out that starts with drinks at one restaurant, appetizers at a second, the main course at a third, dessert at yet another, and an after-dinner drink at some final, romantic spot
3. Going ice-skating together

They exchanged lists, and Lydia selected from Tony's list the progressive dinner date and took responsibility for making it happen. Tony perused Lydia's list and selected the scenic bike ride. Following the basic principles of problem solution, they summarized what they had agreed to and then shook on it.

There are a number of variations to this theme. Some couples enjoy going through an active brainstorming stage and following the basic problem-solving procedures, starting with the targeted question, "What can we do for fun during this coming weekend?" After brainstorming, they compromise until reaching an agreement, then shake on it. We recommend that couples do this periodically. For example, once every three months hold a Couple Meeting and brainstorm about fun things that you generally never do. Select an evening or weekend to carry out your plan. Finally, once in a while, take turns planning a surprise weekend or date for each other.

Sensuality Is Fun

Another approach is to use the fun deck exercise and/or the brainstorming to improve and enhance the *sensual-sexual* side of your relationship. Vanessa and Roy went this route with great success. Their sex life had dwindled so markedly in recent years that they'd come to a resigned acceptance of the loss of the sexual excitement they once had. We encouraged them to be as honest and as creative as possible in generating a list of three sensual-sexual activities they would like to experiment with during the upcoming weekend. Vanessa's list was the following:

1. Go together to a store, buy some lotions, and give each other a full body massage
2. Go to the video store and each rent an adult video to watch together
3. Go to Victoria's Secret and have Roy choose the sexiest piece of lingerie he could find for her to wear

Roy's list was:

1. Go to Woolworth's and buy some cheap underwear to play around in
2. Buy some body paint and paint each other; then take a bath for two
3. Dress in the sexiest clothes they both have, enjoy a romantic dinner in a dark corner of a restaurant, and discretely touch each other

They exchanged lists—Roy chose to arrange for the massage, and Vanessa selected the sexy dinner. They went on to explore both familiar and altogether new terrain in the sensual/sexual sphere of their relationship, and the result was a return of joy and a sense of novelty.

In general, we strongly advise couples not to focus all their sexual attention on intercourse. It is perhaps more important to create a sensual richness in the relationship. Too often, caressing, pleasuring, hugging, massaging, and kissing, occur *only* as a prelude to intercourse. Yet such *sensual* activities are intrinsically enjoyable and an aspect of your relationship that requires tending. Often when sexual activity diminishes—for whatever reason—sensual connections are broken as well. We suggest that every couple put aside time to hug, pleasure, and massage each other, in which they also agree *not* to move on to intercourse. When you create clearly defined sensual times, a physical basis for intimacy will always be available, even when you're experiencing troubles in the sexual arena. Moreover, sensual interactions are often the first step toward repairing sexual problems and generally enhancing sexual pleasures.

Can "Planned Spontaneity" Work?

Many partners rebel at the idea of setting aside times for fun, friendship, and sex. They say to us: "These should occur naturally." Our response is that *time* is the commodity of the nineties, and many couples are not finding or making time for their relationship. *Planning* relationship-enhancing times together is one of the best ways to communicate to each other a sense of real commitment. By planning time for activities you have decided are important, you are translating priorities into actions and avoiding what one of our clients calls "talking the talk, but not walking the walk."

MAKING THE BETTER TALK TOOLS YOUR TOOLS

Bringing fun and spontaneity back into your relationship is one route to revival. Another route involves a form of "preventive maintenance." That is, once you've reduced the obstacles of conflict, destructive talk, and arousal, you must still apply the Better Talk skills, but in a preventive manner. Therefore, moving from repair to revival means turning your once-new and novel skills into well-trod paths of good communication. These paths must take you where you want to go in your relationship, and our goal is to help you stay on course—with love and flexibility.

In the process of using the Better Talk tools that we've presented, each of you will need to tailor these skills to suit your personality. Here are our suggestions for individualizing the Better Talk tools to suit your needs and the unique configuration that is your relationship:

Define Your Rules

You'll be better off if your decisions concerning the use of the Better Talk skills grow out of an active process of negotiation between you and your partner rather than as a result of passive neglect. For example, if you've tried out a suggestion we've made and are quite certain that you don't wish to follow it, we suggest that you and your partner explicitly acknowledge this fact rather than let the idea passively slide away.

In his relationship with Nancy, Gil had become very skilled at avoiding difficult discussions. He was working hard to overcome his tendencies to withdraw from conflict, and yet several recent circumstances had caused him to say to himself, "I know I need to say what is bothering me now, but I just can't do it." His withdrawal set the stage for Nancy (who saw Gil's old pattern all too clearly) to feel that Gil was not committed to working on the relationship as they had agreed. In fact, Gil was very committed to the work and to self-change; he was simply having difficulty with putting new behavior into practice. Had Gil explicitly acknowledged his difficulty, and perhaps explored the reasons for it with Nancy, a problem with Better Talk could have turned into a basis for understanding.

The following are examples of some other general rules that couples in our workshops have found useful. Keep in mind that we're *not* recommending that you necessarily adopt any or all of these particular rules. In order for rules to be effective, they must be tailor-made to fit *your* relationship.

- "We will limit our Couple Meeting times to twenty minutes. If we have not resolved the issue within this time, we will set up another Couple Meeting for a later time."
- "When a spontaneous conversation starts to go bad, we promise to use the Couple Meeting format to continue the discussion."
- "We will not discuss problems after 10:30 P.M. when we're tired and need to wind down. If an issue is pressing, we'll set up a specific time to discuss it the next day."
- "We will not initiate problem discussions during dinnertime or

other times that we have specifically set aside to build positive feelings into our relationship (e.g., during family outings)."

- "We won't deluge each other with 'lousy day' complaints for the first thirty minutes after we have come home from work. After this time, we will limit our 'complaints of the day' discussion to fifteen minutes apiece."

- "If one of us finds that a rule that has been previously set up is not working effectively, that person is to call a stop action and request a renegotiation of the rule."

- "When we find problem issues in day-to-day life repeating in a predictable manner, we will try to 'head these off at the pass' by scheduling a Couple Meeting *before* the issue becomes a problem."

Not All Difficulties Deserve a New Rule

Some couples are tempted to make up lots of new rules whenever a difficulty is encountered. This is not always a good idea. Too many rules can stifle spontaneity and thereby interfere with intimacy. Rules are best constructed when a situation repeats itself enough times that you become quite convinced that limits or structure must be imposed.

For example, Steve and Candy came up with the rule, mentioned above, that they would not discuss any big issues requiring a decision after 10:30 at night. This rule grew out of their discovery that nine times out of ten, whenever they started to discuss something late at night, they were so exhausted that they could not engage in effective speaker-listener behavior. As a result, fights actually became a more likely outcome than calm conversations. This difficulty had called for a rule, which soon served to make their nighttimes more enjoyable, and also cut down on an important source of withdrawals from their bank account.

Steve and Candy also had an experience making a rule that was not so helpful. One night when Candy initiated sex, Steve had difficulty getting an erection. It was the first time that this had happened and was quite troubling to both partners. Candy worried that she was unattractive to Steve, and Steve worried about being able to get aroused in the future. That night, they precipitously made a rule that Steve should be the one to initiate sex and not Candy.

Once we gave the couple more information about sexual performance, they learned that many men in their mid-forties experience the same problem as Steve did, and thus decided that a rule was unnecessary. It also helped the couple to learn that changes in women's sexual capacities do not parallel men's. Armed with this information, Steve and Candy were able to have a relating discussion in which they openly, nonjudgmentally shared how they were feeling about their sexual relationship. They discovered there was no "problem" to solve or bring under rule control. As Steve's fears about his performance declined and Candy was reassured of her attractiveness, the couple's sex life not only "returned to normal," it became even more satisfying and experimental than before.

Know Thyself

No matter how compelling a particular way of relating may sound to you, you may simply be unable to behave as you wish you could. In such cases, it is better to acknowledge your personal barriers and work around or with them, rather than against them. This issue commonly arises for men trying to overcome their tendencies to withdraw from the women in their lives—as was the case with Gil and Nancy.

As Gil worked on knowing himself, he acknowledged that he had difficulties with Better Talk, and he was reluctant to schedule a Couple Meeting. Instead, he asked Nancy for "stew time"—or time to himself. Gil's request was a form of acknowledgment that he was withdrawing. It signaled to Nancy that he realized this problem had more to do with him than with her, and it let her know that this would not be a good time to pursue matters. Gil knew that "stew time" wasn't the best alternative available, but he'd recognized his own limitations and needs. He not only came to accept his needs, he also came to appreciate the space Nancy had granted him.

Once these times no longer intensified conflict between Gil and Nancy, Gil was able to use the time by himself to figure out why he had such difficulty confiding in Nancy. He expressed his gratitude to

Nancy for not pursuing him and openly admitted that his behavior was not what he'd have liked it to be. However, there remained times when he simply couldn't overcome the barrier. At such times, acceptance and appreciation of each other's human limits were a great source of comfort to Nancy and Gil. It is a rule they now live by.

Caring for Your Better Talk Tools

No matter how powerful a set of tools you have, they will require care and maintenance. Periodically, it is good idea to "calibrate" a tool to see how closely to its original design it is functioning. Even world-class athletes and stars of the theater who have achieved outstanding levels of performance will go back to their coaches to practice the basics—complex behavior, like the communication skills you've learned, require this level of commitment, dedication, and practice as well.

For example, Janice and Zack had mastered the Better Talk tools and reported that their relationship was stronger than ever. As we were ending our work, the couple made a pact to have a Couple Meeting using the Floor Exercise at least once every three months to make sure they maintained their skills with the help of this tool. The Floor Exercise was especially helpful to Zack and Janice, and thus they made a wise decision to come back to this exercise. We suggest you do likewise for your personal selection of most helpful Better Talk tool.

An Ounce of Prevention . . .

When things are going well, you'll be able to practice your new skills and move your relationship forward. If you wait until conflicts become set in stone to put the skills to use, then you'll be challenged to deal with your own and your partner's emotional arousal as well as an increased likelihood of destructive talk and thoughts—even though you are now prepared to meet such roadblocks in a constructive way.

Yet many of us find it easier to develop a preventive approach with our cars, rather than our marriages. We take our automobiles in for regular maintenance and oil changes every three months and for tune-ups every 25,000 miles, but we find it hard to apply prevention principles to our relationships. Our research reveals that happy couples who use the Better Talk principles and skills in a preventive mode—having regular Couple Meetings, anticipating problems, learning and applying the simple truths of marriage—successfully increase their chances for an ongoing stable and happy marriage. As noted earlier, in one study, rates of relationship breakup and divorce were 50 percent lower for couples practicing our brand of prevention.

The simple rule of prevention is to practice the essential principles and skills of Better Talk at the very first signs—or even anticipation—of issues that breed destructive thoughts, talk, or arousal. Instead of using Better Talk to reverse patterns of miscommunication, use them to solidify healthy new patterns of communication.

SIMPLE TRUTHS REVISITED

When we complete our seminars or our therapy with couples, we discuss which aspects of our program were most successful. Many partners tell us that they focus on one or two of the simple truths, repeating them to themselves at key moments, such as when a fight is about to break out or escalate out of control.

Each person usually has his/her favorite "beacon" and way of remembering the fact, not necessarily using the same language we used in chapter 2. The partner who uses our simple truths effectively has found some personal meaning in them. Here are some examples related to each of the beacons:

Simple truth #1: *Each relationship contains a hidden reservoir of hope.*

"I know now that we can work it out."
"I know she means well."
"He's not intentionally trying to be difficult."

Simple truth #2: *One "zinger" will erase twenty acts of kindness.*

"With anger, I'll rarely get what I want."
"Criticism is rarely constructive."
"One zinger a day will keep the doctor in business."

Simple truth #3: *Little changes in you can lead to huge changes in the relationship.*

"Partner change follows self-change."

"Make a little behavior change today for a big feeling change tomorrow."

"I don't have to change my whole personality, just little things about my behavior."

"If I know what I'm trying to accomplish, I'm more likely to achieve my goal."

Simple truth #4: *It's not the differences between partners that causes problems but how the differences are handled when they arise.*

"When in doubt, listen and relate—don't suggest and resolve."

"We both feel the same way about things, and that's the key."

"When we were happy, our differences didn't matter. I won't let them matter now, either.

Simple truth #5: *Men and women fight using different weapons but suffer similar wounds.*

"We're both just human."

"We need to work together as a team."

"You can catch more flies with honey than with vinegar—talking is good, fighting is bad."

Simple truth #6: *Partners need to practice relationship skills in order to become good at them.*

"Practice makes perfect, and to err is human."

"Better Talk is a path, not a destination."

"With teamwork, we can work it out."

YOU CAN DO IT

As you've no doubt noticed, we've used lots of sports metaphors throughout this book, because managing relationship conflict is so much like an athletic or acting performance. It takes practice, positive self-talk, control of arousal, and teamwork. At the highest levels of competition, most professional trainers will say that the difference between winners and losers is 99 percent mental, and 1 percent physical ability. We can recall standing around a tennis court watching a highly ranked, but unfamiliar, woman practicing and remarking that with her strokes and speed we were surprised not to have seen her in the big tournaments. We then overheard two coaches talking, and one said: "In practice she's got all the strokes to play with Graf, Seles, Sabatini, Capriati, and Fernandez, but in match play she falls apart. She forgets the basics, gets down on herself, then gets angry, and before long she's out of the match. I wish I knew how to help her."

Throughout this book, we've tried to help you with *both* the "mental" as well as the "skill" aspects of making marriage work. With better understanding of relationships and the Better Talk tools, you are in an excellent position to take charge of both aspects of the relationship. You can achieve your goal.

FINAL AFFIRMATIONS

Some partners see their relationship as it is and ask, Why? We want you to imagine a better relationship and ask, Why not? We want you to feel the sense of hope that you can live your dreams with the person you've chosen as a life mate. That is why we've stressed your ability to overcome all manner of personal differences to find the common ground of relatedness; and it's why we emphasize the reservoir of hope that resides even in many of the most seemingly troubled relationships.

When you imagine the relationship you hope for, give your partner the benefit of the doubt and live out your commitment in words and actions—your hopes will soon give way to reality. Tell your partner "We can work it out" with love and commitment, and you will.

REFERENCES

Baucom, D. "Attribution in Distressed Relationships: How Can We Explain Them?" In D. Perlman and S. Duck (Eds.), *Intimate Relationships: Development, Dynamics, and Deterioration.* Newbury Park: Sage, 1987.

Baucom, D., and N. Epstein. *Cognitive-Behavioral Marital Therapy.* New York: Guilford, 1990.

Baucom, D., C. Notarius, C. Burnett, and P. Haefner. "Gender Differences and Sex-role Identity in Marriage." In F. Fincham and T. Bradbury (Eds.), *The Psychology of Marriage: Basic Issues and Applications.* New York: Guilford, 1990.

Beavers, W. Robert. *Successful Marriage: A Family Systems Approach to Couples Therapy.* New York: Norton, 1985.

Benson, H. *The Relaxation Response.* New York: Avon, 1976.

Burns, D. *Feeling Good: The New Mood Therapy.* New York: New American Library, 1980.

Cherlin, A. *Marriage, Divorce, and Remarriage.* Cambridge: Harvard University Press, 1981.

Christensen, A., and J. L. Shenk. "Communication, Conflict, and Psychological Distance in Nondistressed, Clinic, and Divorcing Couples." *Journal of Consulting Clinical Psychology,* 59 (1991), 458–463.

Cummings, J., D. Pellegrini, C. Notarius, and E. M. Cummings. "Children's Responses to Angry Adult Behavior As a Function of Marital Distress and History of Interparent Hostility." *Child Development,* 60 (1989), 1035–1043.

Emery, R. "Interparental Conflict and the Children of Discord and Divorce." *Psychological Bulletin,* 92 (1982), 310–330.

Filsinger, E. (Ed.) *Marriage and Family Assessment.* Beverly Hills: Sage, 1983.

Filsinger, E., and R. Lewis. (Eds.) *Observing Marriage: New Behavioral Approaches.* Beverly Hills: Sage, 1981.

Fincham, F. D., and T. N. Bradbury. *The Psychology of Marriage: Basic Issues and Applications.* New York: Guilford, 1990.

Floyd, F., and H. Markman. "Observational Biases in Spouse Observation: Toward a Cognitive-behavioral Model of Marriage." *Journal of Consulting and Clinical Psychology,* 51 (1983), 450–457.

Gotlib, I., and J. Hooley. "Depression and Marital Distress: Current Status and Future Directions." In S. Duck (Ed.), *Handbook of Personal Relationships.* New York: Wiley, 1988.

Gottman, J. *Marital Interaction: Experimental Investigations.* New York: Academic Press, 1979.

Gottman, J., and L. Krokoff. "Marital Interaction and Satisfaction: A Longitudinal View." *Journal of Consulting and Clinical Psychology,* 57 (1989), 47–52.

Gottman, J., H. Markman, and C. Notarius. "The Topography of Marital Conflict: A Sequential Analysis of Verbal and Nonverbal Behavior." *Journal of Marriage and the Family,* 39 (1977), 461–477.

Gottman, J., C. Notarius, J. Gonso, and H. Markman. *A Couple's Guide to Communication.* Champaign, Ill.: Research Press, 1976

Gottman, J., C. Notarius, H. Markman, S. Bank, S. Yoppi, and M. E. Rubin. "Behavior Exchange Theory and Marital Decision Making." *Journal of Personality and Social Psychology,* 34 (1976), 14–23.

Greenberg, L., and C. Johnson. *Emotionally Focused Therapy For Couples.* New York: Guilford Press, 1988.

Guerney, B. G. *Relationship Enhancement.* San Francisco: Jossey-Bass, 1977.

Haefner, P., C. Notarius, and D. Pellegrini. "Determinants of Satisfaction with Marital Discussions: An Exploration of Husband-Wife Differences." *Behavioral Assessment,* 13 (1991), 67–82.

Hahlweg, K., and M. Goldstein. *Understanding Major Mental Disorder: The Contribution of Family Interaction Research.* New York: Family Process Press, 1987.

Hahlweg, K., and N. S. Jacobson. *Marital Interaction Analysis and Modification.* New York: Guilford, 1984.

Hahlweg, K., and H. J. Markman. "The Effectiveness of Behavioral Marital Therapy: Empirical Status of Behavioral Techniques in Preventing and Alleviating Marital Distress." *Journal of Consulting and Clinical Psychology,* 56 (1988), 440–447.

Hahlweg, K., D. Revenstorf, and L. Schindler. "Effects of Behavioral Marital Therapy on Couples' Communication and Problem-solving Skills." *Journal of Consulting and Clinical Psychology,* 52 (1984), 553–566.

Hooley, J. "Expressed Emotion and Depression: Interactions Between Patients and High- Versus Low-expressed Emotion Spouses." *Journal of Abnormal Psychology*, 95 (1986), 237–246.

Jacob, T. (Ed.) *Family Interaction and Psychopathology*. New York: Plenum, 1988.

Jacobson, N., and G. Margolin. *Marital Therapy: Strategies Based on Social Learning Principles*. New York: Brunner/Mazel, 1979.

Lerner, H. *The Dance of Anger*. New York: Harper & Row, 1985.

Levenson, R., and J. Gottman. "Marital Interaction: Physiological Linkage and Affective Exchange." *Journal of Personality and Social Psychology*, 45 (1983), 587–597.

Levenson, R., and J. Gottman. "Physiological and Affective Predictors of Change in Relationship Satisfaction." *Journal of Personality and Social Psychology*, 9 (1985), 85.

Margolin, G., and B. Wampold. "Sequential Analysis of Conflict and Accord in Distressed and Nondistressed Marital Partners." *Journal of Consulting and Clinical Psychology*, 49 (1981), 554–567.

Markman, H. J., F. Floyd, S. Stanley, and H. Lewis. "Prevention." In N. Jacobson and A. Gurman (Eds.), *Clinical Handbook of Marital Therapy*, New York: Guilford, 1986

Markman, H. J., F. Floyd, S. Stanley, and R. Storaasli. "The Prevention of Marital Distress: A Longitudinal Investigation." *Journal of Consulting and Clinical Psychology*, 56 (1988), 210–217.

Markman, H. and D. Jones-Leonard. "Marital Discord and Children at Risk." In W. Frankenberg and R. Emde (Eds.), *Early Identification of Children at Risk*. New York: Plenum, 1985.

Markman, H., and S. Kraft. "Men and Women in Marriage: Dealing with Gender Differences in Marital Therapy." *The Behavior Therapist*, 12 (1989), 51–56.

Markman, H., and C. Notarius. "Coding Family Interaction: Current Status." In T. Jacob (Ed.), *Family Interaction and Psychopathology: Theories, Methods, and Findings*. New York: Plenum, 1987.

Markman, H., and C. Notarius. "Coding Marital Interaction." Special issue of *Behavioral Assessment*, 11(1). New York: Pergamon, 1989.

Markman, H., C. Notarius, T. Stephens, and R. Smith. "Current Status of Behavioral Observational Systems For Couples." In E. Filsinger and R. Lewis (Eds.), *Observing Marriage: New Behavioral Approaches*. Beverly Hills: Sage, 1981.

Markman, H. J., S. Stanley, F. Floyd, and S. Blumberg. "The Premarital Relationship Enhancement Program (PREP): Current Status." *International Pro-*

grams of Psychotherapy Research, American Psychological Association—Society for Psychotherapy Research, 1991.

McCarthy, B., and E. McCarthy. *Couple Sexual Awareness*. New York: Carroll and Graf, 1990.

Miller, S., E. Nunnally, and D. Wackman. "Minnesota Couples Communication Program (MCCP): Premarital and Marital Groups." In D. Olson (Ed.), *Treating Relationships* (pp. 21–40). Lake Mills, Iowa: Graphic, 1975.

Minuchin, S. *Families and Family Therapy*. Cambridge: Harvard University Press, 1974.

Noller, P. *Nonverbal Communication and Marital Interaction*. Oxford: Pergamon, 1984.

Notarius, C., S. Benson, D. Sloane, N. Vanzetti, and L. Hornyak. "Exploring the Interface Between Perception and Behavior: An Analysis of Marital Interaction in Distressed and Nondistressed Couples." *Behavioral Assessment*, 11 (1989), 39–64.

Notarius, C., and L. Herrick. "Listener Response Strategies to a Distressed Other." *Journal of Social and Personal Relationships*, 5 (1988), 97–108.

Notarius, C., and L. Herrick. "Psychophysiology of Dyadic Interaction." In H. Wagner and A. S. R. Manstead (Eds.), *Handbook of Psychophysiology: Emotions and Social Behaviour*. London: Wiley, 1989.

Notarius, C., and J. Johnson. "Emotional Expression in Husbands and Wives." *Journal of Marriage and the Family*, 44 (1982), 483–489. Reprinted in D. Olson, and B. C. Miller. *Family Studies Review Yearbook*. Beverly Hills: Sage, 1984.

Notarius, C., L. Krokoff, and H. Markman. "Analysis of Observational Data." In E. Filsinger and R. Lewis (Eds.), *Observing Marriage: New Behavioral Approaches.*" Beverly Hills: Sage, 1981.

Notarius, C., and R. Levenson. "Expressive Tendencies and Physiological Response to Stress." *Journal of Personality and Social Psychology*, 37 (1979), 1204–1210.

Notarius, C., and H. Markman. "Couples Interaction Scoring System." In E. Filsinger and R. Lewis (Eds.), *Observing Marriage: New Behavioral Approaches.* Beverly Hills: Sage, 1981.

Notarius, C., and H. Markman. "Current Issues in the Coding of Marital Interaction." *Behavioral Assessment*, 11 (1989), 1–11.

Notarius, C., H. Markman, and J. Gottman. "The Couples Interaction Scoring System: Clinical Applications." In E. Filsinger (Ed.), *A Sourcebook of Marriage and Family Assessment*. Beverly Hills: Sage, 1983.

Notarius, C., and D. Pellegrini. "Marital Processes as Stressors and Stress

Mediators: Implications For Marital Repair." In S. Duck (Ed.), *Personal Relationships, Vol 5: Repairing Personal Relationships.* London: Academic Press, 1984.

Notarius, C., and D. Pellegrini. "Differences Between Husbands and Wives: Implications for Understanding Marital Distress." In K. Hahlweg and M. Goldstein (Eds.), *Understanding Major Mental Disorder: The Contribution of Family Interaction Research.* New York: Family Process, 1987.

Notarius, C., and N. Vanzetti. "Marital Agendas Protocol." In E. Filsinger (Ed.), *A Sourcebook of Marriage and Family Assessment.* Beverly Hills: Sage, 1983.

Notarius, C., C. Wemple, L. Ingraham, T. Burns, and E. Kollar. "Multichannel Responses to an Interpersonal Stressor: The Interrelationships Between Facial Display, Heart Rate, Self-report of Emotion and Threat Appraisal." *Journal of Personality and Social Psychology,* 43 (1982), 400–408.

O'Leary, K. *Assessment of Marital Discord.* Hillsdale, N.J.: LEA Press, 1987.

Raush, H., W. Barry, R. Hertel, and M. Swain. *Communication, Conflict, and Marriage.* San Francisco: Jossey-Bass, 1974.

Sade, J. E., and C. Notarius. "Emotional Expression in Marital and Family Relationships." In L. L'Abate (Ed.), *Handbook of Family Psychology and Therapy.* Homewood, Ill.: Dow Jones-Irwin, 1985.

Schaap, C. *Communication and Adjustment in Marriage.* Netherlands: Swets & Zeitlinger, 1982.

Snyder, D., and R. Wills. "Behavioral Versus Insight-oriented Marital Therapy: Effects on Individual and Interspousal Functioning." *Journal of Consulting and Clinical Psychology* (1989), 39–46.

Steinglass, P. "The Conceptualization of Marriage from a Systems Theory Perspective." In T. Paolino and B. McCrady (Eds.), *Marriage and Marital Therapy.* New York: Brunner/Mazel, 1978.

Storaasli, R. D., and H. J. Markman. "Relationship Problems in the Premarital and Early Stages of Marriage: A Test of Family Development Theory." *Journal of Family Psychology,* 2 (1990), 80–98.

Straus, M., and R. Gelles. (Eds.) *Physical Violence in American Families: Risk Factors and Adaptations to Violence in 8,145 Families.* New Brunswick: Transaction Press, 1990.

Straus, M., and S. Sweet. "Verbal/Symbolic Aggression in Couples: Incidence Rates and Relationships to Personal Characteristics." *Journal of Marriage and the Family,* 54 (1992), 346–357.

Stuart, R. *Helping Couples Change.* New York: Guilford, 1980.

Vanzetti, N., C. Notarius, and D. Neesmith. "Specific and Generalized Expectancies in Marital Interaction." *Journal of Family Psychology*, 6 (1992), 171–183.

Weiner-Davis, M. *Divorce Busting.* New York: Simon & Schuster, 1992.

Weiss, R. L. "The Conceptualization of Marriage from a Behavioral Perspective." In T. Paolino and B. McCrady (Eds.), *Marriage and Marital Therapy.* New York: Brunner/Mazel, 1978.

Weiss, R. L. "Strategic Behavioral Marital Therapy: Toward a Model For Assessment and Intervention." In J. P. Vincent (Ed.), *Advances in Family Intervention, Assessment, and Theory.* Greenwich, Conn: JAI Press, 1980.

INDEX

Acceptance versus solution, 219
Adaptation, role of change and, 38–40
Agreement
  description of, 98
  examples of, 101–2, 105, 106, 110, 112, 113
Ali and Sam case example, 117–20
Always-never self-talk, 139–40
Anger
  guidelines for handling, 255
  for independence, 248–50
  for personal gain, 242–48
  presence of hidden, 239–40
  for protection, 250–54
  as self-protective, 120–21
  significance of paying attention to, 240–42
  transforming, 240
Anna Karenina (Tolstoy), 43
Arousal
  conversations affected by, 166–71
  gender differences, 171–72, 175–76
  importance of controlling, 51–52
  lack of confidence and the triggering of, 165–66
  low self-esteem and the triggering of, 176–77
  relationship conflicts and, 160–62
  talk and the triggering of, 164
  thoughts and the triggering of, 164–65

Arousal, managing
  accepting responsibility, 182–83
  calming yourself, 186–87
  cooling the arousal, 181–85
  editing, 183
  personal arousal quotient, 178
  stop action, 178–81

Benson, Herbert, 186
Better Talk program
  banning of resolution, 205–7
  blocks to, 237–38
  communication of understanding, 197–203
  couple meeting, 203–5
  definition of, 192
  example of, 213–16
  goals defined, 192–94
  how to use the tools in tandem, 227–28
  importance of knowing yourself, 270–71
  making the tools work, 267–72
  practicing, 271–72
  problem with too many rules, 269–70
  purpose of, 22
  from relating to resolving, 213
  rules, defining your, 268–69
  setting proper goals, 194–96
  speaker-listener tool, 207–13
Biases, overcoming, 143–46

Bodily reactions, relationship
    conflict and, 159–60
    arousal and, 160–62
    sweating, 162–63
Brainstorming solutions, 222–24

Calming yourself, arousal and,
    186–87
Change and adaptation, role of,
    38–40
Character adoration, 139
Character assassination, 139
    arousal and, 168–69
Children
    affected by relationship distress,
    16
    as an issue, 60
Communication
    See also Miscommunication;
    Relationship talk, dictionary
    of; Self-talk, dictionary of
    floor exercise for diagnosing
    problems in, 85–88
    as an issue, 57–58
    pitfalls, 199–200
    sleeper effect, 88–90
    of understanding, 197–203
Competent self-talk, 140–41
Compromising, 234–35
Confidence and the triggering of
    arousal, lack of, 165–66
Conflict interaction
    effects of arousal, 51–52
    expectations can create self-
    fulfilling prophecy, 52–53
    nonreactive to, 51
    physical reactions to, 51
    relationship talk applied to,
    121–33
Conflict interaction, styles of, 44
    escalators/explosive
    boilers/pursuers, 45–46, 47
    pursuit/withdrawal, 48–50
    vicious cyclers, 45, 48–51
    withdrawal/pursuit, 50–51
    withdrawers/silent steamers,
    46–47
Conversations affected by arousal,
    166–71

Couple Meeting
    description of, 203–5
    Speaker-Listener tool in a,
    208
Critical talk
    arousal and, 164
    description of, 98
    examples of, 101–7, 110–11

Dedicated listening, 197
Denial filters, example of, 81–82
Destructive talk. See Thoughts,
    destructive/hot
Dictionary of relationship talk. See
    Relationship talk, dictionary of
Dictionary of self-talk. See Self-talk,
    dictionary of
Disagreement
    arousal and, 164
    description of, 98–99
    examples of, 103, 114
Divorce rate, 16
    for remarriages, 68

Editing, 183
Escalators/escalation
    description of, 45–46, 47
    how invalidation and
    withdrawal can interact with,
    131–33
    invalidation leads to, 123–24
    physical abuse/aggression and,
    123
    relationship talk applied to,
    121–23
Excuses and explanations
    description of, 97
    examples of, 100–101, 104, 105,
    110
Expectations can create
    self-fulfilling prophecy,
    52–53
Explosive boilers
    description of, 45–46, 47
    relationship talk applied to,
    121–23

Feelings, guide to, 173–74
Filters. See Miscommunication

Floor exercise for diagnosing
communication problems,
85–88
Foul-fighting ploys, 211–13
Friendship talk, 260–61
Fun, having more
examples of, 264–65, 266
planning of, 267
sensuality as fun, 265–67
use of the Fun Deck, 262–64

Gail and Fred case example, 99,
100–109
Gender differences, arousal and,
171–72, 175–76
Goals
defined, 192–94
importance of joint setting of,
65–66
monitoring, 241–42
setting proper, 194–96

Health, affected by relationship
distress, 16
Here-and-now self-talk, 140
Hope and good intentions, 26–28
Hopeless-helpless self-talk, 141
Hopeless talk
description of, 99
example of, 107
Hot thoughts. *See* Thoughts,
destructive/hot

Independence, anger for
acknowledging and
understanding, 248–49
example of, 249–50
transforming, 249
Intentions
See also Miscommunication
hope and good, 26–28
using positive intent as an
excuse, 74
Invalidation
how escalation and withdrawal
can interact with, 131–33
leads to escalation, 123–24

Jealousy issues, 59

Kitchen-sinking, 211–12

Listening talk
arousal and listening out, 169–70
dedicated, 197
description of, 98
examples of, 101, 102, 103, 104,
106, 111

Marsha and Will case example,
109–16
Martyr complex, 46
Men, impact of their changing
roles, 39–40
Mind-reading talk
arousal and, 167
description of, 98
examples of, 100, 103, 107, 110,
111, 113
Miscommunication
arousal and, 167
changing from opponents to
team players and reduction of,
83–84
definition of, 79
example of denial filters, 81–82
example of positive filters,
80–81
filters and, 79–80
floor exercise for diagnosing
problems, 85–88
party game "Telephone"
example, 79
why denial filter doesn't work,
82–83
Money issues, 56–57

National Center for Health
Statistics, 16
Negative problem talk
description of, 97
examples of, 102, 103, 104, 107
Negative solution talk
description of, 98
examples of, 102, 106, 107

Partners, reasons for selecting, 69
Pavlov, Ivan, 163
Personal arousal quotient, 178

Personal gain, anger for
acknowledging and
understanding, 242–43
examples of, 243–48
transforming, 243
Personality traits, effects of, 20
Personal Problem Plan (PPP),
developing a, 61–63
Physical abuse/aggression, 123
Politeness, a no-nonsense guide to,
77–78
Positive problem talk
description of, 97
examples of, 102, 104, 105, 106,
110, 111, 112, 113
Positive solution talk
description of, 97
example of, 112
Predict questionnaire
description of, 40–43, 53–54
example of using Relationship
Issues Planner with, 63–66
Problem solving
acceptance versus solution, 219
brainstorming solutions, 222–24
components of, 218
compromising, 234–35
evaluating progress, 226–27
focusing on problem-solving
discussion, 218, 220–22
importance of keeping at it,
229–31
making a commitment, 225
pitfalls, 232–34
recycling workable solutions,
225
selecting the solutions, 224
step-wise approach to, 225–26
timing of, 235–36
Protection, anger for
acknowledging and
understanding, 250–52
examples of, 251–52, 254
transforming, 253–54
Pursuers, 45–46, 47
Pursuit/withdrawal
See also Withdrawal/pursuit
example of, 48–50
Put-downs

case example of learning to
control, 75–76, 78–79
no-nonsense guide to politeness,
77–78
can undo acts of kindness, 28–29

Relationship bank account
description of, 70–71
examples of, 71–73
model in action, 73, 75
Relationship issues, common
children, 60
communication, 57–58
jealousy, 59
money, 56–57
relatives, 60–61
sex, 57–58
Relationship Issues Planner (RIP)
completing the, 55–56
example of using Predict
questionnaire with, 63–66
purpose of, 54–55
Relationship questionnaires,
predicting future happiness,
40–43, 53–54
Relationship revival
becoming better friends, 260–61
having more fun together,
262–67
jump starting a stalled
relationship, 258–60
Relationship riots, 193
Relationships
predicting the future of, 37–38
role of change and adaptation,
38–40
Relationship success
background of couples research,
17–20
reasons for studying both happy
and unhappy couples, 18–19
results of research, 20–22
Relationship success/simple
truths, factors that affect
hope and good intentions, 26–28
how differences are handled,
31–32
importance of practicing
relationship skills, 34–36

no gender differences when it comes to wounds, 32–34
one put-down can undo acts of kindness, 28–29
small changes in ourselves can lead to big changes in the relationship, 29–31
summary of, 272–73
Relationship talk, dictionary of agreement, 98
Ali and Sam case example, 117–20
applied to conflict interaction, 121–33
assessing your own communication by using, 116–17
critical talk, 98
disagreement, 98–99
excuses and explanations, 97
Gail and Fred case example, 99, 100–109
hopeless talk, 99
listening talk, 98
Marsha and Will case example, 109–16
mind-reading talk, 98
negative problem talk, 97
negative solution talk, 98
positive problem talk, 97
positive solution talk, 97
Relatives, as an issue, 60–61
Relaxation, arousal and, 186–87
Relaxation Response, The (Benson), 186
Remarriages, divorce rates for, 68
Resolution
See also Problem solving
banning of, 205–7
premature, 206
Romance, rediscovering, 58
Roosevelt, Eleanor, 137

Self-esteem and the triggering of arousal, 176–77
Self-fulfilling prophecy, expectations can create, 52–53

Self-talk, dictionary of
See also Thoughts, destructive/hot
always-never, 139–40
character adoration, 139
character assassination, 139
competent, 140–41
that douses relationship conflict, 142
examples of self-talk, 136, 149–52
exercise in reading your, 147–49
that fuels relationship conflict, 142
here-and-now, 140
hopeless-helpless, 141
should, 141
situation, 140
Sex issues, 57–58
Should self-talk, 141
Silent steamers
description of, 46–47
relationship talk applied to, 125–26
Similarity, perceived, 69
Simple truths. See Relationship success/simple truths, factors that affect
Situation self-talk, 140
Sleeper effect, 88–90
Speaker-Listener tool
avoid all foul-fighting ploys, 211–13
floor exercise for diagnosing communication problems, 85–88
listener role, 210–11
practice being a responsible communicator, 207–13
purpose of, 76
speaker role, 207–10
Stop action, 178–81
Straus, Murray, 123
Sweating, 162–63

Talk. See Relationship talk, dictionary of; Self-talk, dictionary of
Team work
changing from opponents to

team players and reduction of
   miscommunication, 83–84
destructive thoughts and, 152–54
Thoughts, destructive/hot
   See also Self-talk, dictionary of
   arousal and, 160–62
   assessing your hot thought
      potential, 146–47
   bodily reactions and, 159–60
   feeling what you think, 136–38
   holding your tongue versus
      keeping quiet, 168
   importance of letting change
      happen, 155–57
   overcoming biases, 143–46
   team work and, 152–54
   tuning in to your inner voice,
      138–39
Tolstoy, Leo, 43

Understanding, communication of,
   197–203

Vicious cyclers
   description of, 45, 48–51
   relationship talk applied to,
      126–31

Withdrawal/pursuit
   arousal and, 169
   example of, 50–51
   female withdrawal/male
      pursuit, 128–29
   healing can be accomplished by
      changing positions, 129–31
   how invalidation and escalation
      can interact with, 131–33
   male withdrawal/female
      pursuit, 127–28
   relationship talk applied to,
      125–26
Withdrawers, 46–47
Women, impact of their changing
   roles, 39–40

ABOUT THE AUTHORS

CLIFFORD NOTARIUS, PH.D., is a professor of psychology at The Catholic University of America and director of the Center for Family Psychology. He and his wife live in Washington, D.C.

HOWARD MARKMAN, PH.D., is a professor of psychology at the University of Denver and director of the Denver Center for Marital and Family Studies. He lives in Boulder, Colorado, with his wife and two children.

The authors began their friendship and their studies of marital and family relationships in 1972 while graduate students at Indiana University-Bloomington. They have continued to work together over the past two decades, and are widely known for their work on the treatment and prevention of marital distress and the development of procedures for enhancing our understanding of happy and unhappy couples and families. They have lectured throughout the United States, and in Australia and Europe on the materials presented in this book. They have authored or co-authored over one hundred scientific papers, journal articles, and book chapters, and are co-authors of the *Couple's Guide to Communication* (with John Gottman and Jonni Gonso).

Drs. Notarius and Markman maintain practices in metropolitan Washington, D.C., and Denver and Boulder, respectively. In addition, they offer seminars and workshops to couples and professionals, and audio and videotapes are available. For additional information, please call (303)750-3506.